CHUCKY'S IN TUCSON

Chucky's

IN TUCSON

Brant Vickers

Palmetto Publishing Group
Charleston, SC

Chucky's in Tucson

I have tried to recreate events, locals, and conversations from my memoires of them.
While all the stories in this book are true, in order to maintain their anonymity names of
individuals, identifying details, and places and have been changed to protect the privacy of
the people involved.

Portions of this book have been published in *Stories That Need to Be Told*.
Tulip Tree Publishing, LLC 2016

First Edition

Printed in the United States

ISBN-13: 978-1-64111-161-4
ISBN-10: 1-64111-161-5

Once more, with love to Cheryl Ann, who lived it with me.

And to my mentors, Barb, Mary, and Dr. Bil.
And to those angels, Gay, Chris, Maryann, and Donna.

And to the wonderful memory of John Nelson.

I don't like work - no man does - but I like what is in the work —
the chance to find yourself. Your own reality — for yourself, not for
others — what no other man can ever know.

– Joseph Conrad, *Heart of Darkness*

Prologue

CHUCKY'S IN TUCSON

Teasing a cognitively or intellectually disabled child, teenager, man, or woman is the lowest of lows. I'd give anything to take myself from that time fifty years ago and show the twelve-year-old me who he is today. He could watch his mature alter ego working with Juanita on a simple addition problem as she smiles, claps, and laughs with the delight and success of it; or Jorge, who learned to bounce a basketball for almost a year before progressing to actually throwing up a basket, and then meeting with Jorge's dad and convincing him that it actually happened and watching as tears welled up in his eyes. He'd meet the grandmother who had to raise her granddaughter, who cried when she hugged him at graduation and whispered, "I wish Alisa could stay in your class forever," and the gang banger who was stuck in my class as a student helper because they didn't have anywhere else to put him, who only wanted to say goodbye to one teacher before he transferred to another school so he could play football. I would show my younger self that working with the exact kids I'd been teasing became what my whole life's purpose was pointed toward, that most days I walk around grinning because they pay me to have fun, play, educate, and help those very kids. I now think of it as nothing less than an honor.

We were both looking down the track at Owsley, who had one foot on the top of the waist-high fence and one foot on the track. It was Friday of the first week of school and my second attempt as a special education teacher in Tucson, Arizona.

"The school district pays you too much to be a student's one-on-one!" Mr. Johnson, my principal, shouted at me.

"You don't pay Jill enough to get sued when he becomes a hood ornament," I shot back. "We can't catch him when he takes off. If I just stay here, at least he won't go over the fence."

If we made one more step toward him he would lift himself up over the fence and be gone into the residential streets behind our school. Then we would have no choice but to call the police because a special education student had escaped from campus and was running loose in the neighborhood. He was a student with fetal alcohol syndrome, severely cognitively disabled, and exceedingly violent. Owsley was seventeen and on his fourth or fifth high school, and his teaching assistant one-on-one, Jill, who was tasked to stay with him all day every day, was about to quit, as I was. I had been taking over for her when he'd gotten away, which was so far about three times a day. Owsley weighed about 110 pounds and ran around and around the school, but sometimes onto the track, where we could at least watch him from a safe distance without approaching him – which would make him climb the waist-high fence and take off. We'd had no success getting him to participate in any activities, and I had no idea yet why.

We had already called the police twice that first week. The first day of school we chased him down in the neighborhood, but a motorcycle cop had already shown up. We had Owsley in the principal's office, and I tried explaining the situation to the cop who insisted on talking to him.

I said, "He's severely mentally retarded and can't understand anything abstract about his doing anything right or wrong." The cop was about six five, African-American, and a really nice guy, with a huge heart.

"Well, I have to talk to my main man here," he said.

"Okay, just remember he's severely cognitively disabled, and I think he can be really violent."

"No problem, no problem," the cop talked over me as we walked in and sat down. I let the rest of my speech go.

Owsley was sitting on one side of the conference table and Mr. Johnson was next to him. I sat down next to Mr. Johnson and the cop sat down across from us, about a foot from Owsley. He turned sideways and started talking to Owsley, saying, "You know, son, you can't run away from school. It's against the law. Plus, you want to stay in school and learn all you can, don't you?" I saw Owsley shaking his head slightly, which I would learn in the near future, was a definite antecedent for bad things to come. His speech was muted and barely understandable for those who weren't used to it, but he could speak in short sentence bursts.

"I ganna stheal a bike."

"Now, that's not an answer to the problem either," the cop said. Owsley's head shaking became more pronounced. Mr. Johnson noticed it, too. He, like I, knew something was up; we just didn't know what. He leaned over and whispered for me to have his secretary call the group home. I started to get up and leave.

"I ganna ride it up a Mont Lemmon." I was just out the door leaning in to the office and asking the secretary to call.

"Well, like I said, that is against the law as well," the cop was continuing.
Bam! Boom! Crash!

I learned after the fact, Owsley flipped Principal Johnson's large circular desk over. As the cop must have come up out of his chair, I was pushed out of the doorway and almost knocked down. I righted myself and said, "Call now."

When I walked back in the room, it looked like a bomb had gone off. The cop was standing over a handcuffed Owsley, the table was overturned, a glass-framed poster was broken, and Mr. Johnson was standing there looking stunned and disheveled. The cop had this look like, "What the fuck is going on here?" He later said he couldn't believe how such a skinny kid could be so strong and how hard it was to take him down. I learned to believe it well.

Owsley was yelling, "Fuck you, otherfuckers! You ohtherfucking bitches!"

All I could do was look at them both and say, "I guess he doesn't really need speech therapy so much."

The group home care providers took him home that day, but several times during the next weeks we learned they wouldn't answer their phone, and because we could only suspend a special ed kid for ten days the whole year, we were to learn that day was a mild one, as far as Owsley was concerned. So, I found myself relieving Jill, his one-on-one, when it got too bad, and there I was watching him threaten to climb the fence.

"Well, we can't be sitting out here all day long every day just watching him. Are you coming back on Monday?" Mr. Johnson asked.

"I honestly don't know. This is stupid, and all week we don't have an answer from district on what to do."

"Their answer is what it always is: 'Deal with it.'"

"Jill won't come back. She can retire anytime, and no one else is going to be any better," I said.

I was soon to learn that this principal, one of few I've had, was one of those magic guys who learned after being in the system for many years to manipulate the bureaucracy and get things done that teachers assumed couldn't get done.

"There's this guy. He used to work here. I don't know what he's doing now, but let me make some phone calls this weekend. Can you come back on Monday?" Mr. Johnson asked.

It usually took a month, sometimes two, for a new hire to start work. Monday morning a guy walked in all tatted up with heavy-metal ink, wearing dark shades, and carrying a water bottle. He shook my hand, and said, "Brant, I'm Bruce. How ya doin?" He pointed at Owsley, snapped his fingers, and said, "C'mon Owsley, let's go. I'll stop in to talk to Mr. Johnson, and we'll be back for buses. Later, dude." I recognized I was in the presence of an angel.

I've learned a lot from aides and am indebted not to think that I was above them or smarter than they were just because I was the "teacher." Bruce taught me more about how to handle a difficult student than anything I'd learned from my master's degree program, any peer teacher, administrator, behavior specialist, or anyone I'd run into in the proceeding eighteen years. He simply saved my career that day and schooled me on how to deal with this student – when no one else could.

Shortly after that, we had a meeting with Owsley's team. It consisted of fifteen professionals: his Department of Developmental Disabilities case manager; his counseling center case manager, their psychiatrist; his group home director, their case manager, two of their workers; our school psychologist; our special education director; two school behavior specialists; Mr. Johnson; the head of our school's special education department; and Bruce, and me. Owsley never had contact with his mom; his dad had never been on the scene. A rumor was that Mom had actually showed up at a group home one day several years ago, and Owsley had attacked her and the woman she was with, and she'd never been back. He was on a handful of anti-psychotic drugs and other medicines. His severe attention deficit made sitting at a desk or attempting any kind of activity impossible, and believe me, we and a half dozen other teachers tried over the years.

The team decided two things of great importance that day: Bruce would cruise in his truck with Owsley everyday, all day, and get mileage for it. He ran errands for our teachers, our school, other schools, and even the district. If we needed ice for a party or something to be picked up, like supplies for a class, they did it. Owsley's intense fetal alcohol (all professionals agreed it was the most extreme they had ever seen) and violence would warrant restraint if necessary. His psychiatrist stated Owsley's violent outbursts were physiological, and soon I graphed it to prove it was every three to four days. He needed a physical release, and it was usually accomplished by lashing out at a teacher, group home worker, student, desk, table, window, computer, or basically anything. Bruce and I saw it coming and learned we had to (in special-ed lingo) "trip" him; that meant - God forgive us - we set him off purposefully to get it over with and have a couple of peaceful days.

Owsley would come off the bus most weekends with a mean look and his head shaking, and Bruce and I would just look at each other and think, *Uh, oh*. We rationalized we did what we had to do to keep him safe, as well as other students and staff. By this time at his group home, he had broken windows, every piece of furniture in his room, and several people's faces. If Bruce was absent, I was the only one who could safely take him around the city. When that occurred, and I walked in the door at the end of the day after school, my wife would take one look at me and say, "Bruce wasn't at school today, was he?" That's how exhausted I appeared.

Owsley ran away from his group home many times. We learned at school to control it; they didn't. With the farcical minimum wage and personnel turnover, they never "got" what to do and when to do it. Bruce developed an intense close relationship with Owsley. They actually in some way became friends. Bruce was devoted to him. At times, he had fun with Owsley. He told me how they would be driving around and Owsley would see a patrol car drive by and ferociously jerk around and look back at the cop.

"Don't do that, man," Bruce would chastise Owsley.

"I dno dat pig," Owsley would answer, with both of them laughing. "He dno me do."

One time he broke through his window at the group home and ran away to a park, where he attacked a six-year-old kid playing soccer. They sent him to the state hospital for a week and put him on a heavy dose of Valium. The group home people loved it, but he could barely stand up when he came back. The second day, Bruce called me from the road and said he needed me to meet him in the parking lot – he was coming back in and had to have help. As I went out the back door, Bruce was standing with Owsley, who slipped to the ground.

"Don't worry, Owsley, we'll take care of you. Brant and I love you. We'll fix this."

As we were picking him up, I just looked at Bruce and thought, *Love him*. Well, I guess in a way we did.

I took him to the office and asked the nurse - and by then, another principal - what they would do if a typical kid came in like this. At that point Owsley lunged forward from my arms and came close to hitting his head on the edge of a desk.

"Call the group home and have them come and pick him up, and if they don't answer, leave a message that we're going to call CPS and register a complaint. You can't send a kid to school drugged," our new principal said. I enjoyed seeing him angry and concerned about one of my students as much as the typical ones. They lightened the dosages.

A week after 9/11, we attended a medical review for the Department of Developmental Disabilities and Owsley's group home. Bruce and I went as a courtesy to give input as to what was happening at school. I had learned quite a bit by then. I told them it was a mistake to bring Owsley to the meeting. That many people talking about him would surely set him off. They didn't listen. At least a dozen people were sitting around a conference table. It was after hours and I warned Bruce we couldn't get involved, as there were liability issues after the school day. A group home worker brought him in and his head was already shaking. The psychiatrist said, "How are you, Owsley?"

"Gud," he said, barely looking around. I looked over at Bruce and he was shaking his head. I shook mine and whispered, "Remember, we can't do anything." They took Owsley out, and we continued talking about some of the problems they were having. In about five minutes, a woman burst through the door.

"Is this meeting for Owsley? Is this for that kid outside?!" she shouted.

The psychiatrist said, "Yes, is there something I can help you with?"

"Yes, they're having trouble outside. They're yelling they need help." The group home manager looked around and his eyes landed on us. I shrugged my shoulders and looked at Bruce, who was starting to come up out of his seat. "No, we can't," I said, motioning him to sit. The manager got up and left. We sat there for a minute or two, and I could tell it was driving Bruce crazy. I couldn't check myself either, so I signaled for him to get up and we went outside. We found the group home people standing around with their heads up their collective asses.

One guy was sitting on the curb in the parking lot and whimpering, "I couldn't handle him. He grabbed me and pushed me and knocked me down."

"You let him get away," Bruce said with not a little disgust in his voice.

"Where is he right now?" I asked. They looked at me.

"Is he off this site?" The Department of Developmental Disabilities complex was fairly big, but surrounded by residential areas and a couple of major streets. No answer again.

I pointed at the manager and said, "You need to call the police right now, and we'll help look for him that's all. If we find him, we'll try to call you. If there is no answer, we will call the police. Do you understand?"

He just continued to look at me and I said, "Now. You have a violent client running the streets." He nodded. Bruce and I split up and drove around the streets for about twenty minutes and then we met. I convinced him we couldn't stay involved any more, for liability problems alone.

Later that night, Bruce called me and told me what had happened to Owsley. Bruce had heard the story through a friend of his who also worked in a group home. Owsley had gotten almost two miles away without being found, crossing several large city boulevards and a highway. He started to walk onto the local air force base, which, because of 9/11 having happened only a week before, the gate guards were still in combat mode and carrying M16 rifles. They shouted at him to stop several times and raised their weapons just as two police cars pulled up. The cops restrained Owsley on the ground for a couple of minutes and then asked him if he was okay and would cooperate.

Bruce and I could have told them it didn't work that way. He had to be held down until he had a complete meltdown. It was almost like he'd pass out, and it could be worrisome for those who didn't know how it worked. If we let it go that long, he'd transcend into a coma-like posture for about five to ten minutes, and then he'd pop right up and say, "I thorry, buddy. We need to thalk. I thorry." If not, we could ask him if he was all right and he'd mutter a "yeth," but as soon as he got up, he'd attack, possibly getting a good shot in. I guess they almost tasered him before they just handcuffed him and waited for the group home people to show up.

When I was thirteen, I rode my bike over to Jeff Broman's house after school to get an early start on partying that night. His was one of the few two-story houses in Culver City, California, in the late sixties.

"Wait a second. I'm going to change and I'll be right back down," Jeff said as he ran up the stairs.

I was looking around the living room that had really nice furniture and a beautiful, huge black grand piano. I had never seen one before. I was tinkering on the keys (I didn't play) when I heard this sound from somewhere else deep in the house. It was guttural and feral. I stopped and listened.

"Jeff," I said quietly. The noise got almost imperceptibly louder. I heard slapping noises and raspy breathing. This thing came crawling around the corner, long shaggy hair, Coke-bottle glasses, loose clothes and tennis shoes. It was a person. It came straight for me. I quickly backed up, yelling, "Jeff! Jeff!" I realized it was a he. He came at me and I jumped up on the piano. He started shrieking in a harsh, speechless voice that I couldn't understand. He lunged forward on the piano and banged on the keys. I screamed at that point, jumped off the piano, and ran around the corner into a family room that had a huge couch. I jumped over it and he was right behind me, making an incredible hoarse, barking noise. I ran around and around, while he crawled as fast as a whippet after me. After a few more agonizing moments, Jeff came running into the room and yelled for both of us to stop.

"Brant, stop! He's just playing." We all three looked at each other. The croaky yelping continued, but softer. His head was larger than normal, misshapen; his eyes were askew and his body seemed small. But I couldn't tell – it seemed that if he stood up, he'd only be about four feet tall. "Don't you know my brother? Didn't I tell you about him?"

"No."

"I'm sorry, man. This is Henry. He's cool. He just wants to wrestle. He's laughing; he's playing, dude. I forgot you've never been to my house." Jeff pulled Henry up to a sitting position and hugged him. They were laughing and pulling on each other, and I walked over and sat down on the couch, suddenly exhausted.

Within a short period of time, Henry and I became good friends. As long as I hung out with Jeff, I loved going over and wrestling with Henry. The family accepted him, and his mom walked him around the neighborhood in his walker. Henry loved people and loved to laugh and play "chase" around the house. We'd get tired long before he was ready to stop.

The next year, a family moved in next door to us in Culver City, with its small, cheap California bungalows popular after World War II. The father was the janitor in our junior high school. His nickname was Mr. Green Jeans. He was a hulking, grave, unfriendly guy. I never had any interaction with him. Those who did usually regretted it. He had the late-afternoon shift. His wife had kyphosis (hunchback), as did an uncle and aunt. They shunned any neighborhood friendliness. When they would all congregate, usually on the weekends, for an hour or so, yelling and shouting would commence in an almost incomprehensible congenital language. Their house was dirty, unkempt, overgrown with grass, with the roof and window screens falling apart. As drab and grim as they seemed, on those same weekends, they would dress up in western attire; outlandish bright colors, with ribbons and bows, scarves and hats. The whole group, minus the two sons, would pile into a station wagon and go square dancing.

Jerry and Danny were their sons. They were tall, heavily built, dark-complected, and severely mentally retarded. Jerry could talk, but usually it was just yelling and cussing. Danny was non-verbal, but would constantly make singsong noises. Danny and Jerry never went square-dancing. They stayed at home alone, not only on the square-dancing nights, but also several days and nights a week. Sometimes several days in a row. This was before my family or neighbors – really, even our society – was tuned into Child Protective Services. Most people minded their own business. Danny would stand on the sidewalk outside their house and shake his hands, while alternately lifting his feet and make crooning noises.

Jerry aggravated something in me. I don't know why my parents never noticed. I think they were profoundly dismayed and extremely nervous with the whole scene and chose to ignore it. But my interaction with him wasn't healthy. Nothing, I rationalized, was overtly criminal, but it was still wrong. It started with me coming home late one night, walking up my driveway, and noticing all the lights on in their house. Jerry was in his parent's bedroom. I glanced in the open window and saw him looking in the closet. He was naked. At that young age, I didn't ponder the right or wrong of it.

I leaned my face to the window and hoarsely yelled, "Hey!" Jerry almost jumped out of this skin. He went tearing through the house, running into doors, knocking things over, yelling, "That goddam kid! Oh, that son of a bitch!" After that, he would yell profanities at my friends and me every chance he got - which was often. I always felt his later interactions with the whole neighborhood were tainted by my actions that night. If other kids were playing in the street, he would occasionally throw a glass bottle or jar into the street. Just my shooting baskets in my driveway would be enough to set him off. I did things on purpose at times, just knowing it would. I can't explain why. Whereas Danny would just stand in his driveway or on the sidewalk, Jerry would end up walking all the way down our street, yelling, and we assumed directing traffic. Oftentimes he ended up on Culver Boulevard, only a block from Sepulveda, jerking and shouting swear words. Cops came sporadically, but most of the time the only people not frightened were two of my uncles. They would just chase and shoo him back home, but always talked to him like he was a regular person. I wish I had learned from them.

One day as I was walking home, Danny was in his usual place, and as I went up my driveway, I stopped and listened closer to his singing. I suddenly understood what he was saying: "Illllll beeeeeee baaaaaaaaack in a owwwwwwerrrrrrrrrrrrrrrr . . . " Over and over again. It hit me like a jackhammer. He was repeating what his parents must have told him hundreds of times over the years, and was a habitual lie. "I'll be back in an hour." The profound sadness of that forlorn refrain made me feel wretched to the point of tears. I never again made fun, made faces, or did anything, but instead just waved and took Jerry's cussing as my due.

Holidays were big for Owsley. The week after Thanksgiving, he would start wearing a Santa cap. Owsley knew when his birthday was coming weeks ahead of time, although he didn't know the months or dates. He would start talking about Halloween in September. We would ignore it as best we could, but one day Bruce was walking through the mall with him a week before Halloween, and there was a gift store dedicated to paraphernalia and costumes.

"He freaked out, slammed the plate-glass window, took off running, and then attacked me. I had to take him down right then," Bruce relayed to me. "Just by dumb luck, another group home guy I'd never met happened to be shopping, and helped me, and by the time the cops came, Owsley was cool, but it happened so fast I didn't see it coming." They got back to school okay, and Bruce was laughing. He said he should let Owsley tell me what happened.

He walked up to me sober and morose. I asked, "What's the matter, Owsley?"

In the most serious tone I've ever heard him use, he actually made eye contact with me momentarily and said, "Brannnn, Chucky's in Tucson," nodding his head as if confirming one of the most important pieces of information in the world. We figured one of his group home workers had watched the Chucky horror movies with him, and when they were walking by the store, Owsley had seen a life-size doll in the window and flipped.

I've learned a lot about myself working with kids with disabilities. Most teachers can't imagine doing what I'm doing - the toileting, the feeding, the restraining, but also working with some of the most endearing, sweet, loving people on the planet. Making their lives worthwhile during their school years has been a privilege a lifelong friend said a few years ago. Maybe I'm remembering what I forgot years ago - that I actually had some experience with these kids, and just maybe I'm making amends for some of that wrong time.

Chapter 1

IN PRAISE OF MY MEDIOCRITY

I've been lucky in my life. I've been blessed in so many ways that I feel fortunate and try to remember to be grateful for all the ways life has been good to me. Places I've been, jobs I've had, people I've met, and friends I've had have given me a wonderful, if still incomplete, perspective on living. Much has brought frustration and much pleasure; defining who you are and what you do is a mystifying and difficult endeavor. A couple of things I've done, and continue to do, have been extremely satisfying, enlightening, and maturing, also tempered by a large degree of discouragement.

I ended eighteen years of teaching recently, and at times, wish it were over forty – but it's been the best career I could have had. Not a bad way to pay back some dues to Jerry and Danny. I've recently spent some time looking back and reflecting on some of the choices that have led me here. I needed to put it down for it to make sense to me. I went through some changes before this career came into focus, and learning what I was meant to do in life was a blessing. Being a guitar player, water polo player, runner, and career soldier were things I did and enjoyed, but one thing in my life has been ideal, one thing has been just right, one thing has been perfect.

The art of playing the guitar came extremely slowly and painfully to me. I can't quite remember what motivated me beyond wanting to be a Beatle. Somewhere along the way, the desire to actually play a musical instrument became a factor. When I realized I couldn't emulate what I loved - be Paul McCartney, or later, Neil Young - I still didn't give it up. I play fifty years later, not because I want to be Blind Blake or Reverend Gary Davis (the two players I attempt to master more than any other), but because I wouldn't know what else to do with those hours during the week. It can be described as a passion that one could say I'm still not very good at, considering the time I've invested over the years. I have had friends and one family member who inspired me through their sheer mastery of the skill and beauty of their playing and singing. I've never had the feeling of owning that talent, the reinforcing pleasure of performing and then enjoying the accolades of applause. I experience instantaneous performer's anxiety, and can freeze up directly when beginning to perform, even with fellow guitarists. I haven't played in front of a crowd since 1967, when Jim Gilman and I performed in front of a church group, ironically somewhat successfully. That stage fright haunts me still, and my successive departure from our fledgling rock-and-roll group a few years later was, at best, a blessing in disguise.

I always wanted to be really good at a sport. I remember sitting with my lab partner, Mark Gunther, in tenth-grade biology when he casually mentioned that the new pool was open at night for lap swimming, I had to ask what that meant. I went by myself that very evening. I think that solo venture is why it became so important to me. I met an older swimmer who asked me if I wanted to play water polo. Again, I had to ask what that was. I had quit playing football the year before, and was floundering as far as sports were concerned. Three years later, I became the most valuable player on my high school water polo team, but wasn't interested in continuing in college. I don't think I loved it enough.

I found running by accident. I met a dear lifelong friend through the sport outside my normal circle of acquaintances, but then persisted on my own for years. I can precisely remember the day I realized I wasn't going to be a world-class runner like the heroes I had followed for many years. I was running in college, and had recently run a four-minute, eighteen-second mile, and had finally broken thirty-two minutes for a 10K on the track. My coach came bounding up to me, not even realizing what his words would impart, and said, "Mary Decker just ran four seventeen. She's the first woman to run under four twenty!"

Before I came back to college, I had run and won several races in Germany, and had been on the army's European track and cross country teams, but at that point, I immediately started to rethink dedicating virtually all my time to running. I asked my college coach, Larry Knuth, and Joe Douglas of the Santa Monica Track Club, with whom I trained when not competing in college, what I could realistically achieve in running. I received virtually an identical answer from both of them.

"If you *really* bear down and train," they said, "I mean, *really* start training . . . " All I could think was, what the hell had I been doing for the last three or four years? Running twice a day, going to school, and only working part-time was all I was doing now.

"If you work that hard for another year or so, you'll be able to break thirty minutes for a 10K."

I just thought, *And then what?* I immediately became a fun runner. The dreams I had been harboring for a career, or even just competing in a NCAA Division I final, went away, but I had fun with it for almost two more decades. I still surprised myself a couple of times by accomplishing more than I would have ever thought possible. I truly loved it. I never knew what it was like to *have* to run or exercise. I'd come home from work and immediately start changing into running clothes to go out and run. I never understood what people said when they had a problem getting motivated to run. But I did understand what it was like to be only mediocre at something you loved. With the two things I loved in life, I was only ordinary. It has always been a source of frustration, that little bit of knowledge. I now know it's a valuable lesson, and maturity is gained in that knowledge. The things we love we may not be good at, but if we work hard at them, they can become bigger than life for reasons far beyond the original motivations for having started them.

My love life could have been described as beyond mediocre. In 1995, on leave before heading to Korea, and recently in the middle of a divorce for the second time, my mother looked over at me sitting on the love seat in their house in Lebanon, Oregon, patted me on the arm, and said, "Brant, maybe marriage just isn't for you." Pretty sobering words to hear from your mom.

My first two marriages would best be summarized by saying I married two women I should have dated. It's really as simple as that. I have no hard feelings; afterwards, I just thought I would be better served by not trying anymore. I thought I had an idea of what I wanted in a relationship, and that I probably, at this point, would never be lucky enough to find it. I know that what I thought was love and compatibility was simply infatuation. It never lasted. I was okay with it, and had reconciled myself to a solitary life. It seemed a healthier future than hurting and being hurt again. I have no regrets about any step I've taken or lessons learned, any path chosen differently might have changed where I've ended up.

When I returned from Korea, I was shared a house with a friend in Sierra Vista and we both worked at the Non-Commissioned Officers Academy on Fort Huachuca. I had been back less than a week when Art asked me to accompany him up to Tucson to watch as he and another friend competed in a triathlon. Before I had left the year prior, I'd placed in my age group in the same race. I drove up early Sunday morning and stood around while they got situated for the race. Art's swim heat wouldn't start for another hour, so we went upstairs to watch a couple of the next waves start.

We were looking down on the swimmers going and coming. Triathletes are marked on their legs with the race number and their age, usually on the left calf. Art nudged me, and in his magnificent North Carolina drawl, he said, "Hey, Brant, there's an old gal for ya." Now Art was only about five or six years younger than me, but we always bantered back and forth constantly about that. I was much faster than him, and so he threw my age up at me constantly. We were both Ranger-qualified military intelligence soldiers, and that made us an exception to the rule. Rangers always joke about what Ranger class they attended, and being older, I assumed I'd gone to an earlier Ranger School class than Art. It went like this: "I was in Class 13-83, the last *hard* Ranger class, before they started easing the standards." I lived to regret saying that to Art, who went into the army the day after he graduated high school. He came back with, "Class 15-82, punk. I got you by almost a year. Old man, you suck. *I* went to the last hard Ranger class."

The woman Art pointed out to me was walking to the other side of Hillenbrand pool, and as I watched her, I felt something I hadn't felt in a long time - genuine interest - but I couldn't tell you why. She was beautiful, but I felt something more. It was an indiscernible trace of something mysterious. I couldn't put my finger on it. I shrugged it off and watched as she started her heat and then went down with Art and stood around for another hour until he started his race. I was milling around the finish waiting for our other friend to finish, and thinking Art should also be finishing in another twenty minutes or so, when the woman walked right in front of me. Usually, when an opportunity like this arises. I fail. I had never met a girlfriend without some introduction through either school or work, some commonality and commonplace. I hoped being a fellow triathlete was enough.

"Nice race," I said, feeling stupid, and not knowing if she'd had a nice race or not. We talked for about forty minutes, and I was in love. I know that sounds crazy and my life, up until that point, wouldn't have bore out the possibility of that being real. But I knew it was.

I left without her number, although I had her name. I couldn't get her out of my mind, and drove Art crazy for a day. I can't remember which of us had the idea, but we came up with a plan. I was a good friend with the Fort Huachuca sports director, Les Woods. I went to see him and ask a favor. He agreed, and performed one of the most egregious privacy act violations imaginable. He called the Tucson tri-athlon director and got her number from the entry form. Art and I argued for a day about how to proceed from there.

"If it's unlisted, just tell her the phone company gave it to you," he offered.

"Yeah, that's right, start out a conversation and a new relationship with a lie. No thanks," I said.

In the end, I called, and the first words out of Cheryl's mouth were, "How did you get this number?" I gave up Les in a nanosecond. She was just putting her daughter to bed and asked if she could call me back. I didn't have a phone yet and was calling her from a pay phone on Fort Huachuca. I knew that sounded suspicious, but in the end, it worked out and we started dating. She had looked for me at the awards ceremony, but I had already left.

A couple of the things I've loved in this world I admit to being mediocre at. I was forty and thought I had an idea what love was about, and what learning to care for someone was about, but Cheryl made me realize I didn't have a clue. What I found out at this point in my life, the one thing I've found myself to be truly talented and really good at is loving someone. I am completely and utterly in love with her. I truly can't put into words what she means to me, and from that first meeting at the Tucson Triathlon on October 6, 1996, I only learn to love her more and deeper with every passing year. I love her soul, and the depth of her loving heart continues to amaze me. Even when life seems overwhelming and I have those natural human lows, I have never doubted the destiny or incredibly good luck I had that day in finding her.

I feel as if finding Cheryl was the best thing that has ever happened to me. I felt I had been looking for her without realizing I was searching; I found the girl I'd always dreamed of meeting. She's seen me through a couple of physical changes, the loss of both of my parents, and issues with my son, but has remained my best friend and partner without hesitation. Perfection is in the eye of the beholder, and I know beyond a shadow of any doubt that being with Cheryl Ann is the most important, luckiest, best thing I've ever done or will be good at. But once in a while, people also tell me I've been a fairly good special education teacher. It was a long, unforeseen twisting road to that point.

Chapter 2

BINGO, RINGO

Two years after we met, I was sitting in a doctor's office, and three doctors - a radiologist, an orthopedist, and a rheumatoid specialist - were standing around viewing my X-rays. They were all talking at once and pointing to various aspects of the images of what I assumed were the things wrong with me - seriously wrong with me. I was sitting on their left. I closed my eyes and exhaled. I was very close to getting up and striking one of them, when the orthopedist I actually had the appointment with looked over at me and read my thoughts.

"Oh, man, I'm sorry. I know this is catastrophic for you, and we're talking about you like you're not here, but it's extremely intriguing to us."

He was a young guy. He looked down where I was sitting, thinking for a moment. My doctor in Sierra Vista, where I was finishing up over twenty years in the army, had called him earlier on Monday. My doctor had told me this was a long shot; this doctor didn't see any new patients, or there was usually a six-month waiting list.

"I have a thirty-nine year old who I think has avascular necrosis," he'd said over the phone to this specialist at Tucson Medical Center. He nodded for a moment, looked back at me, and hung up the phone.

"He'll see you Thursday."

As I was sitting there stewing and listening to them talk, I was realizing the reality of over a year of pain and denial, along with hundreds of dollars spent on massage, acupuncture, orthotics, chiropractic, new shoes, and several different orthopedic doctors. As a lifelong runner and new, fairly successful triathlete, I was going to have to admit they were right, and it wasn't an injury from which I could ever recover.

"You're on active duty, right?" he asked.

"Yes, down on Fort Huachuca," I answered.

"I know that's MI, but were you ever on airborne status?"

"Yeah," I reluctantly answered, suddenly seeing where this was heading.

"Bingo, Ringo!" He actually said that. "I was in the reserves. They paid for my college, and I haven't seen anything like this in many years. What kind of units were you in? They don't have airborne units down on Fort Huachuca, right?"

"It's been a while, but before MI, mostly infantry and special operations."

"It's not Marana skydiving, is it?" he said, laughing, I think because he was happy to have figured something out. "Probably a bad jump years ago, and you walked off the drop zone and shook it off. Maybe you were running a day or two later, but unfortunately, you probably microscopically pinched a blood vessel in your hip. All these years later, you're bone on bone, man."

"So, it looks like I'll never run again . . ."

"No, no, no, you're going to need a total hip replacement in a year or two, maybe sooner."

My dreams for a master's running career vanished in a second. I didn't think of much else right then as I walked out to the waiting room and picked up Zachary, my eleven-year-old son visiting from California. We went off to pick up our supplies at home to go on a three-day camping trip to the Chiricahua Mountains. When I opened the mail before we left, I anxiously opened a letter from the University of Arizona Police Department. It read "Congratulations, you have been selected for employment with the University of Arizona Police Department. Please report to the Arizona Law Enforcement Academy on March 18, 1998."

During these last six months before I retired from the army, our office was reconfigured my boss, who was a high ranking Department of Defense civilian, didn't want me to do evaluations on anyone else (if they are of a short period, at my rank, it can be viewed as detrimental to someone's career), so he made it easy for me to continue working on my teacher's certificate on Saturdays. He also didn't know what to do with me, so I started looking for things to do.

"Hey, Greg, there's a police job fair this weekend in Tucson on Friday," I'd tell him on Wednesday, and he'd say, "See you on Monday, Brant."

So before I knew it, I had three hard lines on police department jobs in the area. One hundred people started the process for the University of Arizona Police Department, and I found out later, only three jobs were offered. I had to call the commander and decline the offer. I had shuffled through the run portion of the physical fitness test, but had still done quite well, even though I'd obviously limped. I just told them it was a little bit of bursitis.

I had extreme qualms about being a police officer, although I had two uncles who were cops and had done quite well. I thought how easy it would be for me to fit into that disciplined world, and how nice the benefits were (my son and future step-daughter could go to the University of Arizona for about $200 a semester). Then I realized that wasn't even close to being enough of a reason to be a police officer. I couldn't see myself busting a kid in the dorm for marijuana, or taking stolen-bike report after stolen-bike report, or investigating missing backpacks from the library. I remember what my uncle used to say, and I lived that for my entire army career: "If you take the Republic's money, you do the Republic's work."

Chapter 3

I always wanted to be a teacher. For over twenty years it was always in the back of my mind. One of the best jobs I had in the army was teaching at the Military Basic and Advanced Non-Commissioned Course. I thought I'd be my high school's Mr. Swanson. I'd turn some bump on a log into a lover of literature and stories. He did it for me, and I wanted the opportunity to do it for others. As a junior in 1972, I was on my way to becoming the most valuable player on my high school water polo team, extremely interested in music, playing the guitar, and a voracious reader. The one sure thing in my life was having absolutely no interest in any subject in school. I don't feel I was a student who had lost interest in learning, displayed a lack of motivation to learn, or was particularly defeated and turned off to school. I simply never associated reading for enjoyment with school. As Scout in Harper Lee's *To Kill A Mockingbird* says, "Now that I was compelled to think about it, reading was something that just came to me . . . One does not think about breathing." I had never actually thought it pertained or connected to school. All of my interests were outside of school.

While I was growing up, my parents didn't stress school or academics. My dad graduated from the small Hamlin, West Virginia, high school during the first year of World War II, and my mom had to quit at age fourteen to go to work to help feed the family. It was beyond them to even consider what the proper thing to do for me - as far as pushing for grades and academic achievement - entailed. I wasn't a failure; I just didn't excel.

When I registered for my senior year, I was compelled to see the senior guidance counselor.

"Do you have any plans for the future? And why have you purposely signed up for a number of slower moving [tracking] classes?"

"In 2081, it'll be better than it is now. We'll end the fierce competition that reigns in our society," I said, giving a mildly silly, sarcastic answer by quoting Harrison Bergeron, a short story from Kurt Vonnegut Jr.'s *Welcome to the Monkey House*. The story concerned equality, and purposely handicapping people who were of above-average intelligence so everyone was the same.

"Have you read much of Vonnegut?" she asked me. I nodded. "Tell me about it."

I said I had spent the summer, when not working or swimming, riding my bike to Culver Center and buying - if I had the money, and shoplifting if I didn't – reading all of his novels. One thing led to another, and within a few minutes, she had talked me into enrolling in Mr. Swanson's honors English world literature class. I'm not sure how this was done; I had none of the prerequisites I would have thought necessary. Maybe she just took a chance on me from our conversation. I don't remember ever being as nervous as I was that first day I walked into Mr. Swanson's class. I discovered something after the first couple of readings: We were just reading stories. I had been doing this for years. Mr. Swanson didn't care what your academic background was coming into his class. He only cared what you brought into his class after reading the material.

I more than held my own in the class, and found the other students only had one thing on me, which was an early motivation to excel, and possibly something else called "studying." I'd like to say I caught up and went on to college and finished in four years, and continued in a normal timely fashion. I didn't. I floundered. I sank a time or two, and have continued to struggle, but have in some ways more than caught up with my peers. During that last year I saw what the future held, but still didn't quite realize what obstacles I would face in the arena of academics. I've had a love-hate relationship with school, professors, and teachers ever since.

In May before graduation, my water polo coach sat me down and laid out two scholarship offers, one from University of California, Los Angeles and one from Loyola Marymount College. I knew immediately I wasn't prepared to accept either. I couldn't see myself in a freshman English class at UCLA with several hundred other students, taking notes and maintaining interest, much less passing courses. I just couldn't see myself doing it. I don't think I loved water polo that much, either. I made other choices.

I struggled. I went, in sequential order, to West Los Angeles City College, Santa Monica City College, and Grossmont City College in El Cajon, near San Diego. I spent almost two years signing up for classes, then waiting for one little thing to go wrong and dropping them. I mostly ran and worked.

At West LA, I remember dropping a sociology class because I couldn't understand a word the professor said. I kept looking around the class, wondering if anyone else was having the same problem as I was. No one seemed to, so I got out. I dropped a couple of classes because of asking a girl out – either she refused, or worse, she accepted, and then I was stuck going to a class with a girl I had unsuccessfully dated.

At Santa Monica, where I took many English classes, I remember handing in a final essay exam and not answering the one question on the test, which pertained to poetry.

The professor looked over the blue book and asked, "Aren't you going to answer the second inquiry?"

"No, I don't do poetry," I said.

"But you would have an easy A if you just answered the question. Put something down, anything. I'd hate to drop you a whole letter grade for lack of trying."

"That's okay. I just don't do poetry," I said again, and walked away.

At Grossmont, where I completely failed by dropping all but one class during the semester, I had an especially hard time. I was there mostly to run for Bob Larson and with the offshoot club, the Jamul Toads. He was, and still is, one of the best distance running coaches in the United States. I thought philosophy would be interesting. I took Philosophy I – a survey class thinking to get an overview of the whole thing. The professor had long hair in a ponytail, wore Levis with beach shirts and Birkenstocks, which I actually wore, too, and still do. I also had hair to my shoulders. I initially thought he was cool. He filled up three chalkboards every day - with what, I still have no idea. We only read Plato's *Dialogs*. I understood nothing.

"All other philosophy is bullshit," he'd say, and look around. "Don't talk to me about any other philosopher. They don't mean anything. No crap like Sartre or Camus. Plato is the only thing that matters."

I'd look around and see everyone else taking copious notes. That's what always occurred to me, copious notes, and I still didn't understand what he was talking about.

He'd constantly make fun of the Sophists, who would suck up to the popular philosopher of the day. He'd say they were idiots for listening to the current, hip, fashionable guy at that moment, and believed only Plato mattered. He'd beat us to death with the idea: The Sophists were stupid for not seeing other points of view. One day I couldn't take it any longer and raised my hand.

"But aren't you being to Plato like the Sophists were being to Protagores by having us only read Plato?" I asked.

He stopped writing on the board for a moment, slowly turned around, looked at me, and said, "And you're an asshole for saying that." He slowly turned back around and calmly continued writing.

After class, I was on my way up the registrar's office to drop the class when an older guy ran to catch up to me.

"Hey, hey, man, that's not right. You should do something. Are you going to the dean's office?"

"No, I'm going to drop the class."

"Man, I was in Vietnam, and you shouldn't take shit like that from some fucked-up half-assed dipshit instructor. I'll go to the dean with you. Did you know he has his wife who's an undergrad at UCSD grade our papers?"

I stopped and looked at him. "Thanks, man, I appreciate that, but I don't want the hassle. I'll drop."

"Just remember, he's a punk who's probably never gone anywhere or done anything."

I have remembered that.

At the end of the semester, I did the craziest thing I could think of. I had to get away from friends, and I thought, myself - and I did. To enlist in the US Army in 1975 was scary and strange. Vietnam had just, more or less, officially ended. It was the farthest away from everyone I knew and loved, but all I knew at the time was that I was going to Germany. I continued to read and live, and learned more in those three years than I ever could have in school.

When I reentered school three years later, I was more prepared and enjoyed it more. One day during my first semester back in school at Saddleback City College, my political science professor, Dr. White, taught me something about political bias in the classroom. We were discussing tyranny and the internment camps for Japanese Americans during World War II. No one can defend the camps, and no one should, but to discuss them completely out of context is ignorant. I remember asking my dad, who served on the USS *New Jersey* all during the war, if he ever heard anyone criticize the decision.

"Brant," he said, "our whole fleet was practically wiped out, and Japan had been kicking ass all over the Pacific for ten years. We thought if Roosevelt thought it was the right thing to do, who were we to think it was wrong? Of course, now we can see it wasn't the right thing to do, but we were in a world war."

At one point I thought I heard Dr. White say "concentration camp" instead of internment camp. I had spent the last two years in Germany, and had visited the Dachau concentration camp and several sites around Europe, which gave me, although incomplete, a better view of the war than most Americans'. I had read ravenously about the war when I'd first arrived, and I was, and still am, steeped in its history. It could get depressing, but I saw some of the places firsthand. I remember driving with a sport club running member and friend to a cross-country race near Gunzburg in Bavaria, when Guth Franz looked over and asked, "Kennen Sie Mengele, der Doktor? [Brant, do you know Mengele]?"

I thought for a moment and realized he was asking about the camp doctor at Auschwitz. Joseph Mengele experimentally operated on twins, and conducted unspeakable acts of depravity on kids. He was responsible for tens of thousands of deaths.

"Ja, Ich kenna," [Yes, I know]. I answered. It was one of those uncomfortable moments that cropped up with German friends. Over the next few years, I realized they related to the war and Nazism as much as I related to slave trading.

"Ja, gut, look over da," he said while pointing to the right. On a huge green building the name "Mengele" was printed in letters twenty feet high and across. Several other buildings had the name also. I learned that the family was like John Deere in America, and made farm equipment and tractors. They were millionaires. That's how Mengele was able to stay in hiding for years in South America.

Dr. White continued to refer to the Japanese internment camps as concentration camps - over and over again. I raised my hand.

"Excuse me, are you drawing a parallel between the Japanese internment camps and the German concentration camps in Europe?" I asked.

She looked at me for a second and said tersely, "What's the difference?"

I looked around the classroom for someone to help me. I couldn't believe she'd asked me that question. She had the PhD. I was just getting back in school and already I was fucking up. I really thought someone would jump in and help. Where was the Vietnam vet when I needed him?

"Well?" she said again. "What's the difference?"

"Well, for one thing, we didn't gas and burn them."

An hour later, I was in my coach's office whining about how I had to drop Dr. White's class and that would take me down to only nine credit hours and I would lose my eligibility and lose that semester's GI Bill.

"Relax, relax," he said. "She won't hold it against you. Just ask her out and take her to dinner." He started laughing. I learned about the real politics of college. He was a journalism professor, but more than anything, a crazy-excellent track and cross-country coach. An assistant field coach stuck his head in the door and said, "Yeah, man, she needs to go out with someone like you. It'll lighten her up."

"What?" I said dumbfounded.

"She's so ugly, she's cute," Coach said laughing. "She may not like you, but she won't give you a bad grade just because you made her look like a fool. But you really ought to consider asking her out. She doesn't get around much." This from a NCAA Division I track coach. I was flabbergasted.

I kept my mouth shut after that and received a B in her class. It was the last time I considered dropping a class. I went back into the army, finished college, and stayed for twenty more years.

Chapter 4

WE NEED HELP LIFTING AND CHANGING DIAPERS

At some point during my last few months at Fort Huachuca, I heard through the grapevine there was an opening coming up in the Junior Reserve Officers Training Corp at Desert Hills High School in Tucson. I was almost done with my twenty-two years in the army, and had been working on my teaching certificate on Saturdays for over a year. Cheryl was working as a speech pathologist, and I was increasingly interested in teaching and living in Tucson. In February 1998, I wore my Class-A dress uniform and drove down for an informal interview with Major Bill Young. I had trepidations about Junior ROTC in high school, as I had about becoming a police officer. They were very mixed feelings about young kids going straight into the military right after high school. I relaxed within minutes of meeting Bill. I saluted him, and he smiled and saluted back. He shook my hand.

"We don't have to do that here on campus. I want you to know I don't care if one of these kids actually goes into the military. We aren't a recruitment tool. We have ten boys in the Youth on Their Own program, ten more without fathers in the home, and many of the boys and girls don't fit in anywhere else in school. We give them a home and a safe place with adults they can look up to. With your badges [Airborne, Ranger, etc.] they'll look up to you as more than a teacher. You'll be a role model and confidant - big time."

I retired in March 1998, worked part-time at a local church, and started student teaching in August. I taught two English classes, and in Junior ROTC one military history and two leadership classes. During my first week of preparation before the students arrived, I was walking across campus when an older, disheveled-looking teacher, who I later learned was in his last year of teaching, walked up to me and said, "So you're the new English teacher, huh?"

"Yes, nice to meet you. My name's Brant."

"Yeah, yeah," he said, shaking my hand somewhat reluctantly. He looked me up and down and smiled.

"You're going to hate *To Kill a Mockingbird* before this year is over." I just stared at him and had no idea what to reply.

"And Salinger - that prick - you'll want to fly out to New Hampshire and kill him yourself. These kids will suck the passion out of the very thing you love. They'll suck the soul out of every bit of literature you teach."

I continued to look at him and finally said, "Really?"

"I don't even read for pleasure anymore," he said, and with that, he staggered off. His words were prophetic.

I enjoyed the kids in Junior ROTC, but did in fact hate teaching general English. I have the utmost respect for teachers who plug away at it day after day. I didn't think I could continue. Several days, I almost quit. I had ninth graders, and several didn't know the eight parts of speech. I had several kids who couldn't write a coherent sentence. Throughout the school - and still today in a large high school - most core academic classes were usually twenty-eight to thirty-two students. Out of these, you have two or three students who are with you. They want to learn, they want to hear about Scott Fitzgerald and Zelda. They raise their hands. They care. I had the Goodman sisters, twins, one in each of my classes. They saved me most days. Then you have the bumps on a log, about twenty-six or twenty-seven students – they aren't bad kids, they might even scrape out a B once in a while. I didn't let them bother me. I was one of those kids. You just plod on and hope for the best. Then you have the outright hostile kids. At least one or two, and if you're really unlucky, three. My worst was Ethan; you never forget the name of your first really hard, challenging kid. He took pride in not reading or turning in assignments, ever, not once. Everything sucked, everything was stupid. With Ethan, I realized teaching might not be for me.

One day after hearing him mutter how much everything sucked, I lost it and said, "You know, the only thing that sucks around here is you and your attitude. I heard you say you've never read a whole book. Well, Ethan, everyone has to be proud of something. We'll see how that works out for you." I waited the rest of the day for Dr. Weil, the principal, to stick her head in my room and say, "C'mon, Mr. Vickers, there's something we need to talk about." It never happened. I lucked out. Ethan was probably so used to being yelled at home that what I said to him was nothing. The first time I handed in my quarter report cards with several Fs, I felt sick. I hadn't slept the night before. I had made deals with all the failures and sent home contracts to be signed by parents and the students to make up work and get passing grades. Along with phone calls, I only got one or two back from parents. This was something I was to learn was common. Bill and I were walking through the office, and I almost couldn't put the papers in the office grade-basket. By the end of the year, I remember walking by, engrossed in conversation with Bill, and not pausing a step while throwing them in.

I couldn't have imagined how much one or two fourteen year olds could stress me. I dreaded them coming into the classroom more each time I opened the door in the morning and waited outside for the kids to come in. Once I started working on the lesson, I could cope with the negativity. I handled it - so I thought - fairly well. I had to remind myself hourly that they were just young kids and didn't have any idea what they were putting me through. Ethan was an infection. The boys around him fed off his venomous defiance. Suddenly, I'd have two or three bad attitudes, and no work would come from this group. I was determined to handle it myself and not go to the administration for help. I used all the behavior techniques I could. I even used what later would be called "restorative behavior" before it became the current popular failing technique in public schools. I didn't hand out punitive punishment, but tried to be understanding as to where Ethan was coming from. We talked and tried to come to an understanding. It didn't work.

By late October, I was losing it. I had thoughts of doing something that I was to later witness: teachers just simply walking out the door and not returning to work. Students now know we have no power; they can almost do or say anything, and they might not even get suspended, much less thrown out of school. We have lost all control of our classrooms, and rather than scrutinizing how we got to this point, our society blames the schools. Luckily at that time, Desert Hills still had some things in place. Ethan was suspended for a serious fight for an entire week. It was heaven. The students who normally followed his lead didn't have a leader and were somewhat well behaved, and actually did some work. I think the whole class enjoyed me, also. I was in a much better mood. Monday morning when Ethan came back, within minutes, we were into the old routine. I conceded defeat and reluctantly went to the vice principal for discipline. I started to tell him the whole story, and didn't even finish the first few details or mention a name before he interrupted me.

"You're talking about Ethan, right?"

"Yeah, I've done all I can think of."

"No problem. We all had a bet, highs and lows, on how long you'd last."

"What?"

"Yeah, don't worry about it. You're the last one." He saw the astonished look on my face. "You've lasted longer than any other teacher this year - even teachers with, believe me, *many* more years' experience. Yeah, it's Ethan's second attempt at ninth grade. He's already been removed from all his other classes. He's going to an alternative program, and I wouldn't put much money on that, either. Don't worry, we're actually impressed with your tenaciousness."

I still didn't believe it in the morning when the vice principal walked up to my door as I was welcoming the students into the room. I had a fleeting fear for a moment he was going to tell me it wasn't going to happen for myriad reasons. Right then, I saw Ethan turn a corner and smile as he saw the administrator he knew well. When he got to the door, the vice principal didn't even bat an eye as he was saying good morning to another student, then turned and said in a crisp, curt voice, "Ethan, go wait for me in my office, please. Have a good day, Mr. Vickers." I never saw Ethan again.

I did have days that I prized, where felt I was connecting at least to a few students, and making a difference. Right before winter break, I showed them *West Side Story*, and didn't comment on it. Actually, several got into it, as it was a semester winding down and pressure was lessening. When we returned, we started *Romeo and Juliet*, and I would show parts of the 1969 Franco Zeffirelli film, which I had dragged several friends to because of a crush on Olivia Hussey. I then had the students compare and contrast the 1969 movie with the 1996 movie starring Leonardo DiCaprio. A major success for me one day was asking, "Where have you all seen this movie story before?"

One of Ethan's former acolytes smiled broadly as he shot his hand up and shouted, "That stupid dancing and singing movie you showed us before break!"

"Yes, you can see where Hollywood gets its ideas. Almost all of them come from literature," I said.

After that, we started *To Kill a Mockingbird*, and I played a game I called "Stump the Teacher" with them everyday. They would earn extra points if they could ask me a question about the book and I couldn't answer it. Several kids who I thought would probably never actually read the book proved that they had read ahead enough to try and make me look bad. I didn't care about their motivation; I felt successful simply getting them to read on their own. But it wasn't enough to keep me motivated daily. Something else was occurring.

It essentially started the first week of the year, but without me even noticing it, as stressed as I was about the English classes. Something began to slowly change for me. I was working in one of my leadership classes in Junior ROTC when Jackson, the other instructor, came in my class and asked me to pop into his class next door while he hustled to the restroom. I said sure; it normally wasn't a problem - the Junior ROTC kids were always well behaved. If they weren't, we moved them out. Junior ROTC was a privilege. Things were pretty loose in the classes. I looked in and came back into my classroom, but was only two steps back in my room when I heard yelling and crashing from behind me. I rushed back in and saw two boys grappling with their arms wrapped around each other.

I thought, *What? We're having a fight in Junior ROTC the first week of school? Oh, great.*

They were short and heavy, and as I pulled them apart, yelling for them to stop I was stupefied. I stopped, looked down, and just stared.

Looking back up at me were two round heads, small ears, almond-shaped eyes, and flat noses. I hadn't yet learned to recognize students with Down syndrome, and they didn't have any sign of recognition as to who I was or what I was doing. Right then, Jackson came back in and ran up. He just looked at all three of us standing there and started laughing.

"Brant, didn't Bill tell you?" he asked me. I just continued to stand there. "Randy, Joe, get back in your seats now! Brant, come here for a second." The two boys complied immediately and quietly, and whatever was the problem ceased.

We walked back into my room.

"Didn't he tell you we have special ed kids in our program?"

"Huh, no, he didn't."

"It's okay. We just have to watch those two. They might fight every couple of months. They're in a day program together during the summer, and at the worst, we might have to put one in your room this period. It's okay. We have about four or five special ed kids here. They're great, and they love wearing the uniform."

In November that year, the mass of teachers were complaining about the mandatory Wednesday professional development; the students went home early and we had various meetings, and many times information was put out by the principal. The first one I attended was an eye opener for me. Bill and Jackson and I were there early, of course, and sat through the meeting. At three o'clock the principal was still talking, and I noticed people packing up their bags and leaving. I was shocked. I looked over at Bill, and he just nodded his head as if to say, "Believe it, it's happening." He and Jackson were both chuckling to themselves; they knew I didn't get it.

I flashed back on a meeting I'd had in the mid-eighties with fellow executive officers in our infantry battalion. It was four o' clock on a Friday afternoon, and a part came in for a Jeep. We only had a few vehicles, so it didn't dawn on us what would happen next. It was rarely an emergency when one was down. The battalion executive officer was a man by the name of Deshaw, and he scared me one time by telling me weeks before when he put his son to bed one Sunday night, his little boy looked up at him and said, "See you next Saturday morning if you're here, Dad." During this meeting, he told us a part had come in for the Jeep and he wanted it off the "dead report" by Monday morning. Period. The dead report was what the battalion commander read to see what equipment was unavailable for work or a deployment. That would mean working late into the night – on a Friday evening.

"Get some people started on it and they should be done by tonight," he said.

A newer first lieutenant to the battalion said, "But sir, it's Friday."

He stopped. Looking around the room, Major Deshaw glared at us one by one and in a calm, low voice, said, "Gentlemen, that's what nights and weekends are for."

I looked forward to having a straight nine-to-five job with guaranteed weekends off. I was used to sitting there until the battalion commander finished, and if that wasn't until eight o'clock at night, so be it.

Looking around, I couldn't believe my new teacher peers actually had the gall to just get up and leave. The next day an email went out stating that by consensus agreement, we would start having the meetings at six thirty in the morning on Wednesdays to alleviate the issues people were having staying until the end of the meetings. That way, the meeting had to end at a quarter after seven for teachers to meet students at 7:35 a.m. when the first bell rang.

"It'll never work," Bill said to me.

"It sounds reasonable. Why not?" I asked.

"Just wait. You'll see," he answered.

The next Wednesday, the three of us were sitting there at a quarter after six. For years of my life, I was used to being places at five in the morning for physical training, alerting at two or three in the morning, and then working a normal duty day. Being at school at six thirty was easy for the three of us; it seemed like a break from what our lives had been, having collectively been sixty years or more in the military.

Dr. Weil walked in at 6:20 a.m. and smiled at us. She said, "Of course, I knew you three would be here." We were the only ones there until 6:25 a.m. A few more teachers dragged in at six thirty and they were still coming in at 6:40 a.m. The whole time Dr. Weil stood at the podium and waited, looking down. I glanced over at Bill. He smiled and said, "Now they're on *our* time." The next week we went back to the afternoon meetings.

Increasingly through that first year of teaching, I realized I couldn't continue to teach English. It *was* actually sucking the marrow out of what I had spent a lifetime loving - reading. I couldn't do what most teachers are able to do; that is, take what you can with the few students you reach and let that be enough to get you through the day. I struggled daily. If anyone who has never taught thinks they know what it's like walking into a classroom with thirty-plus teenagers - many with attitudes - they're crazy. I hear talking heads on TV constantly say, "What about schools? Why aren't they doing something?" Everyone thinks they know what schools should be doing because they went to school maybe twenty or thirty years ago. Take a class of ninth grade beginning-algebra students or a ninth grade English class and teach them from August until May, then tell me what you think. And then think about multiplying that times five or six and come up with a class load of 160 students whose papers you have to grade, and have everyone in society blame you for everything from mass shootings to obesity. Then do it for thirty or more years. Then - maybe *then* - you'd have some credibility criticizing teachers and their "Cadillac" retirements they haven't earned.

A columnist for the *Arizona Daily Star* wrote an editorial a few years later scolding the state for allowing teachers to come back after retiring. His name was Jim Kaiser, and after teaching for several years at that point, I was livid at his condescending attitude and ignorance.

He gave me a chance to put my opinion out there. The next day, I had my first letter to the editor published.

Walk in a Teacher's Shoes for a Year

Of course, Jim Kiser left out a few extremely important facts in his column of March 16. Regarding his whine "Teachers: How would you like to make an extra $25,000 and keep the same job?" We can't hire, or keep qualified teachers as it is, young or old. That's why there are openings for retired teachers. Investigate and find out how many math, science, and special education positions go unfilled every year, or are filled with long-term substitutes for lack of interested individuals, precisely because of the low starting and continuing pay. Find out how many leave the profession within a year or two. A few retired teachers who are coming back and finally earning the financial imbursement they deserve will hardly cause, as Kiser says, "a political and financial disaster." Teachers who stick it out do it out of love and concern for our future; they do it in spite of the low pay. Spend a year teaching, not engaging in a fifteen-minute observation, or walking around talking to people and students to get your biased information. Spend it actually teaching the challenging students we want to pass these standardized tests and then come back and complain about "what teachers get."

I got emails from all around the district supporting me and thanking me.

During that first year, I was also having problems with wearing the uniform in a school setting. The program was just what I hoped it would be. Bill was a great teacher and role model. We had several kids with behavior problems who were turned around, and changed their direction in life. They were kids who didn't have a compass, but badly wanted to look up to someone.

Bill was right; I instantly had several kids latch on to me. The trouble was, I didn't have the answers some of them wanted to hear. After a couple of months, I had a senior say to me, "Hey sir, it's like you want to talk us out of going in."

"Yeah, I do. I want you to wait at least a year. I missed several small engagements, just by luck. You see or hear about my working out and swimming at Davis-Monthan Air Force Base and think that it's all about traveling and getting money for college. That's true, but it comes with a price. Just know you owe them, and if you have these aspirations about going into something like special operations, just know that they'll chew you up and spit you out without any qualms. Go to Pima [community college] or even work for a year or so, before you actually go in. Make sure it's really what you want to do."

Like everyone, I didn't see 9/11 coming, but I really felt passionate about their thinking it through before listening to a recruiter and joining because they didn't have anything else going on. I remember one young man clearly; I didn't have any problem with him enlisting immediately after graduating. He lived in a trailer with his elderly grandmother, and to this day we don't know how he did it as a seventeen year old, but when she died he took care of all the funeral arrangements and kept it a secret that he was living alone for several months. He had no known location of his mother or father, and he continued to come to school and get passing grades before some bill collectors and other city officials caught up with his situation. He enlisted, and we wished him well. If someone else had an answer for him, I didn't hear it. I just didn't want to talk about the army or military anymore – I had lived it for twenty-two years. I knew I was done.

What I loved was a few of the kids. It was the special ed kids. I'd come home from work and tell Cheryl how much fun I was having hanging out with Randy, or what Joe had said to me that day. Somehow I connected with them, more than I ever thought possible. When I was working on my teaching certification, a couple of the professors asked me if I had ever thought about special ed. I didn't even really know what that meant, but protested strongly that I had no interest at all with that. Cheryl had twenty-five years' experience with special ed students and would just shake her head when I'd relay situations I'd gone through with the students in our program. "Don't do it," she'd say, smiling. "I see something happening here . . . don't go down that road."

Every day when I'd come around a corner from my second period English class to the Junior ROTC program buildings, Davy would be waiting for me. He was color coordinated day after day. He always had the same color scheme, be it blue or brown or red: socks, shirt, and shorts.

"How are you today, Mr. Veekeers? Mr. Veekeers, good to see you, good to see you. How are you today?"

"I'm doing great, Davy. How are you today?"

"I'm gut, gut. Good to see you today. How are you? Good to see you. Are you going to your office?" That would make him laugh like crazy. He'd bust up every time he mentioned my office. I didn't know if he had some idea, that he comprehended on some level, that I didn't actually deserve an office and it was a big joke that I had one, or if he just liked having the conversation, that he was part of my day and we were having an adult exchange. He was an amazing, wonderful kid, and after two hours of teaching English to sixty-plus kids who, for the most part, didn't want to learn, I needed my Davy shot every late morning. I looked forward to our exchange morning after morning.

I often thought back on one year prior to all this when my student teaching had ended and I had been asked to stay around for the next

August school year to begin English and Junior ROTC. I agreed, and asked to spend the semester as a volunteer in the self-contained special ed class. They did better than that and asked me if I wanted a job as a special ed teacher's aide. I was walking along with another assistant principal when this conversation took place.

"Would you be willing to help toilet students?" He looked over at me to see my reaction. I was assuming that meant keeping an eye on the students we had in Junior ROTC as they went into the restrooms during the day. They were self-sufficient. I think he saw that puzzlement on my face when I was thinking this through.

"No, I don't mean the kids you've been working with. We have a couple of kids - adults actually; they're twenty-year-old men - we need help lifting and changing diapers a couple times a day." I just looked at him.

"I don't know," I finally said. I figured I'd be honest. I couldn't process this right away and needed time to comprehend what it all meant.

"Well, we'll see. If you can't, then special ed isn't for you. You've seen the cool kids and now you seem to want to see the whole show. Welcome to special ed."

Chapter 5

THANKS FOR TREATING ME LIKE A SON, SIR

Our Junior ROTC class spent the spring break down at Fort Huachuca. I still had connections down there and helped coordinate the Leadership Reaction Course, the Rappelling Course, and the pool for a day. We stayed in old, dilapidated, wooden World-War-II barracks with paint peeling off, and open bays with boys on one floor and girls on the other. The kids loved it. I had two special ed students I was in charge of; the other instructors took care of the twenty or so typical students. I learned about how dependent these kids were. Freddy was a young tenth grader with fairly serious Asperger's syndrome. He would nowadays be considered to be on the autism spectrum with a mild cognitive or intellectual disability. He was a sweet, small, thin, bespectacled, extremely nervous kid, who dragged everything he needed for school around in a small suitcase.

"I know everything there is to know about computers," Freddy told me the first day we met. I believed him.

I soon learned his full-time special ed teacher, and several of his mainstream teachers had banned him from the computers in school, as we did in Junior ROTC, because he had a tendency to crash them after a couple of minutes of clicking.

"He's never spent the night away from me," his mom said at the bus when we were leaving. "But he says he trusts you. My only question is, can *I* trust you?"

"Ye-Yes, ma'am," I stammered, hoping I was right.

Joey's mom, on the other hand, had dropped him off in the morning, and neither I, nor the other three adults on the trip, had seen her in the confusion. Bill said this was normal. "Just hope she's here on Sunday afternoon when we return. We've waited hours on other field trips for him to be picked up."

Joey was moderately cognitively disabled. He was a friendly, but extremely strange, boy. Bill had unsuccessfully kept him from cutting his hair in a Mohawk style for the last two years. It was something Joey had seen in a military movie or magazine and thought it looked cool.

"He probably saw a picture of the 82nd Airborne before the drop into Normandy," Bill said. He was also unsuccessful at convincing Joey's mom to keep him from wearing battle dress uniforms daily, which they must have bought at the army and navy surplus store. His mom didn't respond to any phone calls or messages unless it was a problem elevated to the school administration level. Joey ran wild all over the district, and had for years. While running across streets without looking, cars had hit him twice, once seriously, and he spent an entire month in the hospital. He still had a limp. Bill didn't have the heart to exclude him from participating in the program.

"HOOAH!" Joey would scream at me whenever he saw me coming. I was told not to respond too energetically to his enthusiasm, so I didn't. It never lessened his fervor, though.

"You was a Ranger, they said!" he would yell in class, apropos of nothing, showing me a lopsided smile with brown, crooked, decaying teeth.

"Yeah, but we're talking about leadership and community service right now, Joey. We'll talk about that some other time." I would constantly redirect him in class. He really couldn't continue conversations beyond that initial burst.

Joey slightly sprained his ankle the first day on Huachuca. That night, I made him a bag of ice, had him lie down, and got him a couple of aspirins. Every night, I also spent time making sure Freddy's clothes were laid out for the next day, and sat with him during every meal, while never letting Joey too far out of my sight. The class ate in the Military Intelligence Dining Facility (mess hall), and the kids loved seeing the soldiers, men and women. We had several females in our program. They were some of our most motivated and serious students. Inspired kids didn't need our help. They were using the program for their own benefit, either for a college application, or intent on enlisting. Our program makes them eligible for a higher rank upon entering the military, and Bill sent one or two kids to the different academies every year.

Joey needed someone with him to transverse the meal line and make sure he got what he needed. I was hustling constantly. Every night I read to Freddy and settled him in while the other students helped with Joey when they could. I helped dress them both and made sure they took their medications every morning. After reading to Freddy, I walked back down the open bay to see how Joey was.

"Hey sir, hooah! I's kinda wet," he said as I walked up. I had taken too much time reading to Freddy and had forgotten; the ice had melted and soaked the bed and his pants. I moved him and got him changed, apologizing profusely.

The last day was rappelling up in Garden Canyon. A non-commissioned officer I worked with before I retired was in charge. We had three rappel cliffs: two for the students who were capable and motivated, and one short twenty-footer for students who were nervous or not physically strong. Freddy and Joey went with me to the shorter one. Freddy, with much encouragement, went down, and once on the ground, began laughing, singing, and dancing.

While getting briefed and suited up in his harness, Joey was all, "Yes, sah, yes sah, I's unnnerstand." The rappel master was a really nice young guy. He had gotten the correct answers out of Freddy, and I was comfortable he understood what was being asked of him. I had no such illusions with Joey.

Stepping off the side of the cliff took him what seemed like twenty minutes, and the sergeant was as patient as I've ever seen. He was used to people following directions immediately. He was intent on letting this kid complete the rappel.

"*L* position. *L* position. *L* stance," he would say intently. Joey would answer, "Yes, sah."

"He doesn't understand, man. I appreciate the effort." I tried to interject.

"He can do this, sir. You can, can't you? Just remember, knuckle to spine to break, knuckle to spine . . . "

"Okay, sah, I's ready." Joey was finally in perfect position, looking right in my eyes, and for a second I thought, *Maybe he'll do this. Cool.*

"Oh, god in heaven!" he screamed as he lunged forward. "Get me off dis mountain!"

We pulled him up, stood him up, and reassured him he was okay. I felt he was done, and enough was enough. I was done. He'd had a chance, and we could call it a day. The sergeant wasn't so easily convinced, and tried again. I was lulled into complacency with his positive attitude and perseverance - once again. "*L* position. Knuckle to spine," reassurances confirmed.

Lunging forward again - "Oh, Lord Jesus, help outta heah . . . "

At the end of the week I was exhausted. I *was* tired, but strangely serene and inspired. I felt I had accomplished more with these two kids than I had in years of instructing different skills in the army, and more than I had during any minute of any day in my English classes. On the bus ride home, I sat with both Freddy and Joey. "Did you guys have a good time?" I asked.

Freddy looked at me through his thick glasses, smiled, and actually patted me on the back. This, from a kid who pathologically spurned any type of physical contact. "Thanks for treating me like a son, sir. I had the best time of my life."

I fell in love. I knew, somehow or some way, I was going to work with these kids. I didn't completely understand it myself, but knew deep in my heart they had touched a part of my spirit, and tapped into a passion that was profound but also just plain fun. Life is hard enough for any of us, but to go through life with a serious disability is beyond what I can comprehend. These people, now students, traverse life dealing with whatever comes their way, and if I could make their lives a little nobler during their school years, it would be an honor.

Joey looked at me with a meandering head movement and finally focused on me and said, "Yeah, sah, I had a great time." He paused, and I could see he wasn't finished. He then thoughtfully whispered quietly with a nervous laugh, "I didn't care much fo dat mountain though." His mom was there waiting for us.

As the school year ended, I was sure of one thing: I didn't want to teach English, and didn't want to spend another year in uniform talking about the army. I loved the special ed kids I'd met, and treasured something about them I couldn't put my finger on.

People didn't leave Desert Hills. There was no special education job other than a resource position in science. The principal actually offered me the job knowing I shouldn't accept a science position, special education or not but this was when a teacher still could be allowed an emergency certification for two years. I looked her in the eye and said, "Dr. Weil, I'm sorry, but you can't be serious." She giggled with me.

"Well, I'm sorry, but if your heart is set, we wish you all the luck in the world, and don't hesitate to ask for a reference." After my epiphany while I was working in the Junior ROTC program I realized I loved it, so I started my master's in special ed that spring. I finished the year and applied and interviewed at a local middle school, where I immediately got hired for the next fall.

Chapter 6

SILLY, SILLY KNUCKLEHEAD

Our former silly little kitty haunts me. Now and then, I can still look out of the corner of my eye and see her skirting along a wall or passing by an open door. Every so often, I can walk into a room and feel like she's laying in one of her favorite spots, and for a moment sense her actually being there. From time to time I wait for her to jump up on the bed at night and crawl up on my chest for some loving. Occasionally I believe I can feel her rub against my leg in the morning when I'm reading the paper. At times I look for her paw to slide along under the bathroom door when I'm on the toilet, as she was wont to do; she loved being near her people, no matter the circumstance. I can still imagine her head popping up in the front window, standing on the porch bench, looking askew into the living room when we're watching TV. When she was sleeping and my wife or I would walk into the room, she'd raise her head slightly and squeak a tiny meow out in greeting and drop right back to sleep. I still expect that from her, and at times, have thought I've heard it, even though I know she's not there. In the fall of

1999, Cheryl brought her home from work after the school nurse told her some kids were feeding a newborn small kitten in the bathroom.

"Don't let that family take it home. They're completely irresponsible," she told Cheryl.

I came home that afternoon, and on the couch, there was a tiny little orange tabby kitten in Cheryl's arms. Cheryl said when she'd put her on the passenger seat, Autumn just curled up as if she knew she had a home now. I had never owned a cat. I didn't dislike them; I'd always owned dogs. I just never got close to the cats I was exposed to in my life. Cheryl and my stepdaughter Kylin had a Siamese named Blue Eyes, and he had already chased another cat away to go find a new home with a neighbor. He was old and set in his ways, and was Kylin's cat anyway. I had played with him a few times, but never really connected. The day after Cheryl brought the kitten home, Kylin made a bed for Autumn on the couch with pillows, Beanie Babies, and other sundry dolls and such. I was the first one home that afternoon. I sat down on the edge of the couch and looked at her. She looked at me, and I didn't have the faintest idea of how to communicate with a kitten. The usual "good boy" didn't seem like it would work. She just continued looking at me, so I picked up a Beanie Baby and pushed it at her face. She immediately rolled on her back and hissed, smacking at it with her little paws. I did this over and over, and each time I would stop, Autumn would look at me expectantly as if to say, "Hey, do it again. I like this." She stole my heart right then. I never looked back.

I have a picture from that time of Autumn sitting on my shoulder, so small she fits, and I'm looking down at her smiling. That's my main memory of her: her doing something outrageous, me amused, whether it was her in a bag or a laundry basket or the dryer, going through Christmas wrapping paper on the floor, or doing flips chasing a stick with a feather on it around the room, or a million other things. Whatever it was, if we brought it home, she figured it was for her. She backed Blue Eyes off and made her presence known without much of a fight. He was getting on, and she was basically crazy, so he seemed to know it wasn't a battle worth fighting.

Autumn could climb up a tree and onto our roof, which she would do several nights a week. Cheryl and I would be lying in bed and could hear her paws as she ran across the roof chasing who knows what. We didn't have a cat door for her yet, and I couldn't sleep until I knew she was safe in the house. Cheryl had had cats her whole life, so she would just say, "She's a cat. She'll be all right until morning. Leave her alone. She'll learn."

I couldn't, so I would go get the ladder and climb up to the edge of the roof and call her over. She'd saunter over just out of reach, and when I'd grab for her, she'd arch her back and prance away. The game would last for maybe five to ten minutes, and she'd eventually let me grab her. I'd rub her against my face because I could never really get or stay mad at her. I started to call her "Silly." That early summer, we noticed some spots on her ears, just rough patches.

My mom had had a total mastectomy for breast cancer in 1996 while I was in Korea, my second to last year before retirement, and seemed to be doing all right the last few years. I went home to visit early in the summer after we'd gotten Autumn, and my mom didn't really look or feel good. I was just early into my relationship with the woman I have come to love more than I ever thought possible, and early into and a new career teaching, so I thought, or hoped, she would pull out of this relapse. She didn't. By the end of the summer my dad asked me if I could come to their home in Oregon. I stayed almost six weeks. We sat down with hospice about the time I would have started my new job, and I made a deal with my dad. I would stay as long as it took and help out - that meant until my mom died, rather than have him hire a full-time nurse. Hospice in Lebanon was wonderful, but not an around-the-clock care situation. My dad could lose his savings, the house, and everything he and my mom had worked for their entire lives.

"I have my military retirement, but if things get tight back in Tucson, could you pay me a minimal wage to help us get by?" I asked my dad. He said, "Absolutely."

In my next note home, I told Kylin to take care of that knucklehead cat. That name also stuck.

Taking care of my mom around the clock my dad and I made a connection that I never thought we'd attain. I'd never felt my dad and I had much to talk about. When I was about nineteen, I read *War and Remembrance* and realized by serving on the USS *New Jersey*, he had fought in almost every major Pacific battle during World War II. After going to Germany, I read voraciously, and these last years we always had the war to talk about. During my stay and my mom's illness, we talked about things I didn't imagine guys of his generation talked about comfortably.

"Brant, back in West Virginia when I was growing up, old people just died," he said to me one afternoon sitting on the couch in the dayroom while my mom had actually fallen asleep for an hour. "They didn't suffer like this. I don't know if we're doing the right thing any-more. I don't think God intended for anyone to suffer like this."

Two uncles said the same thing to me during this period that I still think about. These were men I'd looked up to my whole life, and they were bigger than life to me.

"Brant, I don't know how you're doing what you're doing. I don't think I could do it."

I didn't see any choice in the matter. I couldn't imagine not staying and helping my dad. I'd joined the army and left home early and really never returned, only to visit once a year from wherever I was stationed. Germany, England, Korea, or the five or six different assignments all over the United States, I always managed to get home. My mom's family was intensely close, and she never lived more than a couple of blocks away from her mom. She talked to her mom on the phone at least twice a day. I was in my thirties when she told me she was over her anger, and proud that I had lived my own life, that she finally understood. She took care of me when I was a child, and there were things I didn't want my dad to have to do with his wife of over fifty years.

When we had called hospice in to help, my mom was still conscious enough to ask, "Brant, is this bad for me?"

My mom was a person who either didn't want to know the truth, or couldn't handle it. It didn't matter to me; I loved her, and if she didn't want to really talk about it, so be it. This was the closest we came to a conversation about what was going on during the whole time of her dying.

"No, Mom, this will help Dad out with the medicine and make you more comfortable."

"I think you need to get back to Cheryl and your work as a teacher, don't you?"

"No, she's fine and understands, and I'll work when I want to. I spent over twenty years in the army and have enough saved for a while. They need special ed teachers more than I need them. I'll be able to find a job anytime."

Not too long after that conversation, she lapsed into a coma. I was thankful for the time with her, and was glad she got to meet Cheryl and liked her. It had been a long hard road for me with relationships and I was pleased she could go out happy for me.

"Please, don't let her suffer," my dad pleaded with me one night. I promised him I would do my best, and thankfully hospice was very generous with morphine. We went from oral to patches to syringes to all three. I was afraid of overdosing her a couple of times and then figured, so what? I did my best to keep my promise to him, but who knows. I was liberal with dosing her, but couldn't believe someone could die a death like that and not feel pain or discomfort. But we were all together those last days.

A week after the funeral, my dad and I talked about me going back to my life in Tucson. I told him if he needed me I could come back in a day. I had a small voice deep inside telling me I was leaving too soon. I suppressed it and left. But that first night home, Autumn jumped up on my chest and looked me dead in the eyes and purred for almost an hour.

The following week, I walked into the most horrible classroom situation I have ever seen or experienced since. I had interviewed for a MIMR/MOMR class before I left which stands for "mild or moderate mental retardation," or now intellectual or cognitive disability. I walked into a class with one aide and a dozen kids, and half were emotionally disturbed. One student was full-blown autistic and had absolutely no reason to be in that class. They had dumped on me pretty good in the interval, and that's why my job was still there. They couldn't even keep substitutes for more than a day or two.

I lasted about a month. Several kids had had their labels changed to accommodate the class, and I now know this to be not only question-ably unprofessional, but illegal. One soon-to-be gang-banger named Darnell would throw his backpack at me almost daily, screaming a ra-cial epithet that didn't even make any sense, and another would run the hallways from first to sixth period. I had to keep control of the rest of the class, so I had to let him go. I called Darnell's home to talk to his mom (there was no dad in the picture) to ask some questions and ask for advice on how to help her son. I identified myself, and before I could finish what I wanted to talk to her about, she said, "I'll beat that boy blue. He'll wish he never was born."

"No, no, ma'am, that's not what I want to happen." I thought, *What the hell is going on?* While talking to her, I could hear a screaming tele-vision in the background and several other kids yelling equally as loud. Before we even had a chance to begin the conversation again about

Darnell, I heard her scream at another boy, "You best shut the fuck up, DeAndre, before I beat you blacker than you already are!"

"No, ma'am, that's okay I can call you back, or you can call me when - "

"You little motherfucker, I told you . . . " The phone sounded muted for the last few words, and I realized she had taken it away from her ear, I then realized with a sickening feeling that she was using it to beat her other son with it. Bam! Bam! Bam! Screaming Thud! Thud! Louder screaming. I could sense - I could feel - the blows through the phone. I cringed every time she hit him. I started yelling for her to stop. The phone went dead. I just sat there, not knowing what to think or do. School had just ended, and I thought Darnell was probably still on the bus. I rushed down to the counselor's office. She was in. She was in, but totally unconcerned with my predicament.

"CPS has several investigations on her and the whole family already. One more won't make a difference. She has a couple of older kids there and they have things going on you don't even want to know about. I'll call them and let them know about this one, but you don't have to do anything else. Don't worry about it."

How could I not worry about it? It made me nauseous. I felt I had caused his brother, and possibly Darnell, to get a beating, and nothing was going to be done to stop it. Darnell came in a few more days and then pulled a fake plastic gun out on the bus, pointing it at other students and threatening to kill them. He was removed from the home and from school, too.

I never once had the principal's support or help. I told the principal several times things had to change, and had a meeting with a district program specialist to see about getting the situation corrected. Both came back and told me nothing could be done.

One afternoon, when the principal had a feeling I wasn't going to stay, he called me into his office and had a phone conference with a district administrator.

"He wants to know if you can handle the classroom. I told him you seem to be doing a good job, but what do you think of the situation in the room?"

"Tell him I was in one of the most stressful, up tight units, in the armed forces, prepared to go to war, anywhere within two hours, and I'd rather be back there than stay in this 'situation in the room.'"

"I guess he's serious about leaving," the principal said to the administrator on the phone.

"Are you going to change the kids and put some of them in classes where they belong?" I asked him.

He looked me right in the eyes and said, "No, nothing's going to change."

"Something is. Consider this my two weeks notice."

I came home the last day of what I considered my teaching career, thinking I should be feeling great, but felt feverish instead. I thought, *Oh, great. Now I caught something from one of these kids as a going-away present.* During the next two to three weeks, I put together my resume, looked over job announcements online and talked to a few people, but many days I would get up in the morning, feeling like shit, and lie back down for several hours. The fever persisted, but never worsened. I went to the doctor, who did some blood tests, but naturally, couldn't find anything wrong. I talked to my dad on the phone several times a week and felt like I should still be there with him. He declined and said he was fine. I finally realized I had left him too soon, not for him, but for me. The fever was probably symptomatic of grief and depression. I couldn't imagine what he was going through. We talked on the phone more and made plans for Cheryl and me to visit that summer, and for him to come out the next winter for Christmas.

But daily there was an incredible bright spot when I would lie down on the bed to read and try to sleep off the fever. I would hear a "rruuuupppp," and Autumn would jump up on the bed. She would crawl up on my chest and look me straight in the eyes and purr. I would caress her head, and she would stay with me as long as I lay there, not sleeping, not resting, just waiting for time to pass, together. A couple of weeks later, Cheryl's parents came to visit. We were looking at putting an addition on the house, so there was some work to be done, and the fever finally broke. Autumn and I always found time to get, what Cheryl came to call, "chest time."

I continued to talk to my dad twice a week until I thought we were both over the worst of our grief. Cheryl and I went to visit him the next summer. Much later, I realized, his was a grief one doesn't get over.

Autumn's ears got worse and worse. Darker and more scab-like patches continued to form. We took her to the vet and he prescribed some cream. It didn't do anything. It started traveling down to her eyes, and he referred us to a specialist. The doctor there told us she had skin cancer. She wanted to remove her ears. We stood there in shock. She said it might give her another year or so. She couldn't promise anything more than that. I saw dollar bills floating away through the air. If I were on the outside looking in at this I knew what the logical solution would be, but Autumn was going to live as long as I could work and make it happen.

She came home from the hospital with a head that looked like a worn-out, badly stitched baseball. Cheryl burst into tears when she first saw her. Autumn toughed it out those first few weeks with the cone around her neck, stumbling around, pissed off. She eventually ended up looking like a furry otter, or some kind of fuzzy seal. She was the most amazing cat I could ever imagine, and many people who owned cats said the same. Autumn would let me hold her in my arms like a baby to either administer medicine or to check on her sores. She would walk down the street with us to visit neighbors, and was expected. It was nothing for Cheryl to come home, say hello to Silly, and then have Autumn wait in the driveway for me to arrive, just to be content all was well.

My dad was devastated after my mom died. I'm almost certain she was the only woman in his life. They met on the school bus when they were fourteen and fifteen, living in the hollows of West Virginia, and after World War II, moved to Southern California and then Oregon. They were the best parents I could have been lucky enough to have. Another summer passed, and Cheryl and I asked him if he wanted to move to Tucson with us. We'd build a guesthouse and he'd have his own space, and I wouldn't worry about him all the time. His health was getting progressively worse. We had several conversations about my mom and how much we missed her. I'm glad for that. He was also having a difficult time understanding my current career choice. It was as foreign to him as it was to me several years before I'd started down this path.

"Brant, does this mean you'll be working with mongoloids?" he innocently asked one day.

I gave him an abrupt snarky answer and immediately regretted it.

"I don't know if the kids are actually from Mongolia, but . . . " The phone was silent, and I instantly joked my way out of it. I flashed on his experience with Jerry and Danny, our next-door neighbors, and also realized he'd probably grown up calling people with cognitive disabilities "mongoloids." It wasn't a denigrating term to him. It was such an unusual choice of a teaching career, I couldn't expect him to connect, and didn't. Several years later when I became a teacher of the visually impaired, I think he was much more comfortable. I had many friends and other family that didn't quite understand either. At times, I wonder if I did.

Autumn's touch-ups were coming more frequently. She would shake her head and blood would fling around the room. We never seriously complained about cleaning it up, such was our desire to keep her going, but one day in September 2004, she had a seizure. When trying to pick her up while she was seizing, I remember asking God out loud to please let her die and not suffer. We rushed her to the emergency vet, and the obvious answer was to put her down; the tumors were probably internalizing. Cheryl had put down too many cats and pets to do it with Autumn. I stayed with her while the vet put her to sleep. I put my hand on her and said, "Oh, little Silly, you were such a good cat." I looked up and the vet had tears in her eyes.

A few weeks after I left the middle-school job, the principal at Harrogate High called and left a message, but that same afternoon, I was also offered a job at a charter school. I felt torn, and didn't want to walk into the same situation I had three weeks before. Cheryl advised me the benefits were always better at a public school and usually you received better pay. I went in to meet the principal and two supervising teachers at Harrogate. A year later, he told me that was one of the strangest interviews he'd ever conducted. It was almost like I was interviewing the school instead of the other way around. At the end of the interview I asked a question: "Can I take a tour? Because if it isn't a good fit, it's a waste of time for both of us." I was shown around, met a couple of teachers and a few kids, and got a feel for the school. The principal turned to me and asked, if I could start the next day. I asked back, "Would you like to know what happened at Nelson?" The principal, Mr. Johnson, replied with a slight chuckle. "No, that won't be necessary. I know Barney from way back. You quitting is a plus in my book."

I finished that year as a long-term substitute shuttling between classes, getting to know the four other special education teachers and the students. At the end of the year, Mr. Johnson caught me in the hallway and asked me if I wanted a permanent position the next year. I stayed at Harrogate on and off for seven years. Since I had started my master's in special education the year before while still at Desert Hills, I felt committed. That first week was shaky with Owsley, but after Bruce showed up and their schedule was set, I decided I was going to give teaching another try. I'd love to say everything was perfect, but what I've found in teaching is something else challenging always pops up. In a special ed class you can count on it; every day is different.

Harrogate School was interesting. It was a small magnet high school; it rarely had over two hundred students. We had four self-contained classes. At one time it was a pure special education school. They had afterschool dances, traded kids for classes, so the students moved around from class to class, and went to academic classes, as well as art, music, and PE. The kids loved it. In the eighties federal law forced Harrogate to integrate. It was intended to be a magnet school with a high academic program balanced with the special ed kids. It didn't come close to filling those expectations, despite the diligence of (during my time) three principals. The district dumped - and I hate using the word - on Harrogate High School with impudence. Due to the small class size, students that had been kicked out of two other high schools would be welcomed. Parents who wanted their kids to be watched every minute thought our school was great. We had no sports, music, or any other extra curricular activities. Harrogate did have an excellent hearing-impaired program, and students who went through it went on to be successful at the University of Arizona program. It was said one time that the definition of normal for our school was that a kid didn't have a parole officer. It was normal to have a police car at the school every couple weeks.

Chapter 7

PRINCIPALS I'VE KNOWN, AND SCHOOLS

It seems simple to say, but principals are only as good as they are. In eighteen years, I've had more or less excellent principals. I've had eight at four different schools. Two times I've moved because of either self-contained classrooms closed, or school closure, and twice for better opportunities. A principal is the school leader. It's all about making influential, sometimes unintended, but important contributions to student learning. Teachers become principals for various reasons: some for money, some for an excuse to get out of the classroom, and some because they truly care about making a difference. Principals are actually more than leaders. Whether they like it or not, teachers depend on principals to resolve all the problems, enforce state and federal (usually unfunded) mandates - dealing with parents, finances, and curriculum - answer for state, federal, and school test scores, and resolve the complications of weak teaching and - one of the biggest for teachers - student misbehavior.

Principals build structure, and make sure those systems work reliably - systems for keeping students from falling through the cracks, systems for helping teachers grow professionally, and systems for dealing with the countless problems that unavoidably happen in a building full of hundreds of complicated, wonderful, but sometimes extremely confused, to criminal, young people. Only one person in a school building has this control over culture and change, and that is the school principal. Their control or change is dictated through training and force of personality. I have witnessed both ends of the spectrum of competence of principals. Brilliant, capable, and competent administrators can encourage transformation and ardent learning, while disastrous ones can damage a school's culture and destroy teachers. I've seen teachers intimidated and burned out without support and help.

A friend asked me if I had seen the movie *Waiting for Superman*. I immediately asked why. It was so much bullshit. A number of things led me to this opinion, not the least of which has been teaching for the last eighteen years in public schools. We, as a society, have been fed a number of lies concerning our schools: American public education is a failed venture. The difficulty is not money. Public schools already spend too much. The talking heads continue to beat the drum that test scores are low because there are so many bad teachers, whose jobs are defended by powerful unions. I live in a right-to-work state with an almost nonexistent union, and if that were true, Arizona's schools would be doing well. The talking heads that opinionate that students drop out because the schools fail them, but they could achieve virtually anything if they were rescued from bad teachers. They would get higher test scores if schools could fire more bad teachers and pay more to good ones. We make some arbitrary decision about who decides who's a bad teacher, and at times, it can be based on test scores. Society, and lately school critics, media, and most politicians from both parties, constantly lament teacher unions, the inability to fire *bad* teachers, poor instruction, and test scores. I'm not sure where our society thinks it's going to accrue teachers in the future. We already get more than we pay for, and I've only seen a few bad teachers in my eighteen-year career. Most bad teachers take themselves out of the equation. If you aren't cut out for it, it can be one of the most stressful jobs in the world.

Ask a parent or concerned citizen what percentage of time a student spends in school. Work it out from ages five to eighteen, six and a half hours a day, 185 days a year: that is, assuming perfect attendance, and taking for granted that they are taken care of and don't suffer from small little problems and disadvantages, such as poverty, homelessness, poor nutrition, unemployed or absent parents, criminal households, or disabilities. Maybe we all believe all children are tucked into bed at night and read to. If you do, you'd probably still guess inaccurately the amount of time schools have our children and young adults. Most people I've asked, including myself when first hearing this statistic, guess wrong. Only about 7.5 percent of their lives are spent in school from kindergarten to twelfth grade. It's amazing we do what we can with kids.

The movie *Waiting for Superman*, I understand, follows five students and their families. The argument is already over in my mind. You mean, you actually have five families, parents, or surrogates caring about how their students do in school? If they care, chances are, the kids will do well wherever they end up. In the worst schools in the United States there are still kids getting into college, and if a single one does, what's the reason for that? Did they slip through the system with the only good teachers in the whole school? Or did they do what has been happening for decades, in the face of the purported facts, that are actually lies about teachers and schools? I've seen students' performances in school be principally determined by their own labors and by the conditions of their family, not by their teachers. There always have been, and will always be good teachers and mediocre teachers, even bad teachers. The ratio of good ones to bad ones is a better percentage than I've seen of lawyers, police officers, judges, doctors, and politicians, and yet all of those professions get paid far better. As they always have and continue to do, public schools present abundant opportunities for an education to those eager to pursue it.

Yearly, we come out with statistics that reveal further trepidation that the nation is falling behind in global competition, and that our math and science scores are ranked in the bottom of every survey or inquiry. If there are no jobs, there is a recession, or poverty continues in large numbers, and the list goes on and on. It all falls back on schools' being to blame. Schools are our permanent perpetrator on which to focus our rancor and annoyance when we sense that something is going askew in our society, that we are going in the wrong direction, or that we are losing the competition for global supremacy. It is not globalization or deindustrialization or poverty or our infantile popular culture or predatory economic practices that bear responsibility; it's the public schools, their teachers, and their unions. How is it that we do rank so low in our national and global test scores? The question is so easily answered; it amazes me year after year that more talking heads don't answer the question honestly. When I was first in Germany in 1977, I was driving with a friend of mine to a cross-country race in a small Bavarian town. We happened to be driving there in a brand-new Mercedes Benz 450 SL, going about 140 miles per hour on the Autobahn. I asked Klaus Dieter where he went to college.

He laughed and said, "I didn't go to college."

"Why not?"

"I was tracked out of gymnasium and sent to Realschule and have been working for Messerschmitt ever since."

"What's Realschule?" I asked.

"It's vocational. That's what happens to you here if you're not an academic student, and I wasn't."

"But you've done all right, haven't you?"

"Yeah, I have a great life."

"Could you go back to school if you wanted to?"

He laughed.

I realized I would have been one of those students tracked out of school by eighth grade if the United States were on that system. We aren't on that system, and we test those students, who aren't academically inclined with everyone else in our schools. That includes students with learning disabilities (auditory/visual processing, ADHD, dyslexia, dyscalculia, dysgraphia, dysphasia/aphasia, dyspraxia, or sensory integration disorder), and students with more severe disabilities such as (autism, emotional, oppositional defiant, and dozens others causing cognitive/intellectual disabilities from mild to moderate to severe and profound if their parents either don't allow testing to identify, or allow their kids to have a label they find objectionable). When these students' test scores go into that school's average, and then the district's, and the state's, and on to the national average, we all scratch our heads and wonder why we purport to do so badly in relationship to the world. In every self-contained class I've had in the last eighteen years, I've had at least one or two students who were forced to take, and through no fault of their own, fail state-mandated standardized tests. This is true in every self-contained class, along with most typical classes with students who are either improperly labeled or not labeled when they should be. If we were able to test only our top, say, 10 percent or even 20 percent of students, we'd rank much differently in the world, as Germany and most competitive countries effectively do, with students like Klaus Dieter, simply routing out students into track programs that suit them. This way, they're only testing the top 10 - 20 percent. This is what we are competing with worldwide.

Chapter 8

TEACHING AT HARROGATE

After my principal Mr. Johnson helped me in an extraordinary way, for which I was grateful, with the Owsley situation, things were moving along smoothly. But then I sadly discovered he was basically a bully. He had driven out several good teachers, who had interestingly found work in other schools and were thriving. His favorite deal was making teachers cry. This was mostly directed at females, as most teachers in schools are still overwhelmingly female. My first year was rolling along, and one of my students was a sweet young guy with cerebral palsy. Jackson was severely and profoundly intellectually disabled, completely quadriplegic. He was non-verbal, made almost no eye contact, and wouldn't engage in any activity. We made his time in school as worthwhile as possible and included him in everything we did during class projects. The one issue with Jackson was noise. He made a medium-to-loud droning din constantly. It would get on anyone's nerves, and it definitely got on all my aides' and other students' nerves eventually. It could, and would, go on for hours.

We made a schedule for all of us to take him on walks in his wheel-chair, and switched off whenever we could see someone was at the end of their rope after hearing him for an hour or two. It was working out pretty well. Jackson, I felt, was as involved in as much as possible and got out in the sunshine and cruised the school throughout the day. His mother was happy with his involvement and how we were taking care of him. She regularly told me if he hadn't slept and needed to nod out once or twice a day. Secretly, some of us prayed he would crash for an hour or two. It never happened. Fifteen to twenty minutes was the only reprieve we ever got. One day I was out of the room with another student, and when I returned, two of my aides were in the room.

"Mr. Johnson was here."

"Did he want anything?"

"He looked around." I was learning most of the aides had been chewed out by Mr. Johnson or treated disrespectfully. They usually didn't engage in conversation with him unless addressed first. I learned to understand why.

"What was happening?"

"We were working with Jackson and Aiden, but Jackson was nap-ping and woke up a minute after he left." Jackson's mom had told me that particular day, that he hadn't sleep at all the night before, and she looked exhausted when she'd brought him in. I thought if Mr. Johnson needed anything he'd get back with me, so I went on with the day. I forgot all about it.

I always arrived at school, and still do, long before most of my peers. Years of being at work or physical training at five in the morning, and never being late for anything, much less a workday, was ingrained into my character and ethic at an early age. As I was walking down the hallway, I was surprised to see Mr. Johnson walk-ing toward me.

"Good morning," I said.

"I'll tell you if it's a good morning or not, and I don't think it is. Ah, I dropped by your room yesterday and couldn't believe what I saw. I don't ever want to see anything like that again. That's totally unacceptable in my school, and if you continue with that kind of thing . . . " As he was saying this, his voice was raising an octave or two with each word, until it was close to yelling.

"Whoa, whoa," was all I could think to say, along with putting my hand up in front of his face. I seriously couldn't think of what he was talking about. Then it dawned on me: He might be talking about Jackson.

"Are you talking about Jackson?" I asked.

"Yeah, and don't think you can - " he started.

"I said, *whoa*," I said intensely. "Are you hungover or something?"

He looked at me with astonishment. I started laughing.

"You don't talk to me like that. You're some rinky-dink principal in some rinky-dink high school. Let me tell you something, I had to deal with professional assholes for the last twenty years. I've had soldiers like General Barry McCaffrey practically spit in my face, and I had to stand there and take it and say, 'Yes, sir' and 'No, sir.' I don't have to do that anymore. If you don't want me here, I'll leave right now."

"No, no, that's not what I mean," he started.

I was on a roll now, though.

"I'll tell you another thing. If I've done something wrong, I can take my ass chewed. But we talk first, and you find out what was going on with that kid before you make a judgment on whether it was right for him to crash for a few minutes."

"Okay, okay." He turned around and walked back toward his office.

I found out later this was his modus operandi. He'd start in on a teacher, and if they didn't, or in most cases couldn't, stand up for themselves, he'd own them. Over twenty years in the army had prepared me for somebody like Mr. Johnson. I also had a luxury most teachers don't have: I really could leave and find either another teaching job, or something else completely different. Teachers who have been working in the job for ten to fifteen years are at times at the mercy of a bad - or worse, *incompetent* - principal. A principal might have moved on from teaching because they couldn't hack the classroom, but have all the bells and whistles, interviews well, and spout the educational philological discourse of the day to get the job, even when they have no business making leadership decisions or simple skills working with people.

Mr. Johnson and I got along beautifully after that. Many times he asked me to join him for a beer after work on Fridays. Our security guard had the same kind of run-in with him. He was a retired sheriff, and after the second time Mr. Johnson yelled at him in front of students, they went into his office. When Sam slammed the door and then slammed his hand down on the desk, Mr. Johnson completely backed off, and never spoke in a loud or condescending voice to Sam again. Mr. Johnson could make things happen, but he was a bully and made many teachers' lives miserable for no reason other than power.

My next principal was one of the best I've ever seen. He was good and fair, and we had an excellent rapport. He was a politician, though. He said he'd stay five years and he lasted two. He'll be a superintendent some day. I gave him some practice at that job by firsthand demonstrating what problems a smart-ass teacher could cause him within a minute. A few weeks into his first year, I was pushing Jackson in his wheelchair down the hallway when I noticed two suits coming in from the opposite direction. Mr. Smallwood stopped and said, "Dr. Tanner, I want to introduce you to one of our excellent special ed teachers. Brant, this is Superintendent Dr. Tanner. He's here for a meeting that seems to be misplaced."

"Nice to meet you. It's nice to see and meet some of our unheralded teachers in the district," he said while shaking my hand. We all stood there for a second.

"Brant's doing a great job for us here, and I'm glad to have him on staff."

"This is Jackson," I interrupted.

"Oh, hi, how are you doing Jackson?" Dr. Tanner mumbled, and I could tell he didn't know what to do or say with a kid as disabled as Jackson.

"I was taking Jackson to the bathroom to toilet and change his diaper. Would you want to help? You can lift his legs in the classic two-person lift?" I said, smiling.

They both stood there staring at me.

"I'm kidding," I said, laughing, and started to push Jackson between them. "It was nice meeting you. Take it easy." Mr. Smallwood came up to me later, laughing, but saying he couldn't believe I'd done that. I told him that since Tanner was an interim superintendent it wouldn't hurt his career.

"That's okay, he was lost and came to our school by mistake looking for a meeting, but please, please, don't do anything like that again."

That same year with all the other problems we resolved one by one with Owsley, we had one we didn't see coming. At the end of the day Bruce would show up and put Owsley on the bus, literally, with a minute or two to spare. The less time he had to sit in his seat and wait for other students (thankfully there were only two other kids on the bus), the healthier for us all. The drivers were extremely nervous with him on the bus, but once they started moving he'd usually be okay. Later in the year we had a new student on his bus, or she had recently moved: Bruce and I never found out. We had no understanding why she was so intent on triggering him to go off. I tried to talk to her and make her understand that it was an immoral and malicious thing to do, but we realized she simply deliberately wanted to set him off. Every student in our school had seen us restrain him at some time during the last couple of years. She would purposely be late to the bus. Bruce and I would stand back and try not to let Owsley see us waiting. After a couple of minutes I would usually go look for her. By this time I found out her name was Saige, and she would either be walking the hallways, or talking to friends who didn't ride the bus. She would blow me off and then saunter slowly to the bus bay.

I went to our principal at the time, Mr. Smallwood, and he said, "The bus only has to wait until three ten, and then they are free to go, unless other arrangements have been made and she has told someone to have it wait - and that's only for special circumstances." I later found out she was having problems with several teachers, and her mother had screamed at him numerous times. He wasn't sympathetic to Saige's issues. We relayed the message to the bus driver the next day.

"Are you telling me I have permission to leave on time today?" he asked after we told him about the time.

"I know that I was trying to be nice waiting for her, but I don't want another take down on the bus, or for that matter, to be attacked again. I'm off, then. It's fifteen after." Bruce and I waved as he drove off. Not a minute later, Saige came running out screaming.

Bruce and I wrote up a statement. It happened a couple more times and Saige's mom would have to come pick her up while she waited in the office, once, for a couple of hours. The district, transportation, and our principal won the battle. Saige stopped being intentionally late for the bus.

I had several conversations with Mr. Smallwood about my future. A couple of times he actually raised his voice to me. It was a good chewing-out, though. He just thought I should look forward to administration.

"You should be a principal. You're wasting your leadership abilities. We need good principals, and with your background, you'd be a great one," he said.

"I've done that already and I don't want to put in the time fighting with parents and bureaucrats. I just want to work with kids and be a classroom teacher. I'm looking at spending less time doing paperwork rather than more. Can't you understand that?" I asked.

"No, I'm always going to think of you as being a lost possibility for leadership." I've always appreciated those words, but have never regretted my choice.

The next year we met Bobby Keeter. He was a first-time principal, and was also one of the best, but had one of the worst first years I've ever seen. He went by "Bobby." He was one of the few African-American principals in Tucson. No biggie to me, I worked with minorities for over twenty years in the service. I liked him a lot. He had a hell of a time as a principal. It started the second day of school. You can't tell what a principal is going to be like from the first meetings. Bobby seemed fine. The same student who purposely attempted to set off Owsley, Saige, started the year with a bang. We would get several students every year that had been kicked out of other high schools, and several gang bangers walked our hallways. Most times they would take themselves out through criminality, truancy, or eventually an act that would get them expelled. That year we started with two Hispanic girls, who anyone with any sense saw as real gangbangers. We later found out their dad, uncles, brothers, and basically everyone they knew was in one of the south side gangs. They were tatted up and only in eleventh grade; well, maybe chronologically they should have graduated several years earlier. For some reason, Saige took it upon herself to welcome them to our school. She did this, and no one was ever able to fathom why, by blowing kisses at them. She did it a half-dozen times throughout the first day of school. Other kids told investigators later, she was able to hear them threatening her in both English and Spanish; she ignored them the same way she ignored me when I was trying to stop her from setting Owsley off.

People think teachers can stop bullying without students' telling them they're being bullied. What most people don't understand is we can't stop it if we don't see it. It can happen in a second, during passing periods, in class while the teacher is focused on actually teaching, and continue for years if a teacher doesn't see it. Most teachers will do something about it if they witness it first hand. Unfortunately, we don't usually see it until it's too late. What would be nice would be if parents raised kids who didn't feel the need to bully other kids. Saige wasn't exactly bullying these two girls, but they thought she was crazy, and at the end of the second day, they caught her in a hallway only a few feet from where two teachers were standing in their doors welcoming students into their rooms. It took all of thirty seconds. They grabbed her long hair, slammed her to the floor, and started kicking her in the face, back of the head, and back. She had cracked vertebrae, contusions, and sundry other bruises. They were out of school, never to return.

Saige thought she'd return a hero. It didn't turn out that way; every opinion seemed to lean toward, "She brought it on herself." Her mom went on a rampage. She demanded Bobby be fired for letting it happen. She organized a protest outside the school and had about four kids in tow, two of which were her own children. The signs stated that safety concerns at our school weren't being addressed, and that her angel was assaulted and there were no consequences for the students who attacked her. Charges had in fact been filed and it was going through the court process. The *Tucson Rag* ran a biased article (without talking to anyone at the school who had witnessed the entire incident, of course) that was published the next week. In the weeks that followed the school was lined up with only two teachers openly judging Bobby and siding with the mother. They were publicly deriding Bobby to the students in their classes. They were spreading rumors about Bobby that I didn't think were either true or substantive. They were accusing him of proselytizing, and everyone I talked to didn't hear it. During this time period, I woke up one morning with swollen wrists and ankles. Within a week I was on an incredible new innovative drug that would put a previously unidentified flare-up of rheumatoid arthritis in submission. I had to miss a couple of days, and when I was explaining this to Bobby, he blurted out, "I'll be praying for you."

I looked at him without offense and said, "Thank you. I'll let you know what they say."

"Please do," he returned. I didn't feel anything other than a considerate, caring man who was genuinely giving me a heartfelt comfort. I was wondering if this was what the assholes were having a problem with. The talk wouldn't die down. He was under a lot of stress and it showed. I felt for him. I didn't think he was being given a fair shake, and couldn't understand why a couple of teachers were doing this. Against my better judgment, I had promised myself that I would never get involved in school politics during my teaching career, but I couldn't stop myself. I sent a letter to the Governing Board.

From: Teachers, Staff, Concerned Parents, and Harrogate High School:
We would like to express our unequivocal support for Mr. Bobby Keeter, the principal of Harrogate High School. The incident (fight) that took place weeks ago has not been allowed to fade or die down due to the efforts of a small minority of parents/students that seem to have lost sight of the purpose of a public school. The real disruption to the educational process and day-to-day routine at Harrogate are these few misguided individuals. They need to move on and allow our school to return to the comfortable, safe environment, it has been and would be, if they would stop propagating what now are untruths and a personal vendetta against Bobby Keeter. We have seen nothing but a caring - at times, emotional, but professional educator doing what

is best for the students and staff at our school. We support his discipline policies and feel they are needed at our school. We have not had proper time to get to know him as much as we need to because of these issues not being allowed to run a natural course. Thank you very much for your time.

My aides carried the letter around and got signatures. The signatures filled three pages and were signed by all but the two teachers, and as many parents as we could find. We received a letter of thanks from the same interim superintendent that I had asked to help toilet Jackson.

In conjunction with this event going on at our school, Cheryl wrote a letter to the *Tucson Rag*.

Don't Like Harrogate? Go Somewhere Else

In response to the piece on Harrogate High School: The last time I looked, Harrogate High School was a magnet school, which means students attend voluntarily. If [Saige's mom] is so unhappy with the school, or feels it is such an "unsafe" environment for her daughter, then she has the option to pull her out and put her back in her neighborhood school. What specifically does she want the school to *do* now? Mr. Keeter and staff followed district-wide procedures. It would have been a better article had the writer interviewed other staff and students at Harrogate High School and had gotten their opinions on how "safe" they feel at this site. Students were actually picketing at the same time he was there, stating that the whole incident has gotten "ridiculous," and indeed things are being done to assure the campus is a safe place. It seems the writer and company has a hidden agenda, doesn't it?

Things settled down after that for a week or two. We still had a tough school with tough students, and every year we were getting more challenging students. Throughout one day a few weeks later, I noticed a preponderance of cop cars and school safety sedans. That evening we got an email asking us to be there a few minutes early the next morning for a meeting. Bobby came in the next morning with a district security officer and two supervising teachers in tow. He told us that yesterday a note was found on a student's car stating the note writer had a gun, and then the note trailed off incoherently. Bobby had immediately called school security and was told to wait before initiating a lockdown. Upon arrival, the security officer called Tucson Police and was told to wait also. Both professional officers determined after interviewing several students that the threat was not real and there was no endangerment for the school. We all sat there in stunned silence and processed the information. It was established that it was bad joke and the students responsible were being dealt with. It gives one a sick feeling to know that teaching could jeopardize one's life and that there are students who continue to resort to such horrendous violence. Suddenly the English teacher who had been at the forefront of trying to undermine Bobby over the fight stood up.

"I have a hard time accepting your continued non-action in these circumstances. Yesterday mid-morning, my students spoke to me about the possibility of a gun on campus and you, *sir*, did nothing!"

For a moment we all continued to sit there processing this outburst, but before I could think about it, I stood up.

"Wait a minute. Let's get this straight. Your students told you about a gun on campus in the morning and you, *sir*, did nothing, much less think the right thing to do was pass that information on!" I shouted back. The room erupted. The clamor took several minutes to die down. I calmly sat down and observed. I saw an ever-so-slight smirk cross Bobby's mouth for a second.

A couple of hours later, Bobby was walking down my hallway and as I was walking toward him, a big smile broke out on his face. He shook my hand and all he said was, "He didn't see that coming, did he?"

Chapter 9

I CAN READ AT A TWELFTH GRADE LEVEL

One morning early before the first bell, from out of the back door we heard a bunch of yelling outside. I walked out the back door of our room and saw two kids fighting right outside. A couple of kids were watching, and the new resource teacher Ms. Adams was yelling and crying as she watched them roll around on the ground. She was bent over like she was going to try to break them up.

"Stop. Oh, please stop. Someone stop them!"

These were the ones I politically incorrectly and inappropriately called the "Chronics," a group of kids who were always late and ditching class. Our security guard, Sam, and monitors would spend all day long trying to round them up and get them back in class.

One kid had the other on the ground in a headlock and was slugging him, not too hard, but hard enough to make it look bad. I surmised it was bad enough to make him sore, or maybe give him a small black eye, but not hard enough to really do any damage. I walked over real slow and patted the new teacher on the shoulder and said, "Don't touch them, and let them fight."

"You don't want to stop it? He's hurting him!" she yelled.

"Don't ever get between two kids fighting," I said. I took a step toward the kids. "Stop, don't do that," I said in a quiet, calm voice. The kids kept fighting and rolling around.

"Please stop," I said again. Then I turned to Bruce and said loudly, "Do you have your cell phone handy? Go ahead and call nine-one-one and get the police here. They aren't going to stop." I winked at Bruce at the same time.

As I hoped, they stopped right away, and one of the kids jumped up, the one on top, and started yelling at me.

"You don't call the police on me, motherfucker."

"Okay, stop fighting then," I said. I turned to the new teacher and said, "I'll help you write up the referral in my room and we can talk about it."

"Bof u' can kiss my ass," the kid said and walked toward us. As the kid balled up his fists and stepped in close, I turned around and stopped. He wasn't very big and didn't even look that threatening – I decided to stand my ground. I wouldn't do this every time, but when I looked at the boy he was beating up, I made a split second decision that he was a punk. The kid still on the ground was small and skinny.

"You don't know me and I don't care what you two motherfuckers do. You don't mean shit to me," he said.

I started laughing. "That's all you got? That's it?" I asked.

"Fuck you, motherfucker!" the kid yelled. He looked like he was coming in closer. I wouldn't do what I did next very often, and probably never again, but I'd decided he wasn't going to do anything. Now, I could have been wrong with a different student and gotten a broken jaw for the wrong decision.

I stuck my chin out and pointed to it and said, "Go ahead, you got one shot. Go for it."

The kid stopped cold and looked at me.

"Go ahead," I said again. "One shot."

The kid abruptly backed up a step and said, "I can read at a twelfth-grade level, I know what you're trying to do."

"You're right. It's aggravated assault, and a class-one felony in Arizona, and you'll leave here in handcuffs, so let's call it over and walk away," I said and started laughing again. That really pissed him off again, but he didn't step up, and the new teacher and I walked into my classroom and I helped her fill out the referral slip and was telling her what to do when a fight broke out.

"Never get in between two kids fighting - you can get yourself in a world of trouble. It's unfortunate, but we can't lay hands on kids. Ever. And you could get yourself seriously hurt."

"What if one is really hurting the other?" Mrs. Adams asked.

"I know it's a hard distinction, but you can't afford to touch kids, especially high school kids who will tell their parents that you tried to hurt them. If one kid is really hurting the other, let them know you're calling the police - not the office, or the monitor, or even school security - they know we can't do anything to them. It has to be the police, and Bobby won't like it - most principals don't - but do what you have to do."

"I know, I heard he doesn't even like to suspend kids anymore," she said.

"Yeah, most principals don't. They're only worried about their stats, and don't even care if kids cuss at a teacher anymore. It's all about looking good and pretending the things that are happening in schools aren't happening. They're calling it 'restorative behavior management,' but what it is, is letting kids get away with violence and attitude, and then later they'll blame the teachers. But remember, don't ever touch a kid, yell, or threaten them. Tell them you're going to call the police, but don't ever touch. I learned that the hard way one time."

"What happened?"

"When I was at Desert Wells, I stopped two middle-school kids one time and pushed them apart. One came at the other again, and I pushed him back again, and the next day I was in the office apologizing to his dad about how I'd used too much force in stopping his kid from pounding another kid in the cafeteria. Not that his kid was a little shit who lied and got in fights every other day," I said, laughing. "These days parents will defend their kid regardless of the facts and how wrong their little darlings were. They'll wait it out, and one day they'll be telling it to a judge."

"What do you think will happen to Tyson for this today?" she asked.

"What? You mean assaulting another student, using profanity at two teachers, and threatening another?" I answered. "Probably not much."

Over a week later, I got a piece of paper in my box. On it written in decidedly *not* twelfth-grade script was, "Mr. Vikeers, i'm sorry what I did. Tyson."

Ms. Adams resigned three months later.

Chapter 10

FLKS I HAVE KNOWN

Having Cheryl in my life has been a gift, personally and professionally. Her decades of experience have been an invaluable resource and help. Her father, Chester, was the inspiration for her career, and as one of the most hard-working speech pathologists she has known, one of the best role models she could have had when starting her career. He witnessed the evolution of the legal system as it applies to special education and it's beginning in the late 1960's that spun from the discrimination and segregation of disabled children from the public schools' regular classrooms. They were excluded from school because of their disabilities. Parents started to petition their legislators about this violation of their children's civil rights. Legislation was written and passed with money behind it to include special students in the public schools instead of separation buildings that housed only handicapped students. The new law, PL194-142, was passed in 1975, and would begin to fund states to educate these students in the regular schools, but mostly in separate self-contained classes.

He told Cheryl a story one time about the first years when he was working on his PhD, and then training other graduate students in rural Ohio in the sixties and early seventies. He was sent to ferret out children who weren't attending public school for myriad reasons, and simply, also, wanted to inform parents that he could and would supply services for them (as he would hunt and rummage for doctor and hospital records for these neglected and ignored students with a multitude of speech and other disabilities). It was hard to find much written, not only schools, but also the medical profession didn't offer much for these children or people, such as services or support. When Chester would find a copy of an examination or page of a medical report or statement describing a visit, he started noticing something written on the bottom of the paper that confused him. Several times he would see the letters "FLK" scribbled at the end of a narrative. He was finally able to ask a doctor somewhere - he can't remember now - who said it:

"What does this mean?" he asked, pointing at the initials scrawled, almost illegible.

"What?" the doctor asked, peering down at the lower part of the report.

"'FLK.' I've seen it several times and don't understand what it refers to."

"Oh, 'FLK' - extreme professional etymological terminology, or maybe simply jargon," the doctor replied, smiling. "It stands for 'funny looking kid.'"

"What?" Chester asked.

"It means we don't have a clue as to what's going on with this kid."

Chapter 11

JULIO RUNS THROUGH THE FIRE
TELLING ME TO JOIN THE UNION

My first day on the job, at Harrogate, after all I'd looked forward to, was traumatic; not for me, but for an aide I was to have the next year. I hadn't even met Owsley yet. That morning when I was walking to the buses after talking to Mr. Johnson for a moment, I saw Julio running toward the nurse's office with a student in a wheelchair, running in a panic. Several other aides were trailing him. Later in the day, after already having dealt with Owsley running around, I learned what had happened. Aiden had cerebral palsy, and was non-verbal, severely disabled, and extremely medically fragile.

He came off the bus with a handkerchief covering his face. Julio, his one-on-one aide, asked what the problem was, and the bus monitor (all special education buses must have a monitor) told him that Aiden's mom thought there was too much dust blowing around. The monitor, Jerry, thought that was strange, but it being Tucson in August, didn't think much else about it, a tragic mistake with over a year of consequences for the school and Jerry. Julio took the handkerchief off immediately and realized Aiden wasn't breathing. He ran him to the nurse, and that's what I witnessed. Aiden was dead. The fire department was called, but to no avail, and he was transported to the hospital. Julio started in my class the next year, and every couple of weeks for over a year he would tell me a lawyer was here and he had to make another sworn statement.

"I tell them the same thing every time," he'd say. "They think I'm going to change my story."

"Well, since you're telling the truth, there's nothing to change," I'd reply.

Aiden's mother was suing the school district and everyone who had had anything to do with Aiden that morning. She finally lost the battle when it was conclusively proven that Aiden had passed away during the night, and when she put him on the bus she must have known he was dead. The handkerchief was - and she was initially successful in that ruse - covering up the fact that he wasn't breathing. I was already struggling with this career choice. When I did finally decide to stick with it, I also decided to join our mostly non-existent union, if only for the help from union lawyers, if necessary.

Chapter 12

BOUNCING BELLIES

After the first week with Owsley, I got to know my other students. I had two boys with Down syndrome. Their names were Mason and Lucas. Both were sweethearts. Lucas could be extremely stubborn at times, but was usually very good-natured. They went swimming one period and had to be monitored - not helped, but motivated to hustle. They would take their sweet time about moving from point A to B, all the time. We had a therapeutic pool with our lifeguard, Jim, monitoring the kids, and gave them activities if they could participate, or let them float around if that was all they could do. The pool was only three to four feet deep, and an aide or two was always in the pool with them, along with the Jim. I already had a different attitude and philosophy than many of my peer teachers, and as a teacher, I helped do everything that I asked aides to do. That included toileting, walking the students to a class when I could, going to lunch with them, and forsaking my planning period if necessary, and sitting down and actually working with the students. Many special education teachers feel they are above those activities, and feel that supervising the kids is their only job. I had to be other places during the pool period, but felt I could easily be back to help Mason and Lucas change after the period ended.

I walked in and helped them get out of the pool. Both Mason and Lucas had the typical large bellies that teenage Down syndrome boys get if their diets aren't closely scrutinized by parents. I took them into the gym locker room, and as it was the middle of the day and we didn't have another physical education class taking place, I gave them some privacy and walked out into the hallway to talk to Jim. We talked about swimming and the pools in the area. I swam laps a couple of times a week, and we knew some triathletes in common, and so we were talking for a few minutes and then I lost track of time. Suddenly he asked me, "Did someone pick up Mason and Lucas?"

"No, they're showering and changing."

His answer was immediate. "No, no, no, you don't leave them alone for a minute in the locker room." He started moving toward the door. I followed closely. We walked in, looked down the corridor, and saw Mason and Lucas standing facing each other, naked, laughing loudly, snorting, and bumping bellies. They would bump and then laugh and stand back and snort and do it again, all while the water was running over them. We both yelled to stop it and get dried off and get dressed. They laughed the whole time they were getting dressed.

"They probably haven't moved on to touching each other, but it's only a matter of time," Jim told me. "You have to know the difference between giving them some privacy and giving them a little too much time to start experimenting." I was to learn these kids have the same feelings other teenagers have, but don't have an outlet or the ability to process that what they're feeling is normal. They also didn't have the ability to process what they can do at school and what they couldn't. There are boys this age with more severe disabilities, who think nothing of masturbating whenever they feel like it, and that can be often.

In the years that followed, I was amazed graduate programs rarely addressed sexuality issues with the cognitively disabled. But then professors, who probably have never actually experienced working with students in a school setting, teach them.

Chapter 13

GRANGER AT THE ELVIS PRESLEY CHAPEL

Halfway through my first year of teaching at Harrogate High School in Tucson, I got word I was getting another student.

"I won't lie to you," my principal said. "He's involved in a lawsuit at another school. His parents didn't think the school prepared him properly for transition. He failed the remedial tests at Pima Community College, so they're demanding he continues in High School. He can stay two more years after this one. He's only nineteen."

"What else should I know?" I asked.

"Too much for you to take in now. He'll be here tomorrow, just take some time and get to know him."

Granger was wheeled in off the bus. I had prepared my aides; I had five that year. We now had nine kids; two kids with cerebral palsy in wheelchairs (not counting Granger), two with Down syndrome, two with Fragile X, one with Angelman syndrome, and one with Coffin-Lowry Syndrome. Granger had cerebral palsy. The brain damage is caused by brain injury or abnormal development of the brain that occurs while a child's brain is still developing — before birth, during birth, or immediately after birth. Cerebral Palsy affects body movement, muscle control, muscle coordination, muscle tone, reflex, posture and balance.

Granger was dirty and he smelled awful. He drooled constantly and he had a real hard time keeping his head up due to weak neck muscles. Granger wore a colorful, but frayed and worn-out bandana around his neck to help catch the saliva, but we had to change it several times a day. His bandana and shirt were usually soaked through within an hour or two. He reeked of cigarettes, and he obviously didn't smoke.

He had no control over his urinary tract or bowel movements. We had to change him two to three times a day. Granger struggled to do most everything; he had no use of either arms or legs, and without intense physical therapy, many quadriplegics collapse in on themselves from lack of use. Granger would only receive these services during school hours; nothing was ever followed up at home. I was later to find out these issues were common, and the parents who took control and added to - even surpassed - what the schools are able to provide have children who are happier. For those students whose physical therapy was followed though, I saw their physical regression decrease and slow down considerably. At that time, Granger used a head pointer (a band strapped around his head with a rod fitted with a tip to press buttons) on a device called a liberator, which had a language of its own, using semantic prediction and picture association, with voice output. Technologies are much different now, and the landscape and technological advances were changing rapidly in 2001. Technology is helping the disabled in myriad wonderful ways. I've said, and still say today, to parents that if having a disability is an unfortunate misfortune, the present is a better time than at any time in our history.

Granger was never tested, and I found out his last special education teacher had been promising his parents that he would be able to attend college and beyond. Nothing was farther from the truth. Promising the parents of a severely disabled student the moon is as criminal as telling them you should just put them in a home and cut your losses (as was done years ago). Many in my profession think, and some possibly really believe, that students can accomplish anything and that technology can overcome any disability. They, too, are influenced by movies: *My Left Foot*, *Rain Man*, or *I Am Sam*, or Stephen Hawking and countless other people who are antidotal, and not the norm. There is a happy medium, allowing kids to attain all that they can in an educational setting, but also by letting them be kids and enjoy themselves. Having a place for memorable experiences with their peers, and if their peers are intellectually disabled, or will be in a day program after school ends – wouldn't that be the proper placement? The attitude that it benefits every student to be mainstreamed into a general education class is wrong. My experience has convinced me some students would benefit and others wouldn't - better to take it case by case and see what the student enjoys. Forcing a student to attend classes that they are not capable of understanding, or thinking that every student should be mainstreamed, is a fable being pushed upon parents and the students themselves. Professors or administrators in special ed and public schools who aren't actually spending any time with the students usually push this new philosophy, or are asking teachers to do something they themselves haven't done in years, or in fact, have never have done.

He was never given a label of MIMR/MOMR (mild or moderate mental retardation), now "intellectual or cognitive disability." Granger should have actually been attending typical classes, and not even in a special education self-contained room. It was physically impossible for that to happen; Granger needed adult support, and the time spent toileting him would preclude his active participation alone. He operated at about a first - or second-grade level in reading and writing. Granger had what I came to call the physicality of cerebral palsy. It can either be environmental (the lack of words, physical experience, ability to form concepts, and other stimuli imprinted on their brain) or the sheer incredible difficulty of attempting to read. While he was reading (pages set up in front of him on a slant board), he would read a sentence and every time he took a breath, the act would expand his lungs and force his head to dramatically jerk up and to the right. Granger would then, of course, lose his place and have to either begin at the start or spend up to a minute or more finding his place. This hampered any effort, and was not conducive to accomplishing an activity or reading assignment. So many things were not imprinted on his brain that he could read a selection and not remember what he read just seconds after he actually completed reading it; however, in conversation he was able to amaze you. Granger simply processed different areas of his brain.

He came in filthy most mornings. He was usually dirty from a bowel movement from the evening or early morning and hadn't been changed. My first lesson learned from a lifesaver of an aide happened the first week with Granger. Granger had soiled himself badly. He had diarrhea. We usually used a two-person lift with him, as he was so weak and medically fragile. Someone had to get his legs as someone lifted his torso out of his chair. There is no way to lift a twenty-year-old man out of a wheelchair properly and comfortably. There is always the possibility that someone could injure their back twisting to lay the student on the changing table. The aide that I helped that day was named Alayna, and after we put on gloves and pulled the cover on the table, we lifted and lay Granger on the table and started to undress him. An overpowering stench hit us like it seemed nothing ever had before in my life. Moving him caused diarrhea to run out of his pull-up and immediately run onto the table. It was like nothing I had ever experienced; I immediately started gagging and turned away.

"Brant, stop," Alayna said. I tried to turn back to help, but involuntarily gagged again.

"Stop, go, get me two towels, wet them, and several more big plastic bags," she said as she pushed me out the door. I stumbled around and got what we needed and brought them back to the bathroom. I handed them to her and stood in the hallway while she finished. Sometimes Granger had a change of clothes, but many times he didn't. We'd put him in clothes that aides, other teachers, and I learned to scrounge, save, and share for such emergencies. The nurse also kept a supply of extra clothes for kids to wear. With Granger, if we sent clothes home, it was unlikely we'd ever have them returned, unless we could trade them later when he wore them as his own. Alayna told me he had a change, so I didn't need to go on a hunt.

Standing in the hallway, I did some hard soul searching and decided then and there, in the event I was in this position again, I would not, under any circumstances, fail to do my job and let an aide finish the work. I had taken on the job and would tough it out, no matter what. Alayna did the right thing, and I didn't say anything to her but a heartfelt thank you, and we let it go. I thought of the first time I jumped from a C-130 aircraft in airborne school. It echoed Jack Nicholson in *Terms of Endearment* on being an astronaut: "I told them I'd do it. You're strapped in, so I might as well sit back and enjoy the ride." I took this job and this was part of it. These kids couldn't help it and they didn't do it on purpose, so I'd better learn to take care of them. I realized I couldn't let my aides do this without doing it myself, as I was always taught to lead from the front. So, I learned to do it. It wasn't my most favorite part of the day. "Oh, good, Granger shit his pants again. Oh boy, what fun!" But I was determined to never let this happen again, and for my karma, almost to the day a year later, I was able to pay the favor back by doing the same thing for another aide. She gagged, and I sent her on her way, and sent up a small thought of thanks to Alayna, who had left to work in another state, for teaching me to do my job that day.

Granger could lay an aide low. No matter that he took several minutes to type out a short sentence; he could type things that were curt and to the point, but delightful or horrifying, depending on his mood. He was obsessed with sex. We learned later that his stepdad watched porn movies with him. Granger was well versed in filthy pornographic dialog. Several times I sat him in a corner without his pointer and let him have a time out, and after about ten minutes, put it back on and took him to the shade of a tree and talked to him about what was appropriate and what wasn't in school.

"Do you know that a woman takes care of almost all your needs?"

"Yeeeessss," Granger would answer with what sounded like a high-pitched moan.

"You can't talk about those things with the aides, especially Alayna. Do you understand? She's taking care of you better than almost anyone ever has, isn't she?"

"Yeeeesss," he would moan, then type for a while. "*I can't stand my life,*" his device would robotically state.

"I'm sorry, but we'll do all we can for you here at school."

"*I wish I would die.*"

"I hope you don't feel that way all the time. We're doing some great things in your classes, and we like you and want you here in school." I didn't know what else to say, and just continued talking about how much we liked him and how valuable he was to us. Some things just couldn't be fixed. He talked to the counselor a couple of times, and then wouldn't talk to him anymore. I don't think our counselor was equipped to deal with it anyway. What could he possibly say to Granger anyway?

"*I'll never have a girlfriend. I wish I could kill myself*" were common refrains from him.

Granger loved music and listened constantly to the radio, mostly retro rock. Other than porn, he didn't have much of an interest in movies.

It was too hard to hold his head up and focus long enough. So, we talked about music, and he was a rolling encyclopedia about sixties and seventies rock and roll. He would yell out in his piercing scream when I told him how many of the old bands I had seen growing up in LA.

"Yeah, man I saw Led Zeppelin a bunch of times, and the Stones when they were at their peak, with Mick Taylor on guitar…"

"*Noooooooooo waaaaaaayyyyyy*," he'd wail, and only a few of us learned to understand and discern that howl.

"My first concert was Jimi Hendrix in '68, man. We didn't even know who he was."

"*Nooooooooo . . .* "

"I swear, Robert Smith's mom drove us the Los Angeles Forum, and Hendrix came out and played for only forty-five minutes and never said a word. We later figured he must have been high, but he played great and then just walked off stage."

"Fuuuuuuuuuucccccccccccckkkkkk…"

"Really, we had to walk a couple of blocks to a gas station and call his mom to come and get us. She freaked; she said she had just gotten home. We had to wait for her for at least an hour."

When I related my rock and roll stories he'd just smile and shake his head. Our discussions about music could go on for hours if I let them. He earned radio time for going to classes and working with his aide and being polite. During the good days, he'd follow the routine and enjoy school.

Those times we connected and I felt close to him, but it was after he witnessed me lose my temper defending him to a math teacher that cemented our attachment. He was assigned a service-learning project that all of our students took part in every afternoon on Wednesday. This teacher was a pure math guy, a former engineer, who had the right reasons for coming into teaching as a second career, but no idea about what teaching entails now. He really thought it was simply all about presenting the information and helping kids understand math. He actually believed that they'd be motivated to learn. He hadn't been in contact with actual teenagers for many years. He had no idea about what to do with kids with disabilities.

"What am I supposed to do with this kid?!" he shouted at me, pointing at Granger.

"Well, first you can use his name. It's Granger, and he can hear, too, so let's not talk about him like he's not sitting right in front of us!" I shouted back.

"I don't have to do this. I don't know what to do with him."

"Actually, you *do* have to do this! And *what* you have to do is freaking nothing; you don't *have* to do anything. Let his aide work with him and let him participate as much as he can. He's actually a lot smarter than some of the dumbasses you have in your classes. Jesus, man, he's a human being. And legally, you truly *do* have to do this, or we could face a lawsuit!" I yelled while cutting him off.

I pushed Granger back to our room, and all the while he was screaming, "Fuucckkkk himmmmmm!" while waving his arm out in front of his body and the tray on his chair, a simulation of giving somebody the finger.

He had a months-long chess game with a student mentor that came to our room. Student mentors got a social studies credit for volunteering in our classroom, and we had some great kids, and a few that were so freaked out they never said a word. I was never sure if Granger totally understood the game, but since it took so long for him to answer on his device, the mentor played along and encouraged him.

At one point, his mom sent a note in saying she couldn't afford his diapers or pull-ups anymore. She said the state was cutting back on money, and free diapers from the City Clothing Bank were in a shortage. I wrote back (they had learned years ago not to answer the phone) that we couldn't supply them and they had to be sent in. After a couple of days, she sent in what I can best describe, as thin cotton codpieces. It only covered his penis and scrotum, and that, barely. Apparently she got these somewhere for free somewhere and that's all he had with him. By mid-morning he was sitting in a pool of urine. We put him on a towel, and that day I scrounged up a couple of diapers from a wheelchair student in another room, and kept them on him until bus time. We changed him back into the codpiece before he left so mom wouldn't think we would supply them continually. I also sent a note stating that we could not continue without diapers or pull-ups. My principal just told me to handle it the best I could. I was learning this was a common refrain, and the response from administrators to problems in special ed was often "Handle it." Granger told us flat out that his mom didn't want to pay for them anymore. His parents spoke freely in front of him, and he relayed much of these conversations to us.

"She has money for cigarettes and booze. They drink every night," he'd tell us. The proof was his odor.

After two days of this, I was done. That night I decided to call Adult Protective Services. Granger was over eighteen. One of my aides came to my help at the last minute. Her name was Braylin.

"I'll call Brant," she said sadly. "They won't know, and if they come back at you -" she started. "Do you think they will?"

"They came here from Hamilton High and a due process lawsuit, so yeah, they will come after me."

"Well, you'll be able to tell them honestly that you didn't make the call and it'll be the truth," Braylin said.

"Thank you."

"Doesn't he get SSI money?"

That was Supplemental Security Income money.

"Yes, it's about six hundred dollars a month," I answered.

"Shouldn't she be using that for these kinds of things?"

"Yeah, she should."

Two days later, he came in with a full package of diapers. They never spoke to me again, and I had him for two more years. They never made a meeting or showed up at school for anything other than his graduation. They always signed his Individual Education Program paperwork in the block that gave us permission to hold the meeting without them present. We had no problem with that. The lawsuit from the other school faded away.

Granger had an active fantasy life. Over the weekends, he would tell us about all the places he went, and would talk to us about his girl-friends and attempt to get graphic. He talked about trips to California and Florida and we just assumed he wasn't aware of the distances. Granger also had the habit of stating that he wouldn't be in the next day or the next week because of an upcoming trip. Granger rarely missed a day of school that I can remember, unless he came in so sick the nurse had to threaten Adult Protective Services before his parents would pick him up. One time they sent a cab, but the driver wouldn't take him, saying he couldn't fit Granger's wheelchair in the trunk. One day Braylin came to me and said, "He keeps talking about this girl, and someone said she's actually a student at Desert Hills High."

"What's her name?" I asked.

"He says her name is Caylee."

I went home that night and told my wife the story. She actually knew the girl and had worked with her years ago. Since she had also worked with Granger and knew his parents, she continuously gave me the right advice for working with him and what to expect. It was her idea that maybe they were meeting at some support group or afterschool pro-gram. Of course, Granger and many kids didn't go straight home after school but were dropped off at another program, and this made sense if the parents worked, but that wasn't the case with Granger's parents – they mostly lived off his SSI money. Caylee was fairly high functioning, could communicate extremely well, was confined to a wheelchair also, and had several medical issues. She was also several years older than Granger. One of the other aides in another classroom knew an aide at another school who worked in the group home where Caylee lived. She called her and found out Caylee was, in fact, spending time with Granger at his home on the weekends. Granger continued to tell us the story of Caylee and talked about them spending the night together. Eventually it evolved into they were getting married. One day a few weeks later, he was wearing a ring on his left ring finger. We all assumed his parents were playing along. The next Friday, he wasn't at school. We all just looked at each other and wondered. No one verbalized the thoughts we were having. Not until Monday – no Granger.

"You don't think - my God, they really are went somewhere to get married?" Braylin asked me.

"I don't think that would be possible," I thought out loud.

The next Wednesday morning when Granger got off the bus, he told us the most amazing story.

"*We went to Las Vegas and the bastards wouldn't marry us,*" he typed. We didn't know if we should believe him or not. But where had he been for three days? He'd never missed a day of school. Every one had different ideas about where he was.

The aide called her friend and got the entire story. Granger's parents had taken them to Las Vegas. At the chapel where they attempted to get married, it seemed even Vegas had some surprising standards – the minister wouldn't do it. They tried a couple of chapels and had no luck.

"Even the Elvis Presley Chapel?" was all I had the energy to ask.

Somehow, they really did get married a month or so later and Caylee moved in with them. She saw what his parents had in mind within a few months. They thought they would be able to control Caylee's SSI money also. She fought with them over it, and someone had the state assign her an advocate and she moved out. We never heard if they got a divorce, but his first - and, most likely last truly romantic relationship ended.

When Granger graduated a couple of years later (he aged out at twenty-one), I was so caught up in the hassles of getting him and two other students through the ceremony, we didn't have a moment until it was all over and I found myself backstage with him and his parents. We all stood there for a moment and looked at each other. Granger looked up at me straight in the eyes, and I think we both realized at the same time we probably weren't going to see each other again. I started to say, "Well dude, it's been great." I choked up.

"Ahhhhhhhhhhhhh nooooooo." He was crying and screaming. I don't know if it was a failing on my part, but all I felt I could do at the time was walk away.

Several years later during a summer break, my wife and I were in the large used bookstore in Tucson called Bookman's. I had taken students there for years, and it was common to see clients from local group homes looking for music, videos, puzzles, and computer games along with books. Suddenly, I heard a familiar wail. I looked over and saw a more mature, slightly older, cleaner Granger, with several other wheelchair-bound people. I wish I could recount that we had a wonderful reunion and talked and enjoyed ourselves during a positive but emotional reunion. We didn't. I had often told my aides to enjoy the time we had with our students; for many of them school would be the best years of their lives. In public school, they have people who will go those extra miles for them and they get all the services they need. I always hope that the group homes, where many of our students end up, provide the same. Unfortunately, they don't have the money or longevity of personnel for that to happen as often. It's best not to think about it and just continue to do what we can when we can. I was a coward and turned away from Granger. I felt I didn't have the strength, heart, or whatever – and I'm sorry for that. I just didn't have it.

Chapter 14

A DOCTOR WITH A HEART OF GOLD

Georgie Boy. That's not his real name, but that's what everyone called him. He loved school; he'd run errands for teachers all day, everyday. His whole life was school, social, emotional, and recreational. It was the only thing he understood or knew. Summers were rough on him. The school arranged for him to attend several programs so he had something else to do, but mostly he had dead time until it started again in the fall. Georgie Boy could barely be understood. A few people who had been with him for several years could comprehend his speech, and he could understand things when people talked to him, but it was real difficult. He'd pick up and deliver all the towels for the self-contained classes. All our rooms had the five-gallon water bottles, and if a room needed water, he'd be the one they called to bring it to the room. We didn't know his background; it was said George was an "illegal" who was dropped off somewhere in Tucson and abandoned. He had always lived in a group home and didn't have any records regarding a family. He had come to Harrogate from elementary school, so was into his eighth year and was only eighteen. Even that was disputable.

I didn't have him in my classroom officially, but Georgie Boy and I had developed a bond. He liked to hang around, and I fit him in so he would have more than one classroom to participate in activities. One morning in the nurse's office, he was lying there coughing, really deeply, and you could hear the stuff inside – it sounded bad. He looked pale and wan. The nurse had sent him home the day before because he was obviously sick. "Home," again, meaning a group home. But here he was back in school again. He would want to come back, but when I saw him lying there, he truly looked miserable. We learn hard lessons on which parents will send their kids to school sick, and a nurse can't send kids home unless the temperature is 101 or above. They have to have diarrhea at least twice before they can call, and parents will send kids in sick for days in a row. But parents rarely have been known to get a note from a doctor when they send kids to school sick. Georgie Boy lived in the group home, and they had been known to do it. This time I lost it and called the doctor on my own without permission or even checking with my principal. The doctor's number was on the note Georgie had come in with. I introduced myself to his receptionist and stated my reason for calling, and after waiting about ten minutes, got him on the phone.

"You sent a sick kid to school with bronchitis?"

"No, I examined him and he has a slight cold."

"No, we know it's bronchitis. You don't have to be a doctor to figure that out. He was sick yesterday, and today he comes in on the bus even sicker with a note from you, saying it's okay for him to be in school." Pause.

"My determination was that he would be fine returning to school," he said.

"No, no, I know the group home doesn't want to look after him because they have to pay somebody to stay home with him all day, so it's a no-brainer for them. But you, I can't understand how you as a doctor could do something so despicable." Pause.

"I don't think you have any understanding, or did you attend medical school yourself?"

"No, but I was wondering how long you've whored yourself out to these group homes." Short pause.

"You can't talk to me like that, I'll have a conversation with your principal, and maybe the district."

"Actually, I *can* talk to you like that. You're far from being my boss, and you can talk to my principal anytime you want to. He's going to see George, and then our nurse is going to contact the state to file a complaint about you, so you do what you think you need to do and keep whoring yourself out to whoever gives you money, and I hope you feel good about sending a sick kid to school, *doctor*!" Click, the phone connection ended.

Our nurse had walked in when this rant began, and simply stood there, listening, staring, and shaking her head as it progressed.

"Did you really talk to a doctor like that? You *are* crazy, but if you need me to vouch for about how sick George is, I'll have my report ready," she said, laughing. "You made my day."

We never heard from the doctor, and Bobby (our principal) called the group home. Georgie was out the rest of the week and the next. Bobby never mentioned my conversation with the doctor, but I'm sure he heard about it, as it spread all over the school within the hour.

Chapter 15

TAKE ME HOME, COUNTRY ROADS

Most people who are adventitiously blind retain a visual memory of things they formerly saw. This memory can be colored by time and distance. For instance, would you remember the exact size or color of a childhood house after one year? Or possibly ten, or even thirty years? Would what you remember just be a puzzling shadow? How about your memories of a place you've never seen, visited, or lived? For over forty years I'd visualized where my parents, grandmother, aunts, and uncles lived in their childhood years in Sweetland and Griffithsville near Hamlin, West Virginia. They literally lived up a hollow. It was years before I truly realized what that was. It was pronounced "holler."

In 2005, my dad died in his sleep from an aortic aneurysm. We were just getting into a routine; he was on oxygen, and the weekend before we talked about getting him a wheelchair just to go out to eat. I went out to dinner or lunch with him every weekend, and it was just getting easier and more comfortable having him there with us. When

Cheryl would join us, she'd ask him something about growing up in West Virginia, and he could talk for an hour. I miss him.

I listened to what seems like hundreds of stories of their lives before they moved to Southern California, where I was raised. Growing up in Southern California in the late fifties, sixties and through the early seventies was wonderful, and I'm extremely thankful for that move. While definitely lower middle class, my friends and I were admittedly so ethnocentric we never considered that people were living someplace other than on the glorious coast of California with the movie studios, beaches, and places like the Sunset Strip, Venice boardwalk, the mountains of Big Bear, and the desert of Death Valley around every corner. I could have been raised in Big Ugly Creek in Lincoln County in western West Virginia instead of running the streets, beaches, and coastline of Culver City, Venice, and Santa Monica. What I really have always wanted to do was visit West Virginia and see for myself what that place was like.

My mom's family consisted of herself, a sister, four brothers, and their mom. My dad's family came from the same area. My dad had been bird-dogging my mom since they were fourteen, and he sent a Valentine to her through his brother on the bus to school. She agreed to marry him after World War II, provided he took her out of West Virginia. After a stopover for a couple of months in Scottsdale, Arizona, she didn't let him stop driving west again until they hit the Pacific Ocean. This was about 1953, and in the next few years, the whole family made the trip, excluding my uncle Bill, who stayed in Cleveland, Ohio. Bill had gone into the navy before World War II and sent money home. About the same time, my mom and her sister Juanita, who both left school at about fourteen, also went to work. Later I came to call them the "Beverly Hillbillies" (the Vannatter clan), albeit, unfortunately, without the oil money.

My grandmother put an extraordinary amount of the effort into raising me and my cousin, Mark. She watched us while our mothers worked. My cousin usually only lived a block or two away from us, and as only children, we experienced life as close as brothers during our early childhood. We called her "Nanny"; I called her "Nanny Button" when I was very little. A lifelong friend of mine still talks about my grandmother's fried chicken - she was truly the best cook, and prepared the best meals I've ever tasted in the world, and anyone who experienced a meal she made would agree. Most of my mom's (and my) favorite recipes came from Nanny: mayonnaise cake, cheesecake, and green beans with several types of meat dishes. An uncle or two lived in the house, along with friends of theirs over the years. I was always amazed at what she lived through in her lifetime, growing up without electricity, indoor plumbing, television, and cars. Nanny saw the creation of all those and hundreds of other amazing technological advances in her life. She left the hollows of West Virginia and was transplanted to Southern California to watch my cousin and me deal with growing up in the sixties and early seventies. She actually took a switch (cut from a backyard tree) to us several times, but it was always warranted. We were a handful, and I can't imagine how she adapted to the social changes she also had to endure in Southern California. She loved to watch Jack LaLane, roller derby, and the first simple incantations of professional wrestling. She was the counselor, steward, and matriarch of the family throughout my early life. After she finally had her own little apartment about a half-mile away, many times when I was fighting with my parents, I'd climb the back fence and head across Sepulveda Boulevard to spend the night, where she would call my mom and make amends between us. I still think about her often.

Once when Mark was driving us around, we dropped in on her unexpectedly and found her eating an early dinner: a small steak, potato, and small salad on a TV tray. She immediately put it away and tried to pawn it off on us, saying she wasn't hungry anyway. We both realized that she never ate in front of anyone and would pick at food as she was cooking and waiting on everyone else to make sure "the kids" were taken care of - a lifelong habit, maybe stemming from the Depression, that she couldn't break. Christmas, Thanksgiving, and most other holidays were always glorious, food-laden extravaganzas. It was an idyllic childhood, and only years later did I realize the adults in my life had issues, not unlike other families, but I miss those carefree days with those strong personalities roaming around. I enjoyed this large, tight-knit family that even after all these years makes *me* envious of my younger self.

My mother rarely talked about her childhood. She didn't seem to have good memories of West Virginia. Receiving mixed messages about my parents' childhood made them more intriguing to me. My dad, when he did talk about it, had what I interpreted as fairly good memories. He usually deferred to my mom, though, whenever I brought up the subject. His memories concerned hunting and fishing and running through the woods in the late twenties and thirties. It seems his farm was more productive than my mom's, hence more to eat, which meant far superior remembrances. I found out when I was about nine how much my mom wanted to control their memories. A relative was visiting California one summer and referred to my dad as "J. D." His name was John, and I had never heard him referred to as J. D., an abbreviation of his full name, John Davis Vickers. A chill frosted the air in mid-July, and I learned my mom had put the kibosh on that nickname early in their marriage - an unwanted throwback to the old days in West Virginia. Early after my grandfather died, I think they had it rough for quite a while. She was always pained to talk about her father. She flat out refused several times, and since Nanny never brought it up, I quit asking. They were enough for me anyway.

I loved listening to my dad and uncles and aunts tell the stories of their childhoods and the tales back in West Virginia. That's how it was always said, "Back in West Virginia." It had a magical connotation for me. I was never bored listening to the stories of places and characters, some many times over, with the laughter and joking that accompanied them. I had no friends in Southern California whose families were comprised of such a cast of hilarious people with such extremely strong personalities, who had such staunch ties to some place. My uncle Bill and his daughters (Eva, Carol, and Sharon) all came out to live with us (Nanny) either once or twice. It's unclear to me now, but I am eternally grateful for those fleeting months, as it gave me a taste of what having sisters would have been like. I know Ohio is their home, but I was always sad when they left.

In the summer of 2007, seven years after my mom died and almost two years after my dad died, I was talking to my Uncle Phil on the phone. He was spending the summer on his farm in Indiana. He mentioned that if I ever wanted to visit him, he'd take me down to West Virginia and show me around. I felt I had missed so many opportunities to do it after a career in the army, and then foolishly waiting until my dad's health was too grim to take him, as we had planned.

"Don't offer that if you don't mean it. I've wanted to see those places, it seems, my whole life," I said.

"I wouldn't offer it if I didn't mean it."

He did.

I made flight plans for exactly two weeks from that day. He and his wonderful wife Rita divide their time between their home in the valley in Southern California, near where their son and daughter and grandchildren live, and the farm in Indiana. She is a retired school nurse and he is a retired Los Angeles homicide detective. Their farm is beautiful, about 190 acres in Vevay, Indiana. The first night, I went to bed in the upstairs bedroom listening to the *clomp, clomp, clomp* of horses pulling the Amish's farmer's buggies heading home after evening visits.

The next morning, we started the almost four-hour drive from Indiana, skirting Kentucky and crossing over the Ohio River. We went through Huntington, West Virginia, and headed down into West Hamlin. I couldn't believe it was so easy and so accessible. I flashed to my first trip to London and finding Abbey Road Studios, where the Beatles recorded all that music, and finding Strawberry Fields in Liverpool, traveling on the London Underground and seeing Waterloo Station; Ray Davis of the Kinks writing "Waterloo Sunset" and thinking there should be more for me to sense, or feel. Yet West Virginia was green, it was beautiful, and it was mountainous.

"You can stand on the road in some of these places and reach out and touch both sides of the mountains," Phil pointed out.

I was there in West Virginia after all those years, and near where all the relatives I held near and dear had lived and grown up. Their memories of these places were the same memories of Culver City that I have, my childhood. My best friend Scott once said, "Brant remembers Culver City the same way that Mark Twain remembered Hannibal." I knew that my relatives had some mixed feelings of Hamlin and Logan, and Sweetland and Griffithsville, but it was home, and the place all of them were born. I always thought of myself as a California boy, born and bred, but I was starting to sense there was more to the story.

Suddenly we were at my dad's high school, where the statue out front was of Chuck Yeager, possibly the area's - other than my uncle - most famous son. It was overwhelming having Phil point out all those places where all those stories happened; swimming holes, hilltops, the cemetery where my grandparents were buried. On the side of a mountain, hollows where relatives lived and died, broken down buildings where there were still ghosts of the forties and fifties floating in the air.

"Is that the old general store where Tom brought -" I started.

"Yes, he brought a fliers cap with earflaps home and said, 'Don't worry, Mom, we don't have to pay for it. I bought it on credit!'" It was a story I had heard a dozen times, and loved it with each telling.

We left the main drag in West Hamlin and started up the hollow, which I saw really was a low, wooded valley set in the mountains near Billy's Creek, where the Vannatters lived.

"In the thirties, they said people came from up some of these hollows, walking hours, to see the first 'hard road,'" Phil said.

Phil had been here with his son the year before and they'd asked directions from an elderly man walking down one of the hollow roads. He looked at them for a moment, seriously took off his floppy hat, and said, "It is right over that thar hill."

I felt like I had seen it before, and I had in pictures, stories, and visions. It wasn't *my* home, but it actually felt like a home from somewhere in *my* long-lost past and memories. On the way back out and on the main drag, the van suddenly stopped, went dead. We pulled over when the first opportunity showed itself, into a parking lot of a small restaurant. We didn't know what to think. Phil had only recently purchased it. It was about two o'clock in the afternoon and we were the only customers in the small but clean mom-and-pop restaurant with the handwritten name "Shirley's" over the front door. The other three people sitting around the large table in front of the cash register were a middle-aged woman, a young girl, and a middle-aged man.

"Honey, can I get a cup of coffee?" Phil asked.

"What would you like, darling?" she asked me. I said a Diet Coke.

"Our van just died on us, and I can't for the life of me figure out what's wrong," Phil said. "Maybe you'd know of somewhere we could call, or the Triple A close by?"

"No Triple A out here," the man jumped in. "I'll take you to a mechanic friend of mine up the road," he added in that unmistakable West Virginia drawl.

"Can we call him?" Phil asked.

"No, no phone. He's just down the road. C'mon, I'll take you."

Just like that, he was out the door with Phil, even offering to take us up to the cemetery we were heading to next. I was left with the lady, who I imagined might have been Shirley, and the young girl, sitting at the table. For a minute or two, I didn't have a clue as to what to talk about.

"Where y'all from?" Shirley suddenly asked, also in that distinctive twang I was quickly getting used to.

I began to tell her the story about my family and who they were. While I was talking, another man walked in, nodded, and sat down, and the women got him a coffee while still talking to me. She asked me my grandmother's maiden name, and when I replied "McMillan," she said she knew some of them. I told her one of my grandmother's brothers was named Cisco and another was named Boyd.

"I knew the woman. She was my second cousin who died with Cisco in that car crash back in the early seventies," the woman said. The man got up and left. I sat sipping my Coke and wondered how very strange everything seemed. The population of this area hadn't changed dramatically for over fifty years, and the economy, according to some, had only gotten worse. Things looked, sounded, and felt like they were stuck in time. The two women continued to talk softly, but loud enough for me to hear.

"I hope Rick is the right one for you I don' know, honey," the woman said.

"Well, he says he likes big girls," the young girl said demurely. I decided to wait outside.

The mechanic couldn't be found, and Phil was back outside. They had started up the van, thinking it might be the fuel pump.

"It might not die on you again for months, or a mile up the road," the man was saying.

We went back inside the restaurant and sat down. The two men had figured out who my uncle was.

"I figured it out when he was talking about California and said 'Vannatter,'" said the second man, who had come in again, pointing at me and smiling.

A local boy had moved to California, but still, a local boy who had become a successful homicide detective, and who would gain national fame for being one of the two lead detectives in the O. J. Simpson murder case. They loved it, and couldn't stop smiling. They were talking to Phil Vannatter and probably couldn't wait to tell their friends about his van breaking down right in front of this local eatery. The first man kept making jokes about buying the van cheap and charging us for rides and things.

"I'll be heading up that way and I'll be looking for you if you have any more trouble today," he said, referring to our trip up another hollow to see my grandfather's grave in a cemetery on the side of a steep hill with other relatives. There was an old white-washed church, where the pastor's name on the sign read "Dave Vickers."

"Do you think this guy could be a relative?" I asked Phil. He just shrugged.

That afternoon, we paid an unexpected visit to friends of my uncle's, a minister named Oshel and his wife Rosemary, who welcomed us in, and even after several refusals, laid a table of food enough for a dozen people; lunch meat for sandwiches, several types of bread, homemade salad dressing, homemade coleslaw, meat loaf, potato salad, chips, and several drinks, topped off with homemade banana cream pie. My uncle told me this man loved my grandfather and had been a regular at their house while they were growing up. The graciousness and offerings without the least bit of hesitation was almost overwhelming. The next day, we visited a cousin several times removed, and went to the Logan County Court House, where I found my mother's birth record, listed by hand in a large 1923, yellowing, decrepit record book. My dad's had been lost in a fire sometime in the 1950s.

Unfortunately, when my dad moved to California, his family rarely visited, and I never had the opportunity to get to know them. Only one sister and uncle came out regularly. Most moved to Ohio for work and left West Virginia themselves. His mom, who I also called "Nanny," did come to stay with us several times, but my family and his family really were the Vannatters. He told me about coming into San Francisco Bay after spending three years in the Pacific on the USS *New Jersey* battleship, for six months as the occupation force in Tokyo. After making his way to Chicago to out-process, his main focus was getting back down to West Hamlin to marry my mom. He left his family and went out west and spent his life with the Vannatters. He was as devastated as we all were when Nanny died in 1975.

My family came out of West Virginia with literally nothing. They worked hard their whole lives, and everyone is doing well and making a good, solid living. Neither my cousins nor I have ever wanted for anything. I've used them as examples of what can be accomplished in our country and how people can raise themselves from extremely rural and dire circumstances to lead productive and extremely successful lives. I'm proud of them and what they gave me.

The Vannatter boys were a tough crew. Everyone has always described my dad as one of the nicest men they've ever met, but he was also timid and quiet. I grew up with uncles who were loud, profane, funny, and sometimes violent. I grew up fearing, admiring, and worshiping them, while at the same time loving them fiercely. My Uncle Bill and my dad both told differing versions of one of the most incredible stories I have ever heard. During World War II, the USS *New Jersey* made a port stop on the island of Maug in the Northern Marianas for re-supply. My dad told me he was walking along a retaining wall the Seabees had built to make a cove for the ships to dock. Several ships were docked with thousands of army, navy, and marine service members all vying for a little peace and fun. They were given two warm beers and two hours to drink and swim in the warm ocean. As he was walking in the sand, some other navy men were sitting high upon the retaining wall, their legs dangling over, and he heard, "Hey, is that John Vickers from West Virginia?"

He looked up and saw Bill. Two Hamlin, West Virginia, boys met in the middle of a world war, in the middle of the Pacific Ocean.

"I'll walk back up and meet you! Stay where you are!" he yelled to Bill.

He had to backtrack, and it took almost twenty minutes or so to get up along the top. When he got there, he asked several of the men if they knew where Bill Vannatter was."

One of them said, "The son of a bitch just got in a fight and was carried away by the shore patrol." That was Bill. He served in the army during the Korean War also. He was my hero. We talked several times, especially after I did a tour in Korea in 1995. He always talked to me like we were equals for having served and wouldn't hear about how I was working in an air-conditioned, heated, beautiful new security building, saving money, drinking beer, and playing my guitar, while he had been slogging through the mud and the frozen wasteland that country was in the early fifties. Bill saw some bad shit in Korea; it's truly the forgotten war, and the returning veterans all had a bad time of it. I admired him and my dad for their service.

After my father died, the three remaining Vannatter brothers (Phil, Joe, and Bill) all said virtually the same thing about him: "We accepted John into our family because he was the nicest and most honest man we knew, and we knew he'd treat our sister well. And he never proved that feeling wrong." I've always respected and always loved the Vannatters, and that was the highest praise I could have imagined bestowed on my dad. I think of him running the hollows and roads and sending that Valentine to my mom in probably 1937 or 1938, and after World War II, spending the next fifty-five years together married.

There was more to the trip than seeing the ghosts and remembering stories and recollections of West Virginia. I got to spend some quality time with my Uncle Phil. I told him some stories of my life I don't think he ever imagined and I'll always remember that as a special trip. No matter how old or experienced I am, I find I'm never too old to bond and make a memory with loved ones or friends. We both talked nonstop for two days and were hoarse when we got back to his farm. My appreciation for that road trip runs as deep as the Ohio River and is as cavernous as the mountain hollows we traversed in West Hamlin. Without quite being fully aware of it, I've carried the legacy from that place in my heart all these years. However, make no mistake, I'm still thankful for that move to the California beach.

Chapter 16

ADVISING MARIO TO DROP OUT

The first time I met Mario was about my third year of teaching. I was following a student at lunch one day; the bell had rung and we were walking back to class. We walked by Mario and a couple of his friends. They were sitting against the side of the building by one of the back doors, then got up and left all their lunch trash laying there on the walkway. I stopped and looked at them for a moment.

"Can you guys please pick up your trash and throw it away?" I asked very nicely.

One guy said, "It's not ours."

"C'mon guys. It *is* your trash. Please think about the fact someone else has to pick it up if you don't, like our janitor or other kids."

"Who cares? Not our problem." They all laughed. "Fuck that," one of them said.

"No problem, I'll have the referrals written up before the next class has started," I said.

Mario walked back over, saying under his breath, "Fuck this school, man. This place sucks."

"The only thing that sucks is you and your attitude. Why don't you take that trash home and throw it on your living room floor? It would probably fit in," I shot back, walking away. I looked at the student I was with and started to laugh.

"Those bozos don't even know my name and won't say anything now, anyway."

The next semester, I couldn't believe what Mario had said to me, but mostly I couldn't believe what I said back, for the second time. I thought Mario would have learned that the first time. Sometimes it slips out, and it always reinforces the reason I don't work with typical kids. It was his second day in our class as a student mentor. Typical students were put in our class as a service-learning project, so they could earn a social studies credit. Every principal used it with me to send a troubled kid or a gang-banger who was having problems in other areas. Many times it worked out great. They worked in our class with our kids to the best of their ability. If they had behavior problems, it could disappear in an instant. They didn't have to be the tough guy; most days they couldn't impress anyone if they tried. It didn't matter if they had severe conduct issues; the kids they were hanging out with wouldn't know it. When you're playing checkers or a game with a kid who can't talk or really understand what's going on, you are the smartest one in the room. It was remarkable how they checked their egos at the door and ended up looking forward to our class. I like to think that over the years it spread out through the school and made our students more accessible to their friends. I think seeing me with our students changed some of their minds about who these kids were; seeing me, some big guy cruising around with the special ed kids. I know it made some of them think.

"You aren't going to be asked to do anything you're uncomfortable with, or simply don't want to do," I'd tell them. "I want you to see that these kids are people, too. You can learn something that most people don't ever learn, or learn very late in life. It's the only lesson I'll try to give you. Maybe twenty years from now when you're walking through the mall with your own kids and they start to shy away, or try to cross away from some guy in a wheelchair - which is what ninety percent of people do; heck, it's what I used to do - you can say, 'Hey, it's not that big of a deal. He has a disability. He's cool.' You might even say hi to him."

At the end of the period that second day, Mario was still complaining, as he had all hour, that the playing field was getting mowed and the workers had the huge field blocked off. I knew the real reason was that Mario and his friends liked to hang out at the far end of the field and get high; they could see anyone coming from a mile away. They couldn't get to the end of the field that day at lunch because the workers were still there. The only people in the class were my aide Jill and two of the wheelchair kids. Mario was saying how stupid school was and how everything sucked.

"Mario, could you play checkers, or maybe cards, with Jimmy here? He would dig it if you would," I said.

"Hey, I know, why don't *you* go mow my lawn like the guys outside? I'll give you twenty bucks if you will," Mario said.

"What are you talking about? What do you mean?" I asked.

"I said, go mow my lawn – that's all teachers are good for."

I started walking across the room. As I did, I brought my wallet out of my back pocket, pulled out a bunch of bills, and shook them in Mario's face.

"Hey, I have an idea. I've got a hundred bucks here, and it's all yours - all you have to do is drop out of school. Right now. You're sixteen, right?"

"I'm seventeen," Mario said.

"Then in this state, you can drop out right now. Today, nobody can stop you. Show me how bad you are, and this is yours. Walk away right now and leave us alone. Get the hell out of here."

Mario looked down for a second

"Hey mister, that ain't very cool."

"Yeah, what's not cool is you thinking that you can say anything you want to teachers and thinking we have to sit back and take it. Your whole life, all you've had are teachers saying" – I changed to a high-pitched whiny voice - "Pleeeease, Mario, don't drop out. Pleeeeeasee stay in school and do the best you can.' Bullshit! Save us all the hassle and take yourself out of the equation. You don't want to be here, well, here's a little secret: We don't want you here either. All you do is cause problems. Have the guts to leave, walk away. We'd throw a party. Leave, or otherwise, shut up."

After that, I walked out of the room, telling Jill I was taking a break. Later, Jill told me in about five minutes the bell rang and Mario simply got up and walked out without saying another word. I later asked if she thought I should apologize.

"No, Brant, that was a harsh little rant, and I doubt he has ever heard anything like that from a teacher. He undoubtedly could get you in trouble, but I don't think he will. He probably needed to hear it."

The rest of they day I waited for Bobby to stick his head in the door and say, "Brant, we need to talk." But once again, I was spared.

After that, Mario took one of our wheelchair kids under his wing and spent the entire hour every day talking to him, and wheeling him around the room, the track, and the entire school, but more importantly, having fun. One day I got permission to take him on a trip to the local air force base. I usually didn't spend much time talking to kids about my military experience, but with Mario I made an exception. All of his family members were gang affiliated; brothers, uncles, dad, and so on. I knew that the closest runway we could drive by had some visiting jets from Britain parked on the tarmac and we could get a good look at them.

"Mario, see those planes? They're called Harriers. They've come all the way from England to fly in our desert," I started.

"Cool," he said. I could tell he actually meant it.

"Yeah, now I could never think about becoming a pilot. I mean, I didn't have the smarts to do that. You have to have a mind like an engineer or something. Hurling a ton or more through space would scare the crap out of me." He laughed, but kept looking.

"Dude, I don't know if you have that in you or not, but from what I've seen, you can do *more* than you think, and you don't have to do what many in your family and friends are doing." He creased his brow, and so I continued. "You don't have to get into the life . . . Now, see those guys walking around underneath the jets?"

"Yeah," he said.

"They're mechanics. You could do that for sure. They make okay money. You'd have to put up with the bullshit of the military, but after that you could get a job at an airline, or maybe stay in for a career like I did."

He looked a little confused, but I drove on. "You would get to travel, but even if you did go to a combat assignment, you'd be relatively safe working on the jets. They have to keep them in a safe area away from the fighting. It's always a risk, but at least a smaller one."

Mario enjoyed the rest of the year in my class, and we didn't have another blow up. I know he struggled in school academically, but didn't exhibit any further serious behavior issues I was aware of, and left quietly for the summer. At the beginning of the next year, I understood he tried to get another semester in my room, but he needed the credits in other places. Only weeks into the next fall, I was standing at buses waiting with my aides for the day to start when over the loud speaker I heard, "Mr. Vickers, please report to the office."

I thought, *What now? School hasn't been going on long enough for me to get in trouble already.* When I walked into Bobby's office, I saw Mario sitting there. Bobby said, "He's leaving and transferring to go to Gateway High to play football."

"Hey, that's great." I said. Mario looked like he was almost crying.

"He only wanted to say goodbye to one teacher, and that's you," Bobby said, pointing at me.

"I wanted to say thanks."

"I didn't do much, but you did great in my class. You're going to do fine, man. Finish school and do whatever you want." I started to choke up, and reached over and shook his hand. "I gotta get to buses, Mario. Good luck."

Chapter 17

BOBBY AND I, LAUGHING OUR ASSES OFF

One day, my supervising teacher came into my room and asked if I minded being observed by a parent. I never minded being observed. I had an open-door policy and welcomed my parents or anybody visiting my room. Once in a great while, a parent was shopping for a placement. It rarely happened, and when it did, it usually was for a reason that wasn't positive. For those in self-contained rooms, many times it had to do with an unhappy parent or a behavior specialist who was going to offer an unwanted suggestion or a remedy that wasn't going to have a chance of succeeding. Typically, the people who are telling classroom teachers what and what not to do have been out of the classroom for years, or have never really spent much time in the process of teaching or managing a classroom themselves. Or worse, they have completely forgotten what it's like and use the old, "When I had my classroom . . ." Most classroom teachers instantly tune out higher-ups when they use this phrase.

Mr. Santiago came into my room in a blue suit, a white Panama dress hat, and a cane. He was introduced to me, and I held out my hand, but he ignored it. He sat down with the head of my department, and I could tell she was anxious with this situation, whatever it was. I was doing a math lesson with four of my students. Two could do some basic addition, with help. I was lucky to have two aides with me. Two students needed to have it done for them, but they could be verbally talked through it. I had gathered menus from a half-dozen restaurants in town. I picked ones that were as colorful as possible, and large. We went through choosing an entrée, maybe an appetizer first, a drink, and then dessert. We then went through attempting to add the price of the items on a worksheet. We always had fun with this lesson. The kids loved it, and we joked around. It was always one of the most successful lessons I taught. Mr. Santiago sat there stone-faced. After a minute or so, I had conveniently forgotten he was there. They left right before we finished up, about twenty minutes into the lesson. I later found out he had a son, Jorge, who was moderately intellectually disabled. Jorge had never been tested, and presented at about first grade in reading, writing, and comprehension. Mr. Santiago became a nightmare for Bobby and the rest of the school. Luckily for me, he said my class was not right for his son, and didn't want him in my room. I was fine with it.

That started about six weeks of hell for our school. Mr. Santiago demanded Jorge be given a one-to-one aide and insisted that he be completely mainstreamed into all of his classes. A one-to-one, or a programmatic aide, was to assist Jorge and escort him to every class, bathroom, except lunch. His son couldn't be independent going from class to class. Had he been in my class, Jorge would have been with students who were actually his peers, and would have attended classes suitable to him. He would have received instruction in subjects at his level of understanding. Several times I would look up to see Jorge standing at our door, longingly gazing into our room as if he knew he belonged there. After his father confronted me twice, shouting that we leave his son alone, I was forced to shout back, "We aren't bothering your son! Please leave the proximity of our room."

Mr. Santiago had requested to accompany his son to every class, and was initially given permission, with us thinking it was to get him settled. After numerous weeks, it became apparent Mr. Santiago did not have a job or anything else to do. He verbally attacked two teachers and went after aides daily. After another aide threatened to quit and went to the union to get support, Bobby realized he was quickly running out of options. Sadly, Jorge couldn't have told you what class he was in. The truth was that he could not differentiate between his science class and his English class. Mr. Santiago made the school uncomfortable. After the third or fourth time he ran over to the district to complain about some perceived injustice to Jorge – (one of the occasions was when I shouted back), the district lawyers limited his time to lunch and one other hour a week. Mr. Santiago and/or his wife would come to lunch with Jorge. What started happening was almost unbelievable.

I ate my lunch with our students in the cafeteria, as several needed to be fed and the others needed to be assisted, if only observed. It took all my aides. I glanced over one lunch period and observed Mr. Santiago sitting what I initially thought was very close to Jorge - then I realized Jorge was in his lap. I slowly got up and walked to the office. The secretary informed me it had been happened several times in the last week.

"It's worse when Mom is here He lays across her and puts his head on her chest."

"We have to stop it. The other kids can't witness this."

"We were told to wait. Mr. Keeter isn't here right now, and I know it's crazy, but don't do anything. Wait for him to get back."

Bobby was aware of it and had informed the district, but they, of course, were being extremely slow to react and had not sent anyone over to observe the creepiness. It stopped in the next couple of days, so someone had done something. Mr. Santiago stopped showing up every day during lunch, so Jorge could pick his own table at which to sit. His aide took a break during lunch so Jorge could eat independently once he got his tray. I had a student, Jason, who liked to sit next to a couple of typical girls, who were fine with it. Jason didn't disturb them; the proximity was enough. I felt the need to thank them and tell them it was nice, and told them if there were any issues, let me know.

Jason loved sitting near the girls and he would try to talk to them when they first sat down. We always arrived a few minutes early to lunch to help our kids get situated. Jason would say hi, but then would be too involved in eating his own lunch to continue trying to connect. One day, Jorge sat down at the end of the same table. I didn't see Dad, so I thought it was a good thing and maybe things were loosening up. After about two weeks went by, and late one afternoon about an hour before school was out, Bobby called me up and asked if I could come up to his office. The day before, he had informed the staff that he was leaving for a high-level administration job, basically a promotion. I walked into his office, and there sat Mr. Santiago with Bobby at his meeting table.

"Brant, please sit down." I nodded and sat across from them both. I couldn't for the life of me imagine what anything had to do with me.

"Mr. Santiago has some concern with what's happening at lunch," Bobby said.

At first, I couldn't comprehend what he was talking about. I looked at them with bewilderment.

"What's happening at lunch?" I asked. Bobby started to answer that there was an issue with where the kids were sitting.

"I don't want my son sitting with that boy," Mr. Santiago jumped in.

"What boy are you talking about?" I interrupted.

"That retarded one. I don't want him around Jorge."

"Wait a second." My voice was raised. I looked over at Bobby and saw his face screw up. He started to shake his head almost imperceptibly. "Wait, you're talking about Jason?"

"I don't know what his name is, and don't care. I don't want him around my son."

"Stop. My student's name is Jason, and he is at that table before anybody else is and he can sit anywhere he wants to. I'm not going to tell him to move, and you sure aren't, either." Bobby's head was moving and shaking back and forth, and he was mouthing the word *no* over and over. I ignored it.

"You're worried about your son sitting next to a student who's actually higher functioning than he is, and with what we've witnessed the last couple of weeks, *you* should have been arrested for some kind of bizarre, incestuous relationship you were carrying out right in front of the whole school." It spewed out of me in one long run-on sentence without having taken a breath. Bobby was freaking out. He was shaking his head more with a look of pure horror, but I don't think he knew what to say. I stood up.

"Don't ever talk about one of my students like that again. You stay away from him and me, and get a life." I walked out.

About twenty minutes later, after the final bell had rung and I was about to go out to busses Bobby burst into my room.

"Can we go outside?" Bobby looked like I had never seen him, flustered, but also disheveled, and he was always impeccably dressed in a suit and tie.

We walked under the ramada, and he stopped and looked at me. He started to smile and said, "Man, I can't believe you said that. What possessed you to say that stuff?"

"Why? Was I wrong?" I didn't even feel frightened or worried about my job.

"No, you weren't wrong, but, man oh, man, I don't know what he's going to do." He started laughing and it was like a volcanic eruption. It must have been weeks and weeks of frustrations bursting out. I started laughing, too. We both stood there cracking up with deep belly laughs. Kids were walking by and we still couldn't stop. Bobby leaned against the wall of my room snorting.

Wiping his eyes, Bobby said, "I don't know. I really don't know."

"Did he go to district headquarters?"

"I don't honestly know. He actually didn't say much after you left and -" He started laughing again. "I called them to tell them to be prepared, but I think they're getting sick of it also, and don't know what to do."

"Well, I don't really care. All I remember is you shaking your head, trying to get me to stop, but I couldn't. The guy annoys me."

"Annoys you?" Bobby said.

We still had a couple of guffaws in us, and really didn't have much else to say.

Bobby put his hand on my shoulder and said, "Don't worry about it. Forget it," and walked away smiling.

Chapter 18

CHERYL WITH LILY AND ABIGAIL

At Harrogate, I was working with a couple of aides who had worked with Cheryl during her career as an itinerant speech-language pathologist. They all had the same thing to say about her work ethic and individualized approach to working with the students in the self-contained rooms. Our rooms were perpetually short staffed, and usually could not be reliant on people coming in, such as itinerant specialists, to help in that capacity, even for a few minutes. Most speech pathologists, physical and occupational therapists, and behavior specialists, were loath to help out in the classroom. They wanted to do their thing and leave. Admittedly, they had a different job than a special education teacher, and a speech pathologist should be working on the things within their field, such as word-finding issues, social communication difficulties, structural language impairments, voice difficulties, and cognitive impairments; attention, memory, and executive function to the extent that they interfere with communication. Some students, like Abigail, had all of these in spades.

If a behavior difficulty occurred with a student, or the room was disruptive, in my experience, not all, but most itinerants would be out of there in a flash. If there were toileting issues or any kind of mess, or another student needed help in the bathroom (maybe simply to be overseen or a little guidance), they'd want no part of it. Things happened in an instant, and three or four adults could be maxed out with immediate responsibilities, pulled in several directions, and a couple of minutes of assistance would be a sanity-saving benefit.

Cheryl was known for helping out in a pinch. She had no compunction about doing the same job as an aide; always with a positive attitude, which was more than appreciated by every aide I ran into that worked with her over the years. She'd help toilet students and change diapers, if necessary, to help the flow of the room, and to facilitate her getting to know the students.

One of the aides at Harrogate, named Betsy, I got to know and liked. She'd worked with Cheryl at Pacifica Middle School a couple of years before I'd gotten there, and loved telling me a story about a student we saw several times a week at the Harrogate therapy pool. At one point after she had moved on from middle school and was in a local high school, her mother demanded and secured a full-time teacher and aide to accompany her to our pool.

Abigail was gnome-like. She was about four and a half feet tall, with Coke-bottle thick glasses, wore a hooded sweatshirt with the hood down constantly, Michael Jackson gloves, and walked stiff legged. She had some albinism; totally pale to the point of shocking-white skin. Since she wasn't my student, I'm not sure, but I'm guessing she had Rett syndrome. Rett syndrome is a rare genetic postnatal neurological disorder. It almost exclusively affects females. Abigail showed the small hands and feet, a deceleration of the rate of head growth, repetitive stereotyped hand movement, such as wringing or repeatedly putting her hands into her mouth, and severe intellectual disability. She had a love and interest in water, hence the pool therapy. Abigail would spend hours in the pool. She would float around constantly stroking her hands in small circles in front of her, barely moving, with her Michael Jackson gloves on. Abigail could be extremely violent.

She also liked small, enclosed areas, and her teacher had set up a tent in a corner of one of the rooms the class used. The aides had known for some time not to actually go into the space she occupied during times when Abigail was in a mood. Betsy always told me this story laughing.

"We shouldn't have let Cheryl go into the tent, but she wanted to help so much, and we actually thought, well, maybe she'd have better luck than we would," she said, smiling. "Then we saw the tent heaving and pitching, and almost come up off the floor, and Cheryl came crawling out of the tent with her glasses askew, her hair messed from having it pulled . . . I guess Abigail clocked her pretty good," she said. "I always felt a little bad about that," she said, grinning.

Nicolae Ceausescu was the authoritarian dictator who ruled Romania from 1965 to 1989. He outlawed contraception and abortion and enacted austerity policies in Romania to pay off debt. During the following economic downturn, the Romanian orphanages were hit the hardest, and lacked electricity, heat, medicines, washing facilities, and food. The children were often tied to their own beds and dangerously restrained by their own clothing. Physical and sexual abuse was widespread. America didn't hear about this until a news report and TV and magazines showed the conditions in full detail in 1990. Americans rushed to adopt the kids. Romania made it easy, more than happy to send these kids far away.

Lily was adopted as a toddler and homeschooled until attending Pacfica middle school. Her parents had no idea of the problems with which they were to be burdened. Our scientists and doctors learned more about attachment disorder from these adopted kids than probably from any other source. Kids showed nearly a complete lack of ability to be affectionate, develop a conscience, form an emotional attachment to others, or adapt to their new lives after adoption. The last and most important tenet an infant needs is to develop a relationship with at least a caregiver for successful social and emotional development. Lily also had severe cognitive disability and was non-verbal. This might have been (now called) familial disability, or retardation from environmental factors. They didn't know. All they knew was it was severe.

Some days Lily would come into the room after getting off the bus and immediately strip. She also had the unadulterated entertaining habit of throwing her feces around the room. Teachers and aides always were on the lookout for antecedents or precursors for aggressive conduct – many behavior specialists were reluctant to concede some students with disabilities didn't have obvious antecedents. Lily didn't. Her antecedents were incidents like grabbing someone's hair and pulling them to the ground, or while working at table with an adult, viciously kicking and watching to see the reaction. Lily loved swinging or bouncing on a stability ball; hence her core was very strong.

Lily attempted communication verbally, but was not able to imitate sound sequences to produce actual words. She had an inability to produce the precise refined specific movements of the tongue, lips, and palate necessary for intelligible speech. Lily could approximate certain words if the context was known (cat, ball, food names, preferences for a reward). This cause great frustration, and Lily reacted by acting out.

Lily's dad never let up with the criticism constantly directed at the classroom and teacher. The dad started bringing in a lawyer to every meeting, and later they all found out his specialty was in real estate. In one of several meetings, Cheryl impressed me with her discernment and courage to say what needed to be said to this clown of a lawyer. He was asking questions about Lily that didn't even make any sense.

"What is Lily reading? And at what grade level?" he asked.

Everyone around the room was so flabbergasted no one spoke for a moment.

"Lily isn't reading," Cheryl finally said. Lily was labeled as severe, and probably more closely to profound, in her cognitive disability. She functioned at pre-kindergarten level. Reading was not even remotely possible. They were working on her identifying picture symbols, such as toilet, hungry, walk, etc.

"Have you ever met Lily?" Cheryl asked him.

"No, but I don't see that as a necessary experience for me to question why she isn't being provided appropriate reading material," he said. Again, a moment passed while everyone tried to process what this jackass was saying.

"No problem," Cheryl said. "We'll have her reading *War and Peace* by the end of the semester."

Lily's parents had had enough, and along with assailing the school for all her transgressions, decided they couldn't handle her at home. She was becoming dangerous to her siblings, so they merely put her in a group home. A group home is a private residence for children or young people who, for whatever reason, cannot live with their families. Usually this might occur after school graduation, and families have given all they could for their children with severe disabilities. Sometimes parents like Lily's would simply throw up their hands and make someone else responsible for their children. Lily's time was now spent with adults, and her parents rarely visited her. Prior to the 1970s and 1980s, this function was served by institutions, asylums, and long before, poorhouses and orphanages. Group homes are a better answer; typically there are no more then six residents, and hopefully at least one trained caregiver there twenty-four hours a day. They run the gamut from bad to good. The staff usually has a high turnover and are normally not paid well, or highly educated. I've seen extremely well-intentioned, kind people, and some I wouldn't leave my child with for anything, but I've never lived with the circumstance. Lily's parents undeniably wanted someone else to manage their child.

Lily was obsessed with circular or round objects; plates, balls, pizza, oranges, soda cans, margarine tubs, etc. One afternoon, Lily was in the middle school playground, always without other students around, and suddenly bolted. The fence behind the school led to a residential neighborhood, and unfortunately, someone had left the small pedestrian gate unlocked. Lily was out across the street before anyone could stop her. She beelined it for the nearest house and another unfortunate occurrence; the homeowners had left their front door unlocked. Lily walked right in, passing the owner in a chair reading the newspaper, and directly to a mantelpiece of decorative plates in stands, grabbed the first one, and held it, looking closely at it. The aide was right behind her, and gently took the plate out of Lily's hand, apologized to the kindly gentleman, and was out of the house within seconds. Lily didn't protest, which was the genuine astonishing facet of the entire incident, and walked calmly back to the schoolyard. After this incident, Lily had two aides assigned to prevent her from running and attacking other students.

Cheryl was involved directly and intimately in every aspect of that classroom, and every other classroom she worked in, for over forty years.

Chapter 19

ANGELS WALKING AMONG US

I've been blessed in another part of my career: I've had some of the best teacher's aides in the business. They can be the bane of a special educator's vocation, or they can be the deliverance. When I had classrooms with four or five aides, there were times when I actually yelled out loud, "How many kids do I have? Nine or fifteen?" Unfair, but I'm human, and it can be extremely difficult to manage the room if you have to manage four or five adults continuously, too. Actually, I've always had at least one aide, and usually two, who were what I have come to call "angels walking among us." They work for just above minimum wage, and school districts justify this by giving them benefits. They take care of students many people don't even realize are in school, much less appreciate having a caring, decent person helping these students with toileting, feeding, mobility, and a host of other personal and educational needs.

Most of the kids in my classes over the years could not attend school without constant, close adult supervision, and these people do this for us as a society without much fanfare or acknowledgement. Teacher's aides truly are angels walking among us. I don't think I can overstate that sentiment.

When I first started at Harrogate High School, after my disastrous first attempt at teaching, I was still wary about being in charge of anyone. I had already done that in the army, and felt I only wanted to be responsible for myself, and myself alone. The problem was, I had learned well what it meant to be in charge. I always flash back to my real first experience in learning and understanding the *real* basics of leadership.

In February 1977, as a private first class, I had charge of quarters (CQ) on a Friday and through the night in a tactical intelligence unit in Augsburg, Germany. During the day, I was a runner (I ran errands) for the first sergeant, and at four in the evening I was tasked with helping a duty sergeant burn all the classified documents produced during the day, or in our case, several days' accumulation. It amounted to two dozen or more paper bags packed tight with material and stapled closed. This was still the dark ages in intelligence work, before large shredders. We burned the bags manually in a pit at the far end of Flak Kaserne (the US military base). It was cold, damp, and getting dark.

The sergeant first class, who was in charge of myself and a CQ from a different company, met us and we started unloading the bags into the pit. It wouldn't hold more than two or three bags at once. We had to manually move the bags around to ensure the burning would continue evenly. The sergeant first class never lifted a finger, just barked orders at us and complained that everything we did was wrong. It was on purpose. Without a word exchanged between me and the other duty CQ, we staged a complete work slowdown. The sergeant had a family waiting for him; we were single and had nowhere to go, except to pull the rest of our CQ duties, which consisted of sitting in an office and answering the phone through the night until six the next morning. If the sergeant had been even remotely polite or helpful, maybe by just helping put the bags in the pit, he would have been home several hours before he was. He had no real power over us, and wasn't a familiar face to us around the Kaserne. It wouldn't have mattered to whom he had complained. After it was all over and he was forced to release us for the last few minutes of dinner, as the chow hall was closing, I turned to him.

"Sergeant, you taught me a valuable lesson today."

"What's that, hot shot?" he said with deep annoyance.

"How to never be or act when you're in charge. Thanks for that."

"Get the fuck outta here."

I've never forgotten that lesson. I've tried to live it in any job where I have been in charge or responsible for anyone.

Jill was in my first class at Harrogate High School. We stayed together for four years there, and then two more years at Culver High School. I became totally dependent on her, and knew without a doubt she had my back, and usually was one step ahead of me. Jill could have easily been an excellent classroom teacher but had chosen to work at this level. She carried the health benefits for her family, while her husband ran the family's business. I found this to be true for many of my aides over the years. She saw me through many challenges, and was always supportive and helpful in calming me down and soothing me when I'd rant about the bureaucracy and stupidity flooding our schools. She loved helping students, and could spend hours not only following my goals, but usually improving and upping the ante of anything I thought of, especially activities with an art pursuit.

I've never had an inclination to celebrate my birthday at school. Teacher assistants love to celebrate anything, and we still celebrate students' birthdays and many other milestones. That first year, I deliberately lied about when my birthday was so it could pass without notice.

"When's your birthday?" Jill asked as we were putting up the student and staff's names on a board, to keep track throughout the year.

"Oh, it was this past July, so it's all right, don't worry about it," I insisted a little too fervently. Jill looked at me askew for a moment and said okay.

This was in August and my birthday is in September. The next day, I noticed the correct date up next to my name. She had gone to the office and checked with the secretary and found me out. It was sweet.

That school year, on January 8, 2002, President George W. Bush signed the No Child Left Behind Act (NCLB), which Congress passed into law with overwhelming bipartisan support in 2001. It was the name for the most recent update to the Elementary and Secondary Education Act of 1965. I didn't think anything of it; politicians pass laws that don't have significant influence on classrooms all the time. This one did. I have come to believe it was the first salvo over the bow to end public education, as we know it. The political left has loaded up schools with the intention of solving every social ill coming down the pike. In the last five decades we have added over forty-five responsibilities to schools involving everything from safety, health, smoking, CPR, drug, alcohol, teen pregnancy, gang education, busing, bicycles, gun, water safety classes to HIV/AIDS training to work programs to ethnic studies to sexual abuse. Jamie Vollmer, a sharp business man who points this out in speeches around the country said, "No generation of teachers in the history of the world has been asked to meet the goals we have laid out for them." The pressure makes education or learning one of the last priorities in the school day. The political right, basically and simply, does not want to pay for it anymore. The schools are caught in the middle. NCLB set such high standards that few schools could meet the criteria and many would end up as a "failing" schools.

This eventually happened at Harrogate. Three years later, the boom came down on us. The law stated that teacher assistants had to meet new conditions by the end of the next year to continue their job. This wasn't merely a job for most of these angels; they lived for the opportunity to take care of these kids. They had to either have two years of college (sixty credit hours) or take a written test online or leave the profession. The next year we lost Bruce, who not only didn't want to take the test, but also was righteously pissed. A full-page article was published in the *Arizona Daily Star* lauding the merits of the bill, and mentioned nothing about the evils or unintended consequences, as usual.

One day Mr. Johnson was walking through our school with the new special education director visiting classrooms. I now know he didn't think I was in the room at that time. I had made my displeasure with the requirement well known.

"Oh hi, Brant. Well, this is Ms. Van Zandt, the new director," he said quietly.

"Hi, nice to meet you. I've heard a lot of good things about you from Mr. Johnson," she said.

We passed pleasantries back and forth for a moment, and then she asked me, "Is there anything that concerns you going on in the department?"

Mr. Johnson looked down.

"Yes, as a matter of fact, very much so." I said.

"What would that be?"

"Well, they way the district is handling the No Child Left Behind requirements is not only wrong, it should be a class action law suit in the making. I'm replaceable, he's replaceable, and I'm sorry, but you're replaceable. I have an aide that we're losing who isn't replaceable. No one can do the job he's doing. Why you aren't grandfathering this test or the college requirement for assistants that have been in this job - some of them decades - is beyond understanding."

Johnson was almost literally dragging her from my room. As she was leaving, she waved her hand and said, "Thank you for your candid opinion. We can discuss this at a later time."

"No problem, I'm here every day. Thanks," I said, laughing.

It really wasn't a funny situation, though, and that night I sent another letter to our paper.

New Law for Aides Will Leave Many Students Behind
The February 4 article "Law Forces Aides to Prove Skills" left out a few important issues. The Elementary and Secondary Education Act, commonly referred to as No Child Left Behind, mainly pertains to Title I schools. (These are schools receiving Federal Funds under segregation laws or due to low economic neighborhoods) The law is quite clear. Tucson Unified School District has blanketed the requirements for all teacher assistants, forcing aides that have been helping students (some for decades) to leave the profession now, which is criminal.

Most teacher aides do not make ten dollars an hour as stated. Most start at between seven and nine dollars as hour. If one has an associate arts degree or sixty credit hours, this pay is unacceptable. TUSD has not mentioned raising pay to commensurate the education now required. Forcing people out without a real possibility of hiring new people must be looked at as a cost-cutting measure. Many schools have job openings, but no applicants are interested in this extremely difficult job for such low pay, especially in the special education fields. In my five years of teaching in special education, I have seen extremely caring, motivated and concerned individuals taking care of the personal needs of severely disabled students; to force them out or require an arbitrary test will, in fact, leave many children behind.

Brant Vickers
Special Education Teacher
Harrogate High School

I never did hear from Ms. Van Zant, and she retired at the end of the year, but several aides thanked me, and I was forced to state the same refrain I had to for more than the next decade: I wish I had the power to double your pay. The only thing I felt I could do for them was make our classroom a comfortable and pleasant place to work - to respect them, and be constantly thankful for their presence, help, and hard work.

The next year, the district finally relented and gave aides another year to meet the requirements, although they had to move aides from Title I schools if they didn't have them. I talked with Bruce until I was blue in the face, trying to get him to not quit flat out, but stay with the district and continue his retirement contributions. He took a job driving buses, and is doing fine. His wife, Sherry, worked in another classroom, and we kept in touch. She constantly reminded me that during one of our endless but pleasurable conversations about music, I had inadvertently agreed to see AC/DC with him by stating they were the only heavy metal group I really liked. The Young brothers have a great act and they don't pretend to be anything other than what they are – you're going to hear rock and roll. I often quote Angus Young from an interview I read years ago, where the reporter said, "You've been accused of having seven albums that all sound exactly the same."

Angus slammed his hand down on the table and said, "*Bullshit!*" He paused for a moment and then softly said, "We have eight albums that sound exactly the same."

I didn't think that they would tour again. I mean, they were in their late fifties, so I didn't really think of it as a possibility. I felt safe.

One day almost five years later, and after I had returned to Harrogate, Sherry, smiling like crazy, walked up to me and said, "Did you hear?"

"Hear what?" I asked innocently, not even realizing what she could be talking about.

"AC/DC just released a new CD called *Black Ice*, and they are going on tour."

I know I looked shocked. She immediately said, "Oh no, you promised. He's been planning on this for years. You said you'd go; you have to."

I did, and we had a great time. I bought the best tickets I could get, and we drove to Phoenix and then I got up the next day and went to work. Actually, they put on a great show. I'm glad we did that, and even gladder I slipped some cotton in my ear without Bruce noticing.

A few days later, Sherry was late to work. She came by my room and said, "I don't have time, but you need to call Bruce tonight. He'll fill you in on what happened this morning."

Bruce had continued working a couple of nights a week at group homes, one of the hardest working guys I've ever known. I called him later and he related the story to me. It seems we weren't quite free of Owsley.

Bruce gets up early or goes straight from his night job to drive the bus, and that's what happened the morning before. I always knew that during the day, for the five years he worked with him, he took Owsley home sometimes, especially when they ran out of things to do around the school and city. My defense was always going to be, that if someone had a problem with it, they could take Owsley for a couple of days and see how they enjoyed the experience. Bruce lived on one side of town, and Owsley's group home was on the opposite side, separated by almost ten miles.

Bruce filled me in. The night before, Owsley had escaped from his group home and disappeared. The next morning, Sherry started walking out her front door to take their daughter to go to school and then work. She walked out her front door and stopped, took a step back inside, slammed the door, and called Bruce, who was on his way to his first bus stop for students.

"Bruce, are you driving?" she asked, distraught.

"Yeah, what's wrong?" he asked.

"Owsley is sitting on our porch," she said.

"What?"

"What should I do? Can you come home?"

"No, don't do anything. Lock the door and call nine-one-one. Do it right now."

"What should I tell them?"

"Nothing. Just tell them some guy is sitting on our porch. Don't tell them that you know him. They're probably looking for him."

They were, and the group home people showed up about the same time the police did. The police had the description and alert that had been out all night. We were amazed to the point of speechlessness that Owsley could remember and had journeyed that much of the city at night without incident (that we knew of). Sherry said he was handcuffed immediately, and we thought that perhaps whoever was working with him had finally learned a few things and passed that knowledge on to the police. It seemed we would probably never be completely free of Owsley.

About this time, Sue Ellen came to me from one of the Title I elementary schools. She was going to have to take the test in a couple of months and needed a home until that time. I immediately recognized a strong German accent. Sue Ellen was extremely nervous and quiet. She had never worked with high school kids, much less big kids. Some of our students could be intimidating, not only because of their disabilities, but their size could be threatening. I waited until the second or third day she was there. She asked me what we did about towels.

"Nehmen Sie die Handtücher nach Hause und waschen Sie sie," I rattled off.

Sue Ellen looked at me in disbelief. "What did you say? I mean, I don't understand."

"Warum Sie nicht verstehen?"

She continued to look at me. "Ya, Ich verstehe. But wait, you speak German?"

"Ja, ich lebte in Augsburg seit neun Jahren."

I had told her to take the towels home and wash them, and then asked why she didn't understand me, I told her I'd lived in Augsburg for nine years. Sue Ellen had grown up in Neu Ulm, just down the road from Augsburg. She had married a soldier and had come to the United States to raise a family. Sue Ellen had worked as an aide for years. Things went much better for her, and she came to enjoy our students. After a while, she studied and passed the NCLB test, and ultimately chose to stay at Harrogate until she retired.

Sue Ellen told me many times how much she enjoyed working with me, and that I was the best teacher she had worked with. It was one of the most treasured friendships in my career. Sue Ellen sealed my loyalty to her by bringing me back a Weizen beer from Bavaria on a trip back from Germany to visit family.

Gillian came to us the next year in 2002, and started in my room. She was a single mom with two teenagers, and was a hard worker. Gillian was there only two weeks when the issue of her sexuality came up. One of my other aides, Julio, asked me to talk to her. Julio was gay also, but said that Gillian was talking about it more than a couple of the other aides felt was necessary, and it was making them uncomfortable. Gillian and I went for a walk with one of our student's named Nastas down the track.

"How's your first couple of weeks going?" I asked.

"Did someone complain about me being here?" she asked.

"No, why would you think that?" I asked, taken aback.

"I was wondering if Julio was having a problem."

"What do you think his issue would be, if he had one?"

"I told him I was gay, and thought it might be a problem. He seems uncomfortable with my talking about it."

"Did he tell you what his sexual preference was?" I asked.

She laughed and said, "I don't think he had to; I can tell," she said.

"Well, you got me, because I didn't know for months, but the thing is, it doesn't matter."

"I thought you might have a problem. Someone told me you were in the military," she said.

"I was. For over twenty years."

"Well, I thought it might be a problem."

"No, I don't care at all. That's the key; there were probably several teachers here who were gay. I don't think you can be in this profession without meeting teachers, and even students, that are gay, and I don't think you can stay in the profession if you have a problem with it. I was in the army, and most of us welcomed Don't Ask, Don't Tell. We were more than happy to get out of the morality business. A couple of the hardest days of my life were being involved in having a young gay soldier, man or woman, get discharged. I'm proud to say, I think I was very helpful in getting people out with honorable discharges, with full benefits. My goal was to let them just move on with their lives, because this was even before 'Don't Ask, Don't Tell.'"

"Well, what is Julio saying?" she asked.

"I think what Julio is saying is that he respects a couple of the people here who do have religious issues, and the best way to handle that is to keep it private, and I'd expect the same from them. They shouldn't be talking about it to anyone, and if they do, or have an issue with it, let me know and I'll talk to them."

"That sounds fine," she said.

After that, we got along fine, and even had some laughs about life and all of our predicaments. Cheryl and I had decided to get married after six years of being together. I was talking about how since neither of us attended church, and we were having a very small wedding in our backyard; it was hard finding someone to perform the ceremony.

"I know a minister who does that. You have to see her a couple times and talk. Not really counseling, but just for her to get to know you," Gillian said. "She performs weddings, or actually ceremonies for gay couples that can't get married legally."

It was perfect. The minister was very kind, and performed a beautiful ceremony for our family and friends. Cheryl's parents and sisters came out, but my dad's health was getting worse. He simply said, "Brant, I've been to two of your weddings and I really like Cheryl, so let's do things differently. I'll pass and it'll work this time." Smart guy. I was grateful for Gillian's help.

We had planned our wedding, and Cheryl's family was due in from Ohio. We had to limit the wedding to a small circle of friends, and I didn't invite any coworkers, but let them know I was sorry. We simply did not have the room at our house or backyard. I was taking a Friday and a Monday off. That was really unusual for me, but I always knew no matter who the sub was, my kids were in good hands with Jill. The next Thursday, just after all the kids were safely on the buses, I was called to the office. When I got there, they said Mr. Johnson was in the teacher's lounge and wanted to talk to me. I walked over thinking, *What the hell? Now? Just before I'm going home?* I walked in and couldn't believe it. The center table was covered with presents and a large cake. A banner stretched across the wall, said Good Luck. Jill had planned the whole thing without me having a clue. I was brought to tears.

"We just wanted you to know how much we appreciate what you do for us and how much of a team spirit you've created here for us," Jill said. Along with my class, several teachers and aides from other classes came by for a few minutes. The next week I got word through the grapevine (the aides all have their own telegraph line, usually quite accurate) that the math teacher was grumbling about the little party my aides had set up. The math teacher had gotten married the week before, and I don't think anyone did anything for her. I never had the chance, but would have liked to explain a few things about a special ed teacher's relationship with his or her aides. If it's done right, the loyalty, and even devotion, to one another can be extremely powerful. We watch one another's backs and have to trust one another.

I treated my aides to, what Sue Ellen came to call, "Sandwich Friday" every few weeks. I wanted them to know I was on their side and they were on mine. If they had to sneak out a few minutes early, I always let them, and was adamant I would take the hit if it were discovered and frowned upon. After my first full year with Bruce, Jill, Julio, and several others, I sent away for a special present for what I considered my team. My old roommate Art was in Korea, and I sent him money and a guesstimate on sizes for silk embroidered dragon jackets with their names on them. It was beyond a success. I wasn't trying to over do anything, I was just was thankful for finally finding my way in this profession and thought, *I'll never have another first year like this.*

Early into the next school year, Gillian, who was working with Granger at that point, was doing fine. NCLB requirements were still being enforced, and another aide told me Gillian was in the lounge crying. The aide said, "She said she finally found a job she liked and was now going to be fired and have to find something else with benefits; it wasn't fair.'" I talked to her and told her we'd get together on the exam questions. There was a study guide available, and I was sure she could pass it. The next week, she was out for two days. When she came back in, she told me she had a note from her doctor, and that she couldn't lift anything for an undetermined period of time. She had a serious back problem.

"Just take the note to the office for the principal," I said.

Gillian said, "I already did."

"No problem," I answered.

One day while she was talking about her missing work the next day for one of her innumerable physical therapy appointments, I asked her a couple of questions; interested in what they had her doing.

"Does he have you do any stomach exercises? I do that in the gym for prevention, too. I've read that's a good thing to do to protect your back."

"No, he doesn't," she said, looking down.

"What does he have you do?" I asked, honestly just curious.

"Just some stuff."

I let it go.

After a couple of weeks, there were several times I wasn't available to help lift Granger. The other aides thought something wasn't right. I had let it go too far, and suddenly Julio braced me.

"Brant, when are you going to do something about Gillian? She's faking, and we're sick of her lying and not doing any lifting," he said.

"How do you know she's lying about her back injury?" I asked.

"She's always talking about going dancing and she went hiking last weekend."

Coincidently, Peggy, who had a class with only one student who had to be lifted as opposed to our three, also had an aide who wanted a change.

"She'll be happy. *Everyone* wants to work in *Brant's* class," Peggy said, laughing sarcastically. "It'll be a good exchange."

I told Gillian the next day and she just had a funny look on her face. I wondered what was really wrong. I found out a week or so later.

Mr. Johnson called Peggy and me up to his office and showed us an email Gillian had sent him. She was quitting, but not before she lambasted Peggy and me for harassing her constantly about being gay, ignoring her back pain, and accusing us of making fun of her discomfort. We had also moved her for no reason, just to get her out of my room. We were dumbfounded.

"We thought we were helping her," Peggy said. It had really hurt Peggy's feelings. I just laughed.

"I don't know what's going on here, but I don't think it really had anything to do with us," I said. "Did she give you anything else from her doctor about her back and limitations?" I asked him.

"What are you talking about?" he asked.

"Any follow-up notes, prescriptions, or whatever you need from her doctor?"

"What do you mean, 'follow-up notes'? I never got anything," he said as he wheeled around and started looking through files. He reminded me of an army company commander, keeping records to be efficient but also cover his ass.

"She told me she brought you the first note from her doctor," I said, already thinking I had been tricked. "This could be on me. I trusted her."

"There's nothing here about her back, much less a doctor's note, prescription for light duty, or anything since she was hired. I was just about to ask you guys why she was missing so much work."

A week or so later, Julio said he had the scoop. I didn't even ask where or why he got it. He said her partner had recently received full disability - falsely - and was telling Gillian that it would be easy; all she had to do was fake a back injury. I guess she thought she could simply justify it by telling us she hurt her back. We didn't believe she ever actually saw a doctor. It was sad, because I thought she was a good worker and got along with the kids; I would have liked to have kept her in my room.

Chapter 20

BILL, BABAK, AND ME

As happened regularly throughout my years as a special education teacher at Harrogate High School, a meeting would take place about a student in another class who needed a male role model, or about a typical student who needed a placement outside of his regular schedule as a "safe place." I seemed to frequently be the chosen one to fill this need. Out of the four self-contained classes, I was the only male teacher. Sometimes I knew it was coming through the grapevine, and usually was prepared. I always attempted to be a team player, and knew many times there was no other answer, though I certainly didn't see Babak coming. I knew he had issues, but none of us saw the projection of difficulties that would develop his last year in school.

Babak's father was Iranian and his mom, Russian. On the surface it wouldn't have been an issue, but combined with his disabilities and some mitigating circumstances, it turned out to be a disastrous combination. Babak was extremely high functioning, and had no business in a self-contained room. He was a senior, and during a brief meeting, I heard he was having trouble in every class he was in, saying things that were inappropriate and acting strangely without any provocation or discernible reason. Bizarre. They asked me if he could have my room as a way station, or time-out place to settle down when things happened. And settle down, they did. Babak was over six feet tall, dark-complected, thin but naturally strong looking, and could be fairly imposing. He towered over many of his female teachers, and would stand extremely close to a person when he was talking to them. He repeated things that were said to him. My first contact with him had been earlier in the year, which was his senior year, when I'd gone to pick up one of my students from the English resource room. I opened the door and saw Babak get up from his chair right at that moment. I still have no idea what prompted it, but he started running around the room. The resource teacher, Ms. Adams, started shouting while Babak picked up a box from a corner of the room, put it on his head, and started screaming from inside it.

"Hit me! Hit me!" he started yelling, sounding like he was underwater. Three students jumped up and began pounding on the box and howling. Everyone was shouting, and Ms. Adams was yelling for them to stop, but Babak kept running around the room waving his arms, with several boys chasing him. Since he couldn't see where he was going, he kept running into desks and tables.

"Hit me! Hit me!" And the other kids were pounding on him and screaming, "Kill him! Get him! Hit him!"

When several students realized the door had opened, everyone slowed down and then more or less stopped. Ms. Adams was crying.

"You guys need to sit down, and Babak, take that box off your head and sit down," I said.

"So, you want me to take the box off my head and sit down," Babak said to me from underneath the box. It sounded muted, like he was far away.

"Yes, do it," I said louder and forcefully.

Babak took the box off and started to walk over to me at the door and go through his whole routine, which was to repeat everything that was said to him about a hundred times.

"Sit down," I said.

"So you want me to sit down and be quiet," Babak said, holding the box.

He leaned forward, holding his hand out with his palm up and cupped, softly repeating everything with different voices, until I, as most teachers did, lost it.

"So, you want me to -"

"No, do not repeat what I said. Do it," I said. "And sit down - now."

Later, Cheryl as a speech pathologist, taught me how to deal with that repetitive speech pattern. I had to simply tell Babak that he could continue to repeat what was said, but I wasn't going to repeat what I had said, and he would eventually fade off. I soon learned that these kinds of incidents were mild compared to what some teachers were going through. He had been through the gambit of every disability label that had been possible for him to have. He was at some point given a diagnosis of autism, specific learning disability, multiple learning disabilities, mild intellectual disability, speech language impaired, developmental delays, and ADD/ADHD. Throughout his school experience, none of them stuck. He was an awfully smart guy when he was on; unfortunately, that was inconsistent and rare. Babak spent a part of the day telling women teachers, "I can smell your sex, and you are inferior to me because you're a woman, and that makes you foolish. You should be subservient to me or any male." Since he was a student with the label of "special needs," he couldn't be suspended more than ten days all year.

Some days he'd been sent home, but then he'd be back the following day. It was getting to be a real problem when they hit on the idea of a safe place "home room" for him. I had an excellent aide that year;

Bill, who took Babak under his care and virtually became his personal guardian. We learned more about Babak and his background the rest of that year than we both wanted to. He usually never made it through the entire day, especially if he had one of his women-are-garbage meltdowns. Babak lived with his mother and sister. He spent the weekends with his dad. Every Monday he would have a fresh, new nuanced take on misogyny riffs directed at his female teachers. Bill started talking to him and found out what we expected: They all came from his dad. What got scary was that he started verbally threatening and acting violent toward his mother and sister. He refused to do any work around the house and told us, "That's beneath me, and I shouldn't have to do women's work. That's what they're for, anyway. I refuse." It got to the point where they had to call the police, and different social services got involved. He was moved to a group home.

He expanded his vitriol to include Jewish people, and asked us at different times quite pointedly if we were Jews.

"Mr. Brant, are you a Jew?"

"Why do you need to know?"

"If you are, my dad says I should be moved to another classroom and shouldn't talk to you."

"Well, I'm not answering that, because if it's a problem I only have one thing to say to you and your dad – and that's mind your own business."

"I'll tell him you said that," Babak said.

"Good, you do that, but right now you need to continue catching up on your math homework," I said.

"So, you want me to ignore that you might be a stinking filthy Jew and do my homework."

I walked out of the room. It didn't matter that I actually wasn't.

Babak probably watched a lot of cable; at least that's what we came to believe, because he could remember whole scenes and dialogue from movies and TV shows. When Babak's teachers didn't know how to handle him, and hoped he would never get completely out of hand, they let him act scenes out for fun. If he got the floor for a few minutes, sometimes he would be calm for a period of time. That led to what I considered the saddest incident in his school career. Another racist fixation popped up before we could stop it. Bill was accompanying him this hour, and we figured he must have watched an African-American comic on a show, and somehow thought it was appropriate and funny for him to repeat it. Babak had been carrying around a Benju, a small stringed Iranian instrument, and playing and breaking into song whenever he got the chance. I didn't allow it in my class, but others let him do the burn-off-energy thing once a day. He got up in front of class and everyone thought, "Oh no, here he goes again." But . . .

"I talk like a black man! I talk like a black man!" Babak started to shout in a low, gruff singsong voice. He was waving his arms around and trying to do some sort of bizarre dance moves at the same time.

"Don't give me any shit, motherfucker. I'm a big, bad, fuckin' sad black man."

Everyone was laughing, and his teacher kept telling him to stop. Everyone was laughing except T. D. T. D. was usually a pretty quiet African-American guy. I'd seen him get in trouble, but when he did, he always got up and walked out of class. Then they dealt with him in the office. His problems were with the teachers and the work he was given to do, rarely with other kids. Today his problem was with Babak. I know they'd had words before about Babak's saying things to him. One time at buses, I heard Babak ask him if it was hard to be a black man in a world that hates him because he's black and crazy.

"What the fuck are you talking about, you crazy, fucked-up Arab motherfucker?!" T. D. yelled that day. He got in trouble and never even told on Babak, or why he yelled it. I tried to intercede on T. D.'s behalf, but unfortunately, he'd said it in front of several other students that didn't hear Babak.

After that, Babak stayed away from T. D., but that day he must have forgotten. He moved closer to T. D. in the front row, and more or less got right up in his face. It must have been something he'd seen in a movie or on TV, but he was twirling around and smiling and singing. Bill started from the back of the room at this moment, but was a second too late.

"I'm a black, black man, you white piss-ant motherfuckers and pink titty suckers."

That's about all he got out before T. D. jumped up and punched him in the face. Babak fell down on the ground and started yelling and crying, and T. D. stood there over him. The teacher was yelling, and everyone was in shock, sitting there staring and trying to process what happened.

"Get up, motherfucker, and I'll show what a black man can do, you crazy piece-of-shit motherfucker."

T. D. was suspended for three days, but Babak was back the next day.

One day Babak was sitting at the computer. When he did, we would only check in on him. He never showed an interest in looking for porn; he was usually looking up strange musical instruments, or Russian or Iranian cultural-related things - music, literature, or history. I slid up to him and wanted to give him a few minutes and show interest in what he was looking at. He had a large map up on the screen. I looked closely and saw it was a map of the former USSR, with large red circles displaying Chernobyl radiation patterns in the northern Ukraine.

"What is the interest in that Babak?" I asked.

"I'm looking at where my mom used to live," he answered.

"When did she live there?"

"Well, she lived there until the Chernobyl nuclear power plant accident in April 1986."

"She lived there then?"

"Yes, she lived in Pripyat. It's right there." He pointed at the map. Pripyat was in the dark red area, indicating the highest level of contamination.

"Wow, what happened?"

"Well, she could see the power plant from her house, and that's why she's here. She was a refugee from Russia. Now, of course, she's an American citizen. She met my dad while they both were coming here from different places."

"I know," I said, looking over at Bill. "That's interesting." We both were flabbergasted.

It was getting down to the end of the year and Babak's behavior was getting worse. I went to the Department of Developmental Disabilities as the school representative, and sat in another meeting with about seven to eight people, which included a psychiatrist who led the meeting. When it was my turn to speak, I stated strongly that his problems did not fit in with any I had experienced in special education before. He didn't fit the pattern of any of the disabilities we normally saw with students. I didn't feel school could offer him any more help, or provide for his educational needs. All I was thinking of were the female teachers and students who would have to put up with his actions for another two to three years. His mom and group home director disagreed vehemently. He was a senior, but as a special education student, he could theoretically stay in school until he was twenty-two. Schools are attempting to change this now, but in the late 2000s it could still be pushed. We talked and nothing was resolved. That night, I received an email from the doctor, his psychiatrist, and the note said, "Mr. Vickers, thanks for your input. It was most invaluable. Click on this link. It fits Babak like a glove. I'm in the process of changing his label again, and I hope it gets him the help he so very much needs."

I clicked on it and this came up: pre-affect schizoid personality disorder.

We had his Individual Education Program (IEP) coming up soon. I wasn't even his case manager at this point, but no one else wanted to do it, so I took on the task. While going over the paperwork, I started formulating an idea. It looked as though his mom and his caseworker hadn't followed up on getting guardianship for him. He was already nineteen, so legally, no one could make decisions for him. We had record of several IEPs where the information was given to Mom and she'd never followed up on it. This comes up often with special ed kids. The parents don't realize the ramifications of this legal issue. The school's hands are tied, and we can only do what we do in the meetings; parents eventually have to take responsibility for their kids. Babak could decide what he wanted to do. Bill and I started working on him. We had several talks about what he desired, and he told us he very much wanted to leave school and graduate with his class.

We'd say, "Babak, what do you want to do? What would a man do?"

"I'm leaving school. I'm a man," he'd tell us.

And so on, day after day.

I was morally at odds about this, but felt the school, my peers, aides, and the other students had to have someone looking out for *them*. I simply, unequivocally, felt I was protecting us from a student with mental illness, and that his placement in school wasn't appropriate or safe.

At his IEP, the group home supervisor yelled and lost control about the decision Babak had made. He was there and it was beautiful; he stood his ground.

"He's obviously been manipulated by you and your staff. He can't leave school. He isn't ready," she all but screamed. She knew the group home would have to pay someone to stay with him all day, every day. He would never work or be trained, and Babak was already in their system. They always wanted their clients to stay in school as long as possible.

"It isn't up to me, it's up to Babak. You have to direct your questions to him and what he wants," I answered.

"Let's ask him." She directed this statement to my department head that was running the meeting. Our job developer was also present; she and I had had words concerning where this was going to go. Her name was Bonnie and she was sympathetic to his staying. I pointed out to her (and usually did to people when these situations came up) that she wasn't going to have to deal with him or spend the day putting out his fires, resolving possibly violent situations, or calming teachers down after Babak told them they should be disrespected and ignored as "it was required." It's easy to sit back and say, "Everyone deserves a public education and a chance to succeed in school, and teachers should learn how to improve their classroom management skills." The people saying that are usually administrators or politicians who aren't actually dealing with the student six and a half hours a day, five days a week, 185 days a year.

"Babak, do you want to stay in school another year or two, or do you want to graduate?" Bonnie asked very quietly.

He sat there for a long minute and thought it over. I held my breath and wondered for the thousandth time if this was the morally right thing to do, but once again, came to the same conclusion. We already had two teachers contemplate whether they would come back again if Babak returned to school the next year.

"He can't not come back next year," the group home representative blurted out.

"Excuse me, let him think," Bonnie started to say.

"I definitely want to graduate," Babak jumped in.

"No, you can't," she started again.

"Yes, I can and I will. My dad told me you women shouldn't be telling me what to do, and you can't make me."

At graduation, which no one from the group home attended, Bill and I stood there and waved at Babak as he left with his mom and sister, all three walking away warily.

Chapter 21

A GRANDMOTHER FROM HEAVEN

Alisa had cerebral palsy. Alisa had it rough. She was in a wheelchair and couldn't move herself around. Alisa was nonverbal, but could communicate some needs and wants, and could definitely show emotion through guttural sounds. She would lift her head and look your way and give the appearance of smiling and nodding if we were right. We tried a variety of picture symbols, but Alisa didn't seem interested in that or picking out what she wanted from visual symbols; she wanted the pretense of vocal communication, if only in perception. She came to me after trying several other classes. One of my professors in my graduate program interviewed these very grandparents and titled the interview "The Angriest People in the World." Grandma visited several times, asked pointed questions, and expressed concerns, and we talked about what I thought we should be doing, but mostly I steered the conversation toward her and what she wanted for Alisa. We talked about her swimming twice a week in the therapy pool, attending music and art classes, and getting off campus into the community at least once a week. She was concerned and then elated that I wasn't opposed to her stretching out on our carpet and bean bags a couple of times a day.

At the intake meeting to change her room assignment and placement, we started going through Alisa's last IEP, which coincidentally was also due. I couldn't believe what they had put down for academic goals. Her last teacher and our department head had her doing things I wouldn't expect some typical kids to accomplish. It was plain senseless. Our department head, Greta, did things like this, and it constantly confounded me. Alisa's last teacher had been a good-hearted person, but not a strong personality, and probably didn't want to fight and stand up to Greta. Greta and I got along for the most part, but had had some differences over the last couple of years. I honestly liked her, but she was a classic administrator who followed the approach, "Do as I say; not as I've ever done, nor will ever do."

I remembered the first week of school several years ago, when she was going to demonstrate and enlighten me on how to handle Owsley. She lasted about an hour, maybe two. He was on the track after leaving several attempts to engage him in activities, and had flipped over a desk. Greta was following him and trying to cajole him back into the classroom.

"Owsley, let's go back into the room and do some picture drawing."

"Uck you, bitch," he said.

"Fuck you, too, you little son of a bitch," she said before he was finished.

I was following her and started laughing.

"Oh my God, I'm sorry," she said to me. This was god's gift to special education and "best practices."

"Don't worry about it. He gets to everybody," I said still laughing. Since then, I'd taken everything she said with a grain of salt.

Luckily that day, halfway through the meeting on Alisa, Greta had to attend to an emergency. As the stand-in for the principal when he wasn't in, she had to attend to the incident. As I started to go over the goals from the last year and introduce my new ones, I was trying to diplomatically tell them that Alisa couldn't possibly accomplish the goals from last year. Grandma leaned forward.

"Oh, honey, you put down on those papers whatever you want to. I've been listening to you guys play this game for a dozen years or more. You can send my little darling to MIT if you need to; I've already seen you're going to do her right. I want her clean, safe, and happy in her classroom, and mostly, not forgotten."

I could have kissed her. It wouldn't be the last time I felt this way. Grandma and Grandpa were a couple of the nicest people that have ever walked the earth. Grandpa was a former construction worker and retired contractor, a down-to-earth, plain-speaking, nice guy. Grandma was the same. Alisa's mom was a drug addict who rarely communicated with Alisa, and only visited one time that I can remember.

"We weren't going to let the state take care of our angel and put her in a group home with strangers. We'll take care of her as best we can, as long as we can," Grandpa told me one time.

They did. I remember asking a counselor what we all were going to do when all the grandparents were gone and couldn't take care of their grandkids with disabilities. I've never understood how we have evolved to a point that parents can walk away from their children because they can't handle it. In every self-contained classroom, there are at least one or two students being raised by their grandparents. If after a divorce, someone has to pay child support to the spouse with custody, why can't the state force parents to pay child support to the state for twenty-four-hour supervision, housing, feeding, health care, and activities?

One afternoon, a couple of us were walking toward the main building after being outside for a walk. I had Granger, and an aide, Alayna, had Alisa, and both Granger and Alisa were in wheelchairs. As we were walking down a slight decline, two students ran by us and bumped Alayna. She lost her balance and went down on one knee. I immediately put on Granger's brakes, but before she or I could grab Alisa, she rolled about five feet, and one of her wheels hit a stone. She came to an abrupt stop, and, her chair spilled over onto the gravelly path. She was still strapped in her chair. As I ran up to her, Alisa gave out a moan I'll never forget. I righted her and ran her to the nurse's office. She had several fairly good-sized abrasions on her forehead and one on her arm, but unbelievably, nothing more serious. Still, I saw my career end right there. Alayna was inconsolable; she spent the rest of the next hour crying, and was worried about her job, also. Grandma was there in less than twenty minutes. She and the nurse had talked on the phone, and when she got there, we nervously stood by in the hallway outside the nurse's office while she looked Alisa over. She walked over to us and stood there for a moment.

"Now I want you both to know . . . " We collectively held our breath. I knew the principal was lurking about, and was also waiting for whatever was going to come next.

"I know neither of you would purposely hurt my angel, and I also know you wouldn't have let something like this happen if it could have been prevented. This is something that all kids go through. All of our kids have had accidents growing up, and Alisa's no different. We treat her like we would any of our babies. She's fine and wants to tell you she's okay."

Alisa came out of the office and we talked. She listened to how sorry we were and she smiled and nodded when we asked her if she wanted to go home with Grandma early. I later learned she found the principal and told him she didn't want to hear anymore about it - it was over and closed - and she surely didn't want to hear of any repercussions against us about the incident.

Alisa aged out two years later. She turned twenty-two, and by law, couldn't stay in school any longer. At graduation, Grandma came up to me and hugged me hard. She didn't seem like she was going to let me go. She pulled me down close to her and whispered, "I wish Alisa could stay in your class forever."

Chapter 22

WHAT THE FUCK, BRANT?!

Juan was a student with profound cognitive disabilities from cerebral palsy. I had him for several years. He was most comfortable in a recliner I had inherited when I took over the class. We had him participate as much as possible, but it was a struggle to have Juan do *anything* other than simply sit and stare straight ahead. The only activity he seemed to enjoy was swimming in the pool, floating around with arm supports, and an aide or teacher supporting him. His dad, Emmanuel, showed up about once every month or two and demanded he be allowed to swim with Juan. He, as far as we knew from Mom, hardly ever saw Juan otherwise. Bobby agreed to the swimming, with or without legal authorization, trying to be sympathetic to a difficult family situation. Juan's mom obviously loved him, but worked long and tiring hours. We never knew if they were divorced or not. A couple of aides at Harrogate provided respite for Juan on weekends, summers, and any time off school.

Juan taught me that on the horizon I might find a niche in the visually impaired world of teaching. Whenever one of us would walk up to Juan in his wheelchair or La-Z-Boy, he would vigorously flinch and cover his face. Most of us were convinced he was, or had been, abused. Juan's relationship with Mom wasn't where we went with our suspensions though. Several aides theorized it was probably Dad, but without any physical evidence or even a hint of proof, there was nothing we could do. I was loath to bring it up to mom, but one day I felt I had to, at least mention what he was doing.

"I was wondering if Juan flinches at home like he does with us at school. I hate to say anything, but it freaks us out," I said.

"I know he's been doing that since he was an infant. No one has hurt him that I've ever seen or witnessed," she said. "I'm glad you told me, because it shows you care and notice things about him."

One day as I walked toward him from across the room, I realized he only flinched when I came within about two feet from the front. He energetically jerked and recoiled as usual. I waited a few minutes and came upon him from the side slowly and cautiously, and gently put my hand on his shoulder and spoke quietly.

"Hey there, Juan, how's it going? It's Mr. Brant. Just seeing how you're doing."

It worked; he didn't flinch, startle, or jump. I realized he flat out couldn't see us. He was probably close to blind. I later learned this was common with severe cerebral palsy. We were just shadows coming out of nowhere; hence, why we constantly scared the shit out of him, especially me, a big hulking figure with a loud voice barreling down on him out of a haze or darkness. The flinching never went away 100 percent, but we learned to talk softly to him and it cut it down dramatically.

Juan's mom went away on business once or twice a month. When she did, she had respite bring him to school and pick him up. Other times, he rode the bus. Having a student not ride the school-provided transportation was, and still is, a major problem for special ed teachers. I can't count how many times I waited for a parent, guardian, foster parent, group home, respite, or for myriad other reasons the responsible person was late picking up their student. We can't simply dump a special needs student in the office. Most principals require the teacher to wait, and that might be an hour or more. I have never understood how especially a parent can undeniably be so imbalanced and mean as to let their kids sit and wait at school. The special needs students know that they are being disregarded – I've seen the forlorn look on their faces too many times to know it's a thoughtless thing to do to a kid. Not to mention, teachers aren't caregivers or babysitters, but so many times it doesn't seem to bother parents. It's happened too many times for me or one of my peers to keep track.

Emmanuel loved to come in our classroom and show off; telling us everything we were doing wrong, and how much he communicated with Juan, and why couldn't we? He always dressed in old faded Levis, with lots of turquoise jewelry, long hair, sandals, tie-dye shirts (right out of the sixties/seventies), and, of course, Birkenstocks. I didn't mind, and found a middle ground to let him vent, and told him we would take his suggestions to heart. I actually found we had a lot in common with music and having grown up through that period.

"I can't believe you're into the Dead, Brant," he said one day.

"Well, I grew up in the same era and loved it also," I answered. I neglected to tell Emmanuel I still wore Birkenstocks around the house.

This next week, Juan's mom was going to be gone Monday through Friday on a business trip. Dad had sent word in he was going to have Juan several of the days. He never did. Respite was late picking up Juan on Tuesday, Wednesday, and Thursday. We had Bobby talk to them on Tuesday and it didn't do any good. Harrogate had a late start - one of the experimental testing high schools - to see if a late start at nine o'clock, instead of the traditional seven thirty or so, would have any impact on student performance. It didn't. We dismissed at three o'clock. They picked him up two or three days out of the school week and he rode the bus the other days. We could leave after the students did. This week I waited. On Friday, the respite caretaker dropped him off – late, also - and informed us Dad was going to pick Juan up that afternoon and spend the weekend with him. I felt uneasy about that.

Three o'clock came and went. At four o'clock, we attempted to call Dad and got no answer, but left a message. At four thirty I called again. The office manager also called respite and attempted to call Mom on her cell phone, as well as an emergency number (we thought it was her sister's). At five o'clock, the office and the school was making an effort to close. I was still sitting in the foyer with Juan in his wheelchair. I had a complete view of the parking lot. I had also changed him at four o'clock, just in case. The office manager and Bobby approached me.

"If Emmanuel or respite doesn't show up in ten more minutes, we're going to call the police and CPS and invoke an abandoned student," Bobby told me.

"Will he know that?" I asked.

"I've already left that message to both Dad and the respite worker," our office manager said.

They went back to closing up the school as I continued to wait, and I thought about calling Cheryl to tell her we'd be late eating sushi tonight. Suddenly, two cars came screeching into the front parking lot from both ends. They both slammed on their brakes only a foot or two from each other. Emmanuel was out in a flash as I was pushing Juan through the front door and down to the curb. The respite workers didn't even attempt to exit their vehicle. Dad spitefully grabbed the wheelchair from me without a word. I thought, *Cool, a clean getaway* - just as Emmanuel stopped and turned.

"Really, Brant, the fuckin' police? What the fuck, Brant?!" he said as he scooped Juan up and put him in the car, then started to fold up Juan's wheelchair. I merely shrugged, and left to meet Cheryl for our sushi and Friday night Asahi beer celebration.

Chapter 23

A FLASH FROM THE PAST

One Saturday evening after one of Kylin's ballet recitals, we went to Fourth Street in central Tucson to one of the most popular pizza places. It was early, but still crowded with university students. As we started ordering I noticed one of the girls behind the counter looking at me somewhat strangely. I immediately did one of those second looks. I knew her, but couldn't for the life of me place her. Suddenly, she yelled out, "Mr. Vickers, how are you?"

It was one of the Goodman sisters from my first year of teaching at Desert Hills High School. I said, "Hey, you, how're you?"

"I'm doing great, I'm at school and an English major. You were one of my favorite teachers," she said.

I was shocked. I hadn't thought of that year in a long time. I thought of myself as a purely special ed teacher, but once in a while, did wish I could talk to students about literature and the stories I loved reading. The rest of that year had been efficaciously blotted out of my mind. In fact, I rarely mentioned that I had taught English to any of my current peers, or anyone.

"I, I, um, didn't know that," I stammered. I felt strange.

"Yeah, you did some great things. I loved talking about your letter to Harper Lee, and some of the stuff you knew about other writers, and movies you could quote. I know you didn't like it, though. My sister and I always felt bad about that. We were sorry some of the kids were so hard. What are you doing now?" she asked.

"I'm teaching special education and really like it."

"I'll bet you're good at it. Take care," she said as she started to help another customer. I walked away, dazed, and realized the platitudes and clichés we read about the teaching profession are absolutely true - and how we affect students without even appreciating it.

Chapter 24

JUSTIN AND FEET

The next year, I picked up Justin from another class. We traded difficult kids every few years so teachers and aides wouldn't get burned out on the same demanding behaviors, which was easy to do. I alone kept Owsley for four years until I asked for a break, but Bruce went with him and I picked up the slack whenever Bruce was absent.

Justin was a short, thin, good-looking black teenager. He was a student with a textbook case of autism, but was also was an extremely exhausting young man. He had a couple of behaviors that were admittedly disturbing. I agreed to have him in my class and met him at the bus the first day of school. We were walking down the hallway and I was trying to talk to him. I had helped restrain him a couple of times during the last year, and didn't want to have him only know me from those experiences.

"Justin, did you have a good summer?" I asked.

"Good, good. You had a good summer?" he responded.

"Do you mean *my* summer?" I replied, trying to keep that pronoun agreement thing going.

"Yes, yes, how was Mr. Brant's summer?" he asked. I noticed he was suddenly breathing hard as we were walking. To keep the conversation going in the right direction, I went with it.

"My summer was fine. I'm glad to be back at school," I said.

"It was good, good, it was good," Justin picked up the pace.

"I'm glad you're in my class." His breathing was increasing in severity. As we were walking, I saw one of my aides and asked her to accompany him to class; I said that I would be there in a minute. I immediately went to Justin's room from last year. I stuck my head in the door and found his last year's teacher, Toni.

"Does Justin have asthma?" I asked her when she looked up from her desk.

She started laughing and said, "I'm sorry – I know you know about everything, but I did forget to mention how it manifests itself walking down the hallway."

"How what manifests itself?" I asked interrupting her.

"The toes thing."

"What?"

"Let me finish, Mr. I'm-Going-to-Handle-It."

"Okay, sorry, go ahead," I said.

"It's not asthma, you goof, he's hyperventilating. He's looking at girls and their toes and getting exited. I'd watch him for a while, and don't let him go to the bathroom for a while, either." I didn't hear any more as I was rushing humbly to my room.

Justin simply freaked out on girls, mostly toes, or open-toed shoes, or at times, merely girls in general. He'd walk down the hallway singing the warning his teachers always gave him: " No toes, no toes, don't look at toes, no toes."

Later that day, I was walking down the hallway again and saw one of my female aides standing outside the bathroom. I saw a look of horror on her face and immediately asked, what was wrong.

"We were walking by and he bolted into the girls restroom. I didn't have a chance to stop him. He's been on edge all day. I'm sorry."

"Who's in there with him?" I asked. "Or is he in alone?"

"No one," she answered. "At least I don't think so."

"Okay, I'll go in alone at first. If I need help, I'll call you."

I knocked on the door as I eased it open and yelled, "Is there anyone in there?" No answer.

"I'm coming in," I said as I went in the door. I didn't come out for a while, and then stuck my head out and asked my aide to go get the nurse and bring some towels with her when she came back. I stood in the door and didn't let anyone else in until the nurse came rushing in. Anyone passing by could easily hear Justin yelling, "No, no, no, I didn't do it, I didn't do it! No diapers, no diapers, no toes, no diapers . . . "

Later, I learned a new aide from one of the other classroom's had thrown a dirty diaper in that bathroom by mistake. She was new and wasn't told that we didn't put them anywhere but in the special ed bathroom. They were put into the covered closed container. This was one of the other bizarre aspects of his disability, only this crossed over into disturbing. He could find a dirty diaper anywhere in the whole school – by smell. You don't really want to know what he did with them. I immediately instituted a routine for his bathroom breaks, and for anyone accompanying him to always be on the inside while walking past the girls' bathroom.

Dozens of stories have been told about Justin over the years. My favorite was mine alone, one that showed his obsessiveness but also displayed his incredible high-functioning memory and cleverness. Justin could find inappropriate material on the internet within seconds. I stopped him by simply not letting him on a computer alone – ever - but several of his teachers had to learn the hard way. He was usually a really quiet kid, but one who freaked out over blonde girls. Justin could click to sites and bypass the school buffers in a couple of seconds. For example, a major movie star's site was too obvious. Justin would go to her co-star's site, who may not have such a respectable site yet, and may have pictures in a bathing suit that are pretty revealing; maybe not X-rated, but enough to rattle Justin.

Justin loved to look through mounds of magazines; aides and teachers brought them in by the dozens. It was an activity that he could stay with, and I could make into social studies activities. One day he was wigging out looking at a *National Geographic*, and I was fearful I wouldn't get him to put it down to get on the bus to go home. I finally got him to by convincing him he could read it the next day. I came back to the room and expected to find in the magazine the usual African girls washing clothes by a river topless or something, but found a picture of a beautiful, young, white blonde girl from a story on Iceland. I tore it out and put the magazine back in the pile for kids to look through. The next day, first thing in the classroom, he found it and looked through the magazine for almost an hour, saying something weird over and over again. He kept saying, "Brender Finsdoper, Brender Finsdoper, Brender Finsdoper." I couldn't figure it out, and kept trying to talk him out of the freak-out. At lunch, Justin had finally settled down, and I went to the recycling to find the page I'd torn out. The girl's name was on the bottom of the picture in the caption; it was Brybhildur Finnsdopttir. I was amazed at how close Justin was, and how he had remembered it overnight.

His grandmother told me at a meeting one time, "Oh Lord, help him, he do like them white girls."

"Well, ma'am, I don't want to fight him all the time. If he finds a picture of a girl in a magazine, and if it's not too inappropriate, I'd rather let him have it and take it home," I said.

"Yes, yes, that's the way to do it," his grandmother said. "I let him go in his room and have at it, because it won't he'p to fight with him, 'cause he loves those white girls," she answered, laughing. "I agree; you have the right idea."

"Can I ask you a question about the music?" I asked. I had discovered that Justin could name and tell you the recording date of almost any Motown song from the sixties. It was what many of us came to call the "memory trick." It wasn't someone with autism being a savant. That's in the movies. But they could do memory tricks and fool you into thinking they had a special talent, and it was a special talent in a way. You just had to give Justin a small amount of information and he could blow you away. All you had to do was say the song or the artists and he could finish the rest. If you started "Under the Boardwalk," Justin would answer, "The Drifters, 1962." Or say, "The Temptations" he'd answer, "'My Girl,' 1965; 'Just My Imagination,' 1971; 'Ain't Too Proud to Beg,' 1966," and so on. He could do it all day long.

"Oh, Lord, that's his grandfather. He listens to that music all the time, and they talk about it. Justin will listen to it with him all day and night if we let him."

During that year, if he was leaning toward a meltdown, and I had the people and time, I would reward Justin by taking him to a fast food place and buying him some chicken nuggets. Of course, on the way, we'd have the radio tuned to the golden oldies station. He loved them, and I realized how much fun I had with him, and how much I loved this job. Those days in special ed are gone. You legally can't take a student in your personal vehicle, and you have to have a lesson plan, goals, and objectives tied to the curriculum to accompany any activity that you do. I caught the tail end of the times when teachers could load students up in their cars and go wherever they and the kids wanted to for a couple of hours without worrying about molestation charges or lawsuits. Maybe it's a smarter, more protective time for teachers and students both, but something glorious was also lost. I will always cherish and remember those days of eating chicken nuggets and talking about and listening to music with Justin.

Chapter 25

ROBBIE AND I TALK INSANE ASYLUMS

Walking down the hallway with Justin, we passed another teacher's special ed class coming from music. Robbie walked over to us and started talking in his wonderful, outrageous autistic banter, but as always, looking straight down at the ground, as he did even when talking to people he liked. Robbie spent time with me to give his classroom teacher a break. He'd accompany me on walks with other students, or he'd take part in the activity he normally wouldn't stand for. After a week or so, his mom came to school to meet Mr. Brant, who Robbie was talking about and having these unusual conversations with. She approved, since he rarely talked to anyone. He conceived the conversation topics based loosely on the daytime soap operas they watched together in the evenings on cable.

"I wanted to meet you, as Robbie talks about you at home," his mom said.

"I love spending time with Robbie, ma'am. He's a great kid and we have a fun connection, as long as you don't mind me joking around with him," I said.

"No, no, it's wonderful that he has a male teacher to talk to about his stuff, as long as it's not too much for you."

"I look forward to it everyday," I said.

"Thank you for being his friend," she said as she left.

"My pleasure," I answered. I thought once again that I was lucky to be paid for this job.

Robbie and I really liked each other, and our conversations followed a definite pattern every time we saw one another in the hallway.

"Don't take that tone with me, mister."

"Are you exhibiting maniacal behavior again, Robbie?" I'd say.

"Yes, but don't you worry about me."

"Have you been released again?" I'd say.

"Yes, I've been temporarily released from the asylum," Robbie'd say.

"What kind of asylum?"

"The asylum for the criminally insane, and in particular, homicidal maniacs."

"How long have you been committed for this time?"

"I have been committed for the rest of my natural life because of my paranoid schizophrenic tendencies."

"Are you going to be okay?" I'd say.

"Yes, don't worry about me, I'm going to be okay. But you have turned against me with a vengeance and it will be your undoing."

"Are you sure?"

"Yes, and if you ask me again I'm going to be forced to sue you for everything you got," Robbie said.

"What exactly are you going to sue me for?"

"Don't play dumb with me, boy. Drop the innocent act!"

"Why shouldn't I play dumb with you?"

"I'm going to sue you for defamation of character and take you for everything you got," Robbie said. "Because in the end, I must get back at you the only way I know how, and justice must be served."

"Are you sure you're going to be okay?"

"Yes, don't worry about me. I'm going to be okay."

"Okay, we'll see you later, Robbie."

"Yes, okay, once again, don't worry about me, I'm going to be okay."

I always made time for Robbie. Even if I was in a hurry, I'd stop and pass a few moments of teasing. His current teacher said it always made his day, and he would go over the conversation in detail later maybe several times. It might go something like this: Even while walking, I'd pass him and he'd intuitively know we didn't have much time, but I'd swap a few sentences with him.

"Don't play dumb with me, mister."

"I won't," I said.

"I have friends in high places and this type of behavior won't be tolerated."

"Tell that to our principal, Robbie. He's the one who needs to hear it."

"You're always trying to make him look bad, aren't you?" he asked.

"I've never tried to make anyone look bad, except maybe you."

"I'll throw you under that bus, to make me look bad."

"You mean it'll make *me* look bad, Robbie?"

"No, it's going to make me look bad. Don't embarrass yourself. I promise I'll be in compliance from now on." His teacher told Robbie to keep going, so he walked away down the hallway muttering about "Don't play dumb, and you're all I have left, and don't tell me, I'll tell you."

Chapter 26

JUSTIN AND I TALK TO A MOM

It's probably painfully obvious I didn't always keep my cool or be politically correct. At times, I fully admit to losing it and having my bad days. Teachers are human and see the best and at times the worst in students, but many times the best and poorest in parents. Leslie, was a new student who had been coming to school for a week, and since we were about four months into the school year, transportation for her bus wasn't set up yet so her mom had to drop her off. I was assuming that's why she was late every day. One morning, I took Justin with me to meet Leslie's mom. Justin and I were sitting outside on a bench in front of the school, waiting for Leslie. I had to see her mom that day. The late bell rang, but kids kept coming in late. I kept muttering under my breath about how these parents thought nothing of bringing their kids to school late every single day, and then wonder why they weren't doing well in school.

"They aren't doing well 'cause they're late everyday," Justin would repeat. Actually he would repeat everything I said, so I could enjoy his agreeing with me.

It was always the same kids constantly, and the parents had to sign them in and then they complained about how much time it took instead of getting them here on time. Justin could've told me it was because they didn't care any more than the kids did, and that most of the teachers had given up, too, so if the kids came rambling in late, they didn't care. It was funny; it was one brand-new late-model SUV after another for twenty to thirty minutes. I kept mumbling that most of these kids were on free breakfast and lunch, and would be looking for something to eat, but the cafeteria was closed now that the bell had rung. Several of them came out of their SUVs with big bags of Flamin' Hot Cheetos and a two-liter bottle of Mountain Dew sticking out of their backpacks. I would grumble about how everyone thought it was the school's fault most of these kids were pudgy.

I *had* to wait today to see Leslie's mom. I had sent several notes home and had tried to call, but had never gotten an answer. She needed to fill out paperwork or send in some money so Leslie could eat lunch. Many parents assumed the school would take care of it, but the school simply can't; the parents have to. I had made up my mind to wait and talk to her. Justin wanted to come with me, and I thought it would be a nice buffer if things became ugly. Leslie was nonverbal. She had a communication device that she could barely use, and was content to sit and draw all day long. She couldn't read or write, but was a sweetheart, and hadn't caused any difficulties and seemed to be enjoying our activities.

At last we saw a black SUV park and Leslie get out of the passenger side. They were walking up to the school when I stood up.

"Good morning," I said. "How are you doing, Leslie?"

"Yes, I'm a little late, and Leslie isn't feeling good today," her mom said over me. "So could we get her something to eat?"

"Well, the cafeteria closed about a half hour ago, so the only thing we have in the room is a juice or two, and maybe an old leftover bagel."

I continued. "But Leslie is doing great. She seems to be adapting to our room and school very well."

"Oh, you don't have anything else for her to eat?"

"No, speaking of which, can you talk to Maureen, the cafeteria supervisor, because you need to fill out some paperwork for Leslie to eat; or you can pay her in advance to cover both breakfast and lunch."

I didn't bother to tell her that the day before, I'd bought Leslie lunch because her mom hadn't taken care of this.

"Well, yes, I guess I can," her mom added. "I'm in a little bit of a hurry and I was wondering if I could have your phone number to call you if I have any questions."

"Yes, the room's number is on that welcome letter I gave you. I put it in Leslie's backpack, and you can always call the school and the office can put you through to my room."

"No, I mean your number at home so I can call you if anything comes up."

"I'm sorry, I don't give out my home number. It's something I don't do. If you need to talk, I can always make time to talk during the day, and I can call you back if I'm unavailable during that time."

"Oh, I need to be able to get in touch with you in the evening if I have to."

"I'm sorry, again, I don't give out my home number. There wouldn't be a need for you to call me at home." I shrugged my shoulders and smiled. Leslie's mom wasn't smiling; she was frowning and kept talking.

"What if, what if there's an emergency and I need to talk to you?"

"If there's an emergency, I would hope you would call nine-one-one or the police. I'm not the one to handle an emergency at your home," I said, still smiling.

"What if Leslie's sick and can't come to school?"

"If Leslie is sick, think about calling a doctor, and if she can't come to school, you can call the office and let them know, but I'll know when she doesn't get off the bus."

She probably had had that relationship with another teacher, and I have always felt that was their choice. Some teachers get that involved in their students' lives. I don't have the energy to work with the kids all day and then talk to the parents socially after hours and become their friend. By this time, I was leading her mom into the building. I walked her to the cafeteria door and pounded on it. Maureen opened the door. I looked over at Leslie's mom and said goodbye to her, and turned to Justin and Leslie and said, "C'mon guys, let's get to class. So long. Thanks for coming in, and we'll see you later this afternoon. Remember to be here a few minutes early – two fifteen - because we have all the other students to get to buses at two-thirty."

I walked away, and Leslie's mom was standing there confused, looking from us to Mrs. Maureen, who started talking a mile a minute about how much Leslie owed, and how to fill out the paperwork if they thought she could get reduced or qualify for free meals.

We were gone.

Chapter 27

SAM TELLS A STORY ABOUT LUCAS' BROTHER

Sam was our only security guard due to the low number of students. A retired sheriff, he got along great with the kids. He was all at once a helper, a guidance counselor, an enforcer, and, most of all, someone they could talk to without incriminations. In short, they trusted him to always be fair and cordial. He hung with students I couldn't stand to be around, and was always patient. Many of these kids he befriended, it was possibly the last time an adult would have patience for them.

We had a student who gave every teacher he ever had a hard time. His name was Lucas, and he of course came from a broken family. He had a younger brother who was equally difficult. They both were suspended every other month or so, and probably should have been more often, but through two principals, they didn't want them to miss more school than they did routinely. Lucas had a learning disability label and read at the fourth- or fifth-grade level. Kids in resource classrooms have a common profile: sliding through elementary school and most of middle school. Their commonality with peers is usually perceived as limited, but they are accepted nonetheless. Suddenly, though, not being able to read or solve simple math problems isn't cool, and this creates huge behavior problems for themselves and the teachers who try to help them, especially in high school. Acting out is a better alternative than being made fun of or seeming, in their minds, stupid. Lucas acted out a lot. He was a classic bully. He came close to getting permanently kicked out of school several times for fighting kids who were, for the most part, smaller, and therefore easier prey than boys his own size or age.

One of his better moments took place in the computer lab. It was the early 2000s and schools were beginning to have buffers placed on the computers. Sally, our computer lab technician, was continuously keeping an eye peeled for students like Lucas. He was usually not working on the assignment required, but looking at something inappropriate. He was in the back row one day when I had Babak, and we were looking up some musical history sites. I saw Sally (she was a sizeable woman, and unfortunately couldn't really move fast) jump up several times and attempt to get back to check on Lucas. Every time, she would walk away muttering. I left but was back a couple of hours later with another student, and talked to her about what he was doing.

"I don't have it on our administration computers yet to see what they are doing in real time, but I knew that kid was doing something," she said.

"What was it finally?" I asked.

"It was unbelievable. I was able to go back through the history - even though he erased it on his, I *can* look at it through mine after he logs off. He was looking at porn; really bad stuff."

"How can he get around the buffers?" I asked.

"What a smart ass - literally. He was looking at stuff in foreign languages; Russian, Japanese, and German. The buffers don't stop that, yet. I let the district and Mr. Johnson know. Lucas is going to be suspended for a week."

"Yeah, he's learning disabled all right," I said laughing.

Lucas graduated that year. The Friday after Thursday night graduation is called "grading day." We have four of them a year at the end of quarters; no kids, and Sam frequently needed to chase a couple of kids out of the school throughout the day. I always had fun with a couple of my verbal, higher-functioning students who endlessly wondered what teachers did on those days without kids. They couldn't conceive of the teachers here at school without students. I've also had kids in my class who believed we *lived* at the school. I came up with this answer for them every time they asked.

"Do you promise not to tell? I could get in big trouble if I tell you what happens on grading days." I'd say to them.

In a chorus, they answer, "Yeah, we promise."

"Well, when you guys aren't here, we throw a huge party."

"No way!" they'd yell.

"Yeah, really, we have a band and a huge all-you-can-eat buffet, and we eat and run around the hallways and go swimming and scream and yell."

"You're lying!" they'd yell back.

"Please don't tell on me. I'd get fired."

Lucas was there on grading day talking to Sam, and I walked up and put out my hand for him to shake. He looked at me.

"Hey, I'm congratulating you," I said.

"Yeah, be polite," Sam interjected.

Lucas was probably thinking about the last conversation we'd had. He was picking on a kid in the computer lab, telling him how stupid he was for having a hard time on a simple computer exercise Sally had them doing. I was checking on one of my kids who was able to navigate some Disney programs and listen to the stories. Lucas didn't know I was sitting in the back. Right before I walked up behind him and bent down, he had poked the kid hard in the throat.

I poked him in the arm and said, "This kid here, and almost everyone else in this entire school, are worth more than you'll ever be. They're worth more than you, and a thousand of you and your friends put together. If you think you're such a bad ass, why don't you go down to the Bashful Bandit this weekend and run your mouth to one of the bikers there like you have been to him. They'll kick the eyeballs out of your head. You'll leave here and do nothing and go nowhere."

It wasn't the brightest thing to say to a high school kid, and I realized once again I was much better working with my kids than typical students. I had this problem all during the course of my interactions with the general population. Lucas never said anything else to me, but always looked meanly at me in passing for the last few weeks of school, so he couldn't understand why I was shaking his hand and asking him how graduation was the night before.

"Was it nice?" I asked.

"Yeah, I guess," he more or less whispered.

"Well, I wanted to say welcome to the party," I said.

"Huh?" he asked as he shrugged.

"For almost twelve years – well - maybe more, you've been giving teachers and everyone at every school you've been to a hard time. Calling us names, being a real pain in the ass, haven't you?"

He looked down.

"Yes, that's correct, and he was about to leave now," Sam said.

I said, "Yeah, you can't stand it here, but you come back to hang out, and I wanted to welcome you to the real world. Now one day, and probably soon, you'll realize those teachers you've been harboring so much animosity for - that means 'hostility' - are just a bunch of schlubs trying to make a living, and maybe help kids like you. Welcome to the party."

Sam started laughing. We all three stood there. Lucas continued looking down.

"Have fun working at Circle K," I said, walking away. "If you're lucky."

Sam told the story to more than a few teachers the rest of the day, and before I left, two went out of their way to shake my hand.

The next year, Lucas's brother Carl was following the same path. He got in a fight in his history class. Mr. Raul had had enough of him and sent him to the office. In the meantime, he let the student Carl had sucker-punched call his parents on the way to the nurse. Sam told me all of this later that evening after the police had left and everything had calmed down. Mr. Raul knew that Mr. Johnson would undoubtedly not do anything to Carl, so he let the boy call home so Mr. Johnson would be forced to require some consequence for Carl. Sam and Mr. Johnson also had words about the doing-nothing attitude. Sam told him it was obvious kids were learning not to worry about any consequences.

"Mr. Johnson sent him back to class after our blowout in the office, probably to pick up his back pack or something. As Carl was walking out the door, he elbowed Mr. Raul in the chest and almost knocked him down, and Mr. Raul called the police."

"Why'd he elbow him? Wait, I know that's a stupid question. Never mind. What did Mr. Johnson say?" I asked.

"Well, of course with everything else going on, as a principal, he wanted him to use 'restorative behavior discipline' and have Carl write Mr. Raul a letter of apology."

"Is Mr. Johnson pissed Mr. Raul went ahead and called?"

"That's what they say."

Sam missed what happened in the office once the police got there, but the office manager told him Carl had started cussing them out and had gotten up in one of their faces, so they threw him on the floor and handcuffed him.

"Well, he started to give the cops a hard time, just like he talks to teachers," Sam told me, laughing.

Sam was in front of the school trying unsuccessfully to get a group of kids to leave and go home. They'd been arguing with him about their right to stand on the sidewalk, when the side door to Mr. Johnson's office opened and Carl came out with his hands handcuffed behind his back. He was between two policemen, with one behind him. Some of the kids had started cheering him.

"He looked over and saw all of us watching and started to struggle by jerking back and yelling," Sam continued. "'You assholes can't do this to me, I didn't do nothin' wrong. Fuck you.' Carl was screaming so loud we all stopped and stepped back," Sam said. "The cops moved him forward fast and kind of ran him toward the car, but when they got close to it, they picked him up off the ground. When he was close, about three or four feet above the car, they slammed him down on the hood. It made a huge, loud thumping noise. The cop, who was walking behind them, came over and pulled something out of his waist belt. He put it in Carl's face and said, 'If you offer any more resistance, I will mace you. Do you understand?'" Sam related.

Carl had started crying and nodding his head.

"'Good,' the cop said, 'because if I have to mace you, I'll hog-tie and hobble you also.'"

They picked him up and put him in the back of the car and got in. The kids behind Sam were silent. It was something I guess no one had expected to see or hear. As the cop cars drove away, Sam had looked around him at the kids standing, looking dazed, and he smiled.

"This is a great learning moment for you all," he'd said really loud, waving his arms around and then pointing back at the school. "This is when the artificial world of school meets reality. Carl was under the mistaken impression he could talk and do things to police officers that he could do to teachers. We have to take it; cops don't. Have a nice day."

Chapter 28
NASTAS' BIA CASE WORKER

Nastas lived in the same group home as Owsley, rode the bus with him everyday, and spent the days and nights with him over the summers, weekends, and vacations. He didn't go home, and Mom didn't visit him more than once or twice a year. I had him for five years until he graduated. I only met Mom twice, and even then, I didn't really meet her, only tried to talk to her in passing. She would usually drop him off the first day of school sometime within the first few hours of the day. She would leave him in the office and walk off without waiting for me or an aide to meet her. For two years, I sent her self-addressed envelopes enclosed with invitations to his Individual Education Program meetings. She never responded, and we would have to reschedule the meetings, for the first two years, up to three times. That's how many times a parent gets to stiff school personnel. By federal law, we have no recourse but to reschedule the meeting. After the third attempt, we can hold it without the parent present. I always wondered what she did with the stamps on my envelopes; I even paid for the letters to be certified, hoping that would help her get them back to us. She lived on the Navajo reservation.

I was told Nastas had fetal alcohol syndrome, and he had all the physical and intellectual appearances: an abnormal look that fit the characteristics of fetal alcohol, short in height with low body weight, a small head, poor coordination, severe intellectual disability, and behavior problems. Nastas was extremely thin and had a long, dark ponytail almost to the middle of his back. The back of his hand had a large, nasty, circular, reddish, callous sore. He stood and would put the back of his hand to his mouth and at the same time pick at it. He would cross his legs and stand bent at the waist while picking and make guttural sounds. It's called an excoriation condition, and is an impulse control disorder characterized by the repeated urge to pick at one's own skin. With Nastas's other physical characteristics, he frightened other typical students.

Something about him got to me. He could be a very nice and funny guy. Nastas got things. He didn't talk, but wasn't completely non-verbal; he could make guttural sounds and a whining noise that at times let you know what he wanted. Mostly, he kept to himself. He was unable to attend to any activity and couldn't participate in any endeavor other than tearing pages out of magazines. Alternately, we found he loved looking at and tearing the pages out of old phone books (when we were still able to get them). At least once a day, I would try to find him a newspaper from the day before, and Nastas would sit in a comfortable chair, cross his legs, open the newspaper, and pretend to read it. He would smile and nod as if he knew you were watching him (he did), and put on a show for us.

"Nastas, what's going on in the Middle East today? What's the stock market doing?"

He would nod again and make a soft cantankerous noise, and then shake the paper, as if straightening it out, and continue reading.

We only had trouble with Nastas at lunch. He seemed to feel he didn't get enough to eat, and we, for the most part, concurred and gave him treats throughout the day, along with supplementing his lunch with snacks and juice a couple times a day. If Nastas finished lunch, which he did quickly, and got away from the table, he'd beeline it for the lunch line and quickly freak out some of the students waiting, or the ones leaving with their lunches. He had been known to grab food from other kids' trays. I had to restrain him and take him outside maybe once every other week or so. We had a plan to get him in and out before the other students were eating, but the best-laid plans don't always work out in special ed. When I did take him out, I usually took him to the ramada and crossed his hands in front of him (he had been known to scratch and bite), and held him for about five minutes. Then he would calm down and be back to his ordinary self.

One of the first times I had him in the ramada, an aide I grew to really like was walking by and asked, "Do you need me to get Sam to help?"

"No, Nastas and I are getting to know one another. We're okay."

"Someone told me you used to be in the army. What would your army buddies say if they could see you now?" she asked laughing.

"I really don't know," I answered. "Wait, it probably makes perfect sense. All that training being put to perfect use."

Today in education we hear about many kids being lactose intolerant, and many times most of us agree it's an exaggeration on a parent's part. We obviously have to follow their instructions, but we also sometimes see nothing happen when they actually ingest a dairy product. We watched Nastas closely, and monitored his diet anyway, but with Nastas we experienced what true lactose intolerance looked like. At one of the few times Owsley stayed for breakfast (he was usually gone by then with Bruce), he sat with Nastas. Since they were roommates, we didn't think anything would happen. Owsley had lulled us into complacency more than once. As soon as we were all distracted with other students, he slipped Nastas a milk carton. We talked about it, and most of us thought, *Well, we'll just wait and see.*

We did. In our room we had a large (donated) oriental rug, about twelve by twelve feet. It was beautiful and really tied the room together. Nastas exploded. His diarrhea ran down his legs, out his pants, and onto the rug in seconds. He flopped down and we couldn't get him up. It was a mammoth struggle with him fighting and screaming unintelligible gibberish, which only reflected his misery. The whole time, other aides were yelling and getting the other kids out of the room, and gagging. I finally got him up and to the nurse's office, where he stayed the rest of the day. The rug looked ruined to me. Luckily Bruce had returned from an errand, and I asked him to help me drag the rug out.

"Don't throw it out, Brant. We can salvage it, man," he said.

"What?" I asked. "What can we possibly do?"

He had an idea. We hung it on a low fence near the shop class and ran a hose from there. They had industrial-strength cleaner and we washed and rinsed the rug for several hours. The Arizona sun dried it out and we'd start the process again. Several of my aides smelled it closely before allowing us to bring it back in the room. We made damn sure Nastas's never ingested a milk product again.

After the first two years, I realized Nastas' mom wasn't going to attend a meeting, communicate with us, or send any paperwork back. Every year, we also had a problem with our district's Native American Studies office. They were scheduled to attend his meetings, too. We always gave them several weeks' notice, but many of us experienced that their attendance was as pitiable as Nastas' mom's. From the group home, we discovered she got a ride from tribal transportation from the reservation in Tuba City every year to see him for a day or two. She didn't drive, but could have had a ride to see him regularly, and he could have spent the summers with her.

The third year, I waited for her in our foyer on the first day of school. When she showed up, I braced her and introduced myself, with the paperwork ready. She tried to walk away, but I stood in front of her and had her sign the Individual Education Program (IEP) invitation without dating it. A man got out of the car that I presumed had brought Nastas and her to our school. He stood there and watched as she signed where I told her to. As she walked away, I waved to the man. I later checked the box that gave us permission to hold the meeting without her. I would date it later when we had the IEP meeting. It was the only right thing to do, and I did the same thing for the next two years.

Into the third year, Nastas went home for December break. When he came back, he was bruised and his ponytail was shorn. The group home was told he'd been bad and Mom's new boyfriend had done it. They were investigating on the reservation. As far as I knew, he never went home again. I kept thinking something wasn't right about the whole thing with Nastas. I was wondering about the fetal alcohol label, and was actually wondering if we had some shaken baby syndrome or something else. He didn't have all the exact same attributes as Owsley, and I looked into his accumulation files at the district. We called them "cum files" for short. They went back to his first attendance at school and contained his complete background and medical history. It turned out he didn't have fetal alcohol. It was a stereotype every one of us bought into without question. The acceptance was because of the high incidence of it on the reservation, but Nastas wasn't one of the statistics.

Nastas had Coffin–Lowry syndrome. It's a genetic disorder that causes severe intellectual disabilities, and is also sometimes associated with abnormalities of growth, cardiac abnormalities, and kyphoscoliosis (an abnormal curvature of the spine). Coffin-Lowry can also cause auditory and visual abnormalities. I felt vindicated for him. I don't know why, but I believed Nastas deserved better. His disabilities remained the same, and he received the same services, but I was happy for him for some reason that I still can't explain today.

The fifth year, I got an unusual visit from Nastas's case manager on the reservation. She was from the Bureau of Indian Affairs. This was a complete surprise, as I didn't know he had one. Her name was Ms. Thompson. We were walking that day on the track. Every day, when I had the time, I took Nastas out around the school; he loved to work the trash and litter pick-up stick. I carried the bag. It got him out, and we also helped clean up the school from the dirt-bag typical students who littered constantly. I wouldn't have done it regularly with my students, but Nastas loved it. As his case manager was talking, I could tell she didn't really think much of his situation any more than I did. Nastas was graduating, he was aging out, and turning twenty-two during the summer, so school was ending for him in a month.

"If you need anything for him, I can supply you with materials and anything you think will help him in school. I have almost unlimited funds," she said.

"I can't think of anything now, but I could have used the help four or five years ago," I couldn't help saying. I couldn't believe it; she'd showed up after five years and was now interested in helping him.

"Well, if you think of anything, let me know," she said.

"What's going to happen to him now that school's over?" I asked.

"I don't know. We don't have the proper facilities for him on the reservation. He doesn't have any skill - like so many of our fetal alcohol kids."

"Nastas actually has symptoms that are not synonymous with fetal alcohol. He has another syndrome called Coffin-Lowery," I said.

"No, he must. He has all the physical characteristics, and I've seen it so many times."

"No, it's Coffin-Lowery. I looked in his cum file, and it's been in there since his birth."

"His mom has told me that she drank while she was pregnant. She thinks it's fetal alcohol."

"Well, I'm sure it didn't help, but has she ever taken the time to go to one of his IEP meetings?"

"I don't know if she has or not."

"Well, she might learn some things about her son if she attended a meeting about him. She hasn't in the last five years here."

At graduation, a group of about ten people showed up to see Nastas walking across the stage with Bruce, Owsley's one-on-one. Both Bruce and I tried to talk to a couple of the people in the group. No one paid any attention to us. Bruce certainly made the attempt; he had spent several years with Nastas and Owsley, taking them into and around the community. He ended up swearing under his breath at what we assumed was the stepfather or boyfriend. After the small graduation ceremony, we let it go, and we watched them whisk Nastas out to the parking lot, and all then pile into several cars. They never even glanced at us, much less said thank you for spending untold hours with Nastas, playing and working with him, feeding him, buying him clothes and food, taking him to the nurse, and even supplying him with magazines; no "Thank you for taking care of my son for the last half dozen years or more."

You're welcome.

Chapter 29

MUNCHAUSEN BY PROXY, APPROXIMATELY

Munchausen by proxy is a name often used when a parent, caregiver, or spouse fabricates, embellishes, persuades, or induces mental or physical health problems in those who are in their care. We saw this with parents of special needs kids. The primary motive is to gain attention or sympathy from others. Most of us couldn't count the number of times we've sat in meetings and had trouble getting a parent or guardian to actually stay focused on the student. We all were empathetic about a parent's struggle, and I tried to always refrain from thinking I knew what it was like to have a child with a significant disability. It's the lowest presumption a teacher can have to think they know what's best for a student, but we do know what we'd do because of our years of experience. Sometimes we could see what was not right – maybe not *illegal*, but simply not good - for the child. And unfortunately, at times we saw something that *was* flat-out wrong, and had to call CPS. The name Munchausen by proxy is derived from the term Munchausen syndrome, a psychiatric disorder where those affected feign disease, illness, or psychological trauma to draw attention, sympathy, or reassurance to themselves. Our situation was that of a parent or guardian who sought to procure attention through their student with disabilities. They demanded the team or doctor give their child a label the child may not have needed. Most of the time it was somewhat benign, but at times it was downright sinful.

Willie was a selective mute. He refused to talk to adults. His foster mom acquired the label of autism for him as a middle-school student. She browbeat the system and the district autism team into giving him the label. I, and several teachers before me, had objected vociferously with no success.

Of all of the students with autism I've had over the years I can point out at least one, in every classroom who didn't have the three or four stipulations most psychologists check off a list to give the diagnosis. Students with autism fluctuate in personality as much as we do as individuals. There is a quote usually attributed to Dr. Stephen Shore: "They say if you've met one person with autism, you've met one person with autism." Willie didn't have any of the checks on the list. His so-called autism spectrum disorder didn't present on the accepted range of conditions characterized by challenges with social skills, repetitive behaviors, delayed or nonexistent speech, or by unique strengths and differences. Willie wouldn't communicate or do work; he'd just calmly sit and look down. But he wouldn't hesitate to look you in the eye if he was interested in what you were saying.

During his tenure at Harrogate, Willie was busted several times destroying school property (computers, mostly, and he was barred from using them), bringing bullets and a knife to school, and stealing small useless items from classrooms. I caught him talking to other students on numerous occasions, scoping out girls by hanging closer than was appropriate, and actually laughing at ordinary jokes, or yelling out in a few of the typical classes we had him attend - all of which deviate from autism as we understand it.

I was in the office one day talking to my department head.

"What asshole doctor gave Willie that label? He's no more autistic than I am," I said.

Our psychologist was also sitting there and sheepishly said, "Well, it wasn't a doctor this time. We actually gave it to him." She was a member of the district's autism team. This partially explains, along with improved identification or misdiagnosis, why the number of autism cases has exploded over the last couple of decades. Doctors have no compunction labeling a student/person autistic, even when another obvious disability might be involved. Autism is the label du jour. Most parents would prefer their child to have the label of autism as opposed to another label they might consider an inferior. Every special ed teacher I know has had at least one student, sometimes several, who was diagnosed with autism but actually had another disability, usually one of the approximately 250 forms of cognitive disability.

Willie clearly had deep-seated emotional issues and wasn't getting the help he needed. During an IEP meeting one time, the school speech pathologist, who was required to see Willie once or twice a month, was literally shouted down for thinking about approaching the subject of his incorrect label.

"I don't see any reason to continue therapy with Willie if he won't verbalize to us," she said.

"He gets the services he needs because that's your job," Willie's mom barked.

"Again, as a speech pathologist, without any speech taking place, it's difficult - if not impossible - to work with Willie," she tried to say.

"You'll not drop that service, and you'll have to figure out a way to make it work. That's your job, and I'll talk to whoever I have to to make sure this isn't dropped just because you don't want to do your job," his mom said.

"It's not about wanting to do my job or not, it's about Willie not wanting to participate."

"Welcome to the world of autism." Mom always pulled that line out when she was done discussing something. I got so sick of hearing it, I would almost start to gag every time she pulled it out of her self-protective baggage.

"If selective mutism was an aspect of Willie having autism, I'd agree, but it's not, and -" our speech pathologist tried again.

"We're not changing a thing."

"Selective mutism would better be serviced by, say, an emotionally disturbed label. Willie might get the services that would be more beneficial for him."

His mom finished up with, "Just try dropping this service, lady."

Let's not forget that a foster or actual parent gets more SSI money and services if there's a label of autism.

One day our school got one of the most interesting cases I've ever seen, for sheer, bizarre controversy. Caster came from another high school, and her mom was in due process for not having services provided to her satisfaction. Our school initially felt horrible for her. We were told Caster was blind from medicine she was taking for lupus. Chloroquine and hydroxychloroquine are drugs used in the treatment of a variety of diseases, such as rheumatoid arthritis and lupus.

This was a year or so before I started studying in my graduate program for visual impairment, so I didn't have as much knowledge about the subject as I was to acquire. But I didn't need it to see that something wasn't kosher. Caster walked around the school. She'd had only one or two orientation and mobility lessons, when the instructors more or less refused to schedule her again. They, and the teachers of visual impairment demanded to have an ophthalmological report before continuing services. The reason behind this is was to discount anything else that might have been going on with a student's brain causing vision loss.

Visual impairment teachers aren't doctors, and that report is essential and a legal necessity. That didn't stop mom from sending Caster in with a cane that she had no idea how to use, especially how to *fake* using it.

Immediately, I (along with everyone else) saw her walking briskly around the school like she was born blind and had been attending school for years and knew the layout and position of every class, door, desk, bathroom, office, table, curb, corner, turn, sidewalk, and marked walkway. It was amazing to see. Sam, our security guard, and I were standing in the bus bay one day right before the bell rang, waiting for students. We were close to the curb, when down at the end came Caster, moving like always, faster than we would normally walk. During this time, the buses were still pulling in, and as they did, Sam and I both stepped back. A bus is a large vehicle, and makes a loud noise, specifically when it's pulling in and stopping. As we stepped back, Caster walked between the curb and us, seemingly dangerously so.

"Hey, hey," Sam started to say. I grabbed him and motioned for him to stop.

"She's fine, man. Watch this," I said as she promenaded daintily like a ballerina, perfectly poised between a bus pulling in and the curb. As she reached the end of the bus bay, the sidewalk angled back across the street toward the schools portables. Caster flawlessly traversed wheelchair-accessible curb drop-offs and the markings for the crossing.

Sam and I looked at each other and laughed uproariously as we walked to meet the other students. Sam said, "She doesn't need an early release to get anywhere. Hell, her eyesight is probably better than mine." Later I realized I never actually witnessed her sweeping her cane, but just pushing it along in front of her, which is a basic bad habit that students with visual impairments do and learn to correct after running into obstacles, sometimes painfully.

Caster was a constant topic of discussion among the teachers, as one after another saw her using her vision in dozens of situations. The sad part was that no one could actually do anything about it until the legal due process played out. Bobby set up a small office room, usually set aside for private meetings, for her to work in and take the statewide tests that were coming up. Mom had her learning Braille, a task that normally takes several years with a qualified teacher of the visually impaired, but Caster was learning quickly. Of course, she didn't have to learn from a teacher of the visually impaired (TVI) which would have had her learning tactually - if Caster would have actually had a visual impairment. I was walking by one day when our department head grabbed me and said, "Brant, take a look at this."

She motioned for me to look in the window of the office. They had covered up the window with paper, but had left a tiny hole that we could see through. I pressed my eye to the crack and saw Caster looking from the computer to the braille writer she was working on, and then check another piece of paper (probably the braille alphabet), and precipitously back again.

"Does her mom say she has some sight?" I asked Bonnie.

"No, no, they are saying she is totally blind. As soon as the legal stuff is done and we're keeping record of all this bullshit, she'll be busted," she said. "I feel sorry for Caster. It's hard to because she's playing along, but Mom must have her completely bamboozled into thinking this is a right thing to do."

"Unbelievable," was the only thing I could think to say. Not only was Castor not blind, she had full use of her vision. The term Bonnie was looking for that applied was "without any light perception."

One day, Castor was just gone and I never did hear what transpired with the whole incident. We also heard the lupus label was as false as the blind label. A couple of years later when I was on the TVI team, I asked and one of my peers about it. They simply said they'd told Mom to either to get an eye exam or leave the district. She apparently left.

Chapter 30

MARY'S DAD

My last year at Harrogate I took a trade for Owsley for another extremely challenging student. I thought I was making a good swap. Restraining Owsley was making me physically ill. When I see depictions of either police or healthcare workers (working with mentally ill) criticized for using disproportionate force or restraint, most times it's obviously a talking head who has never come close to actually restraining an out-of-control human being. I had had enough. I frankly didn't want to be involved with it any longer. We weren't trading baseball cards; every one of us had our limits with difficult behaviors, so we needed to have a change. I knew I would be called upon to help with Owsley, and I was, but the trade was a mixed bag. I took on one of the most challenging kids in my whole career.

Mary had Prader-Willi syndrome. It's a difficult disability; some of the things that go with it are low muscle tone, short stature, incomplete sexual development, cognitive disabilities, problem behaviors, and a chronic feeling of hunger that can lead to excessive eating and life-threatening obesity.

Mary physically looked like most kids with Prader-Willi syndrome, exhibiting the characteristic facial appearance, including narrow temples, an elongated face, thin upper lip, and a prominent nose. Mary would eat anything. She'd eat until she would blow up; she'd eat until she literally would vomit and desire more. They say if you have Prader-Willi, your life is an endless meal and search for food. I mean it when I say Mary would eat anything. Some of the things she stole, snuck, or hoarded and ate at different times included a raw frozen pizza, a huge jar of peanut butter, a bag of flour, two six-packs of soda, a whole roll of raw cookie dough, a whole container of syrup, and many other grotesque things out of the trash - and this was all at school.

One day, she got caught eating raw bacon. Two girls had brought each other joke gifts for Christmas, and one had the bacon in her backpack. Nobody saw it - at least no other teachers did - until Mary had stolen it out of one of their backpacks, gone into the bathroom, and eaten it all. They had to call her parents to take her to the hospital to have her stomach pumped. It had happened before. Most Prader-Willi syndrome students are stubborn, but Mary's stubbornness was legendary. Part of the syndrome is obsessive-compulsive behavior. She'd argue about anything. It didn't matter if you saw her steal another kid's milk on the cafeteria table; once she had it in her possession, she'd argue that it was hers, that she'd brought it from home or bought it. Mary would talk endlessly about her schedule, what classes she had, what TV shows she was going to watch, and always, always, exactly what she was going to eat in the next couple of days. She counted how many chips she had in her lunch. God forbid she was shorted a couple; she'd talk about it all afternoon and into the night at home. This compulsive need to repeat things over and over again can drive a person crazy. She'd go over things again and again and again and again. Now, I really mean she'd go over things again and again and again and again, until aides, other students, or her teachers wanted to scream, "SHUT UP!"

Mary's parents insisted that she be mainstreamed, which I concurred with for the most part, but I also felt there was a limit to what classes in which she could successfully function. She operated at about a third-grade reading level, and maybe a tad lower for comprehension skills. Mary's dad was a complete asshole. I let it go, mostly. During one meeting after she'd snuck a soda while at school, he was ranting about how we weren't doing our jobs. I pointed out we couldn't actually stop her from purchasing a soda (this was when schools still had a few junk food vending machines on campus) with her own money. A better answer would be to not send her to school with money. I took his wrath. Next, he demanded we buy her a diet soda daily as a reward with our community-based instruction money. I was getting something like thirty dollars a month for the whole class of eleven students that year.

"That's fifty cents a day, two fifty a week. Monthly, that could add up to a disproportionate percentage to spend on one student."

"That's what I want, and that's what I want to happen!" he yelled.

"Well, that's not going to happen. Sir, if you want your daughter to have a soda everyday, that's fine, but we can't watch everything she does, and we can't spend that kind of money on one student."

Mom jumped in. She realized that Mary was in her last class and had been moved several times already from a couple of schools. At this point there was nowhere else for her to go.

"We can probably send in -" she started.

"I said, that's not going to happen. She should be able to get a soda here." Her dad was yelling at this point. I started to laugh. He was turning beet red and glaring at me.

Our department head, Greta, jumped in and made the concession to defuse the situation. Dad was about to blow when she assured him Mary would get her sodas. We never discussed it, but Monday morning,

Greta brought in two cases of cheap soda from either the Dollar Store or Food City. I took them without a word, and that afternoon, tried to give one to Mary. She wouldn't have anything to do with cheap soda. She screamed for an hour, lying on the floor.

"I want my Pepsi! I wannnnnt myyyy Pepsiii !"

It was never brought up again.

She was quick, too. One day in her student council mainstreamed class, she was standing at Mr. Monica's desk, the librarian, with Mrs. Joni, the student council teacher, while they were talking. Mr. Monica had a sub sandwich lying out in the open on the back corner of his desk. While they were discussing the progress of some event, he noticed his sandwich was gone. It was a foot long, and he hadn't had time to eat it during the normal lunch period, so he was saving it for later. It was gone. Poof!

"What happened to my sandwich?" Mr. Monica asked. They looked around.

"I didn't see it," Mrs. Joni said. She looked at Mary for a moment.

"It was here a second ago. I mean it couldn't have disappeared," Mr. Monica said.

Mr. Monica was a heavy dude, and wasn't thrilled about missing a meal. Mrs. Joni looked at Mary another moment. Mary always looked incredibly guilty when she stole something. Mrs. Joni's glance fell down to Mary's pants. Mary always wore the same gray sweat pants, day in and day out, along with a dirty, gray hooded sweatshirt. She tried to keep the hood up all day long, and nobody fought to have her take it down. Sometimes it helped with another gross habit she had. Joni noticed the bulge in her crotch area.

"Did you take Mr. Monica's sandwich?" Mrs. Joni asked.

"No, no," Mary said.

"What's in your pants, then?"

"Nothing. No, no, nothing," Mary said, shaking her head.

"Mary, come to the bathroom with me, please," Mrs. Joni said.

"No, no, no, no." Mary started to cry.

"Mary, you have to come with me and give me that sandwich. It's not yours, and you can't eat it."

Mary followed Mrs. Joni to the restroom and gave up the sandwich, which was brought back to Mr. Monica and placed on his desk.

"Would you still like to eat your sandwich?" He said no.

Mary's mom had to count her calories and monitor her intake stringently. It's common for children with Prader-Willi syndrome to become huge. It was a constant fight at home; they locked up the cabinets and refrigerator, but would occasionally forget. Mary's brother was a constant issue. He didn't want his life subjugated to such a degree, and caused conflict in the household.

Greta called me during a passing period one day, and I walked down to the cafeteria to find Mary on the floor. She had tried to grab a student's Power Bar as they were walking by, but had gotten caught and then pushed away. She was lying on her back screaming. Greta was concerned about Mary apparently slamming her head on the floor and being hurt. I walked over and slid one shoe underneath Mary's head so she wouldn't actually hit the floor. I immediately knew exactly what she was doing. She wouldn't hit her head, anyway; she could bounce and slam her shoulders off the floor like a real-life RAW champion and make people think she was hitting her head by the sound of the thud, but she wasn't really. Every once in a while, she misjudged and actually banged her head against the floor or a wall, and then she *really* started screaming. It was an ugly thing to see one of her meltdowns.

I told her, "Mary, you can't steal other people's property and expect to keep it. You aren't going to earn your soda this afternoon or be able to work on your puzzle if you keep this up."

By this time that class was almost over, and not many kids saw the spectacle. I always preferred the meltdown not to be witnessed by that many other students. Mary kept yelling and crying and banging her head.

"Oh, noooooo, I want my tweet, I want my tweet! I need my tweet! I earned it!"

Soon, she sat up and rolled over on her stomach. We tried to get her to sit in a chair. This whole process could take up to two hours. It was difficult to realize at times that Mary was intellectually disabled; she was emotionally about four years old. She could read a little bit, but could barely write. She could do a five-hundred - or thousand-piece puzzle, though, like nobody's business. She'd go through about two or three a week, only working on them an hour or two a day. If you would let her, she'd sit at a desk and do puzzles from morning till night. I bought her dozens at the thrift store and traded them into our local used bookstore throughout the year.

But the worst thing that she did was something nobody could handle, not my aides, not really even her parents, her teachers, and none of the kids in school. When she did it, everyone was repulsed, and it made people actually hate her. I tried to get this behavior back in our classroom as soon as it commenced, but was not always successful. Her brother, who had his own issues and attended our school, ignored his sister and walked by her without acknowledging her presence. We were instructed to never use or ask him for assistance, which I would never have considered.

Mary picked her nose. Not picked it, but ran her fingers so up into it, ran her fingers so far up into it, it looked like they must have been going up into her brain. Mary's deviated septum was self-induced. After her fingers ran up into her nose cavity, she'd lick and suck them. She could do this for hours. No one could stop her. We could yell, we could be polite, we could bribe, we could beg, we could threaten, we could scream, and all that only made it worse. We'd have had to tie her hands behind her back to make her stop. We had to let her do it. Mostly when she was upset, she'd do it for about twenty or thirty minutes and then calm down and stop for a while. That's why I tried to keep this performance art from the other kids, and why her brother kept his distance. They called her "The Nose."

One afternoon while waiting for the bus with Owsley to leave, I saw Mary's mom walking along the sidewalk. I was about to say hi to her and wait for whatever indignation was coming my way. She never got to me. Out of the side door, came Mary with her hood up and her finger in her nose. I had been thinking about the coming weekend, and somewhat dreading the ballet recital I was going to have to attend for my stepdaughter; not really, but it was a passing thought. Mary's mom immediately changed direction, and through the crowd of kids, I could hear them distinctly.

"Mary, hi, how was your day, honey?" her mom asked.

Mary immediately turned away with her finger still jammed up her nose and said, "What are you doing here? I don't want you here. Leave me alone."

I could see any high school senior saying something that incredibly rude to their mom, but looking at Mary and seeing her with her worn-out, ugly sweats, hood up, ramming that finger up her nose, and walking away, scowling, muttering, and having other students part like the Red Sea as she approached, killed me. I saw her through her mother's eyes.

Her mother stood there, dispirited, and sad. She put her head down as Mary continued to walk away. I immediately thought of my stepdaughter and how beautiful she would look tonight, and how graceful the whole dance company would attempt to be, and all she would accomplish in the future. Mary's mom would never have an experience like that; her world was so different, and about 180 degrees away from those normal teenage, and even moving into adulthood, milestones, like college, a career, marriage, or grandkids. I vowed never to argue or be sarcastic, even to Mary's dad, again. I took their anger and wrath. The day of graduation, working with the seniors and all during rehearsals, Mary's dad never said a word to any of the teachers helping prepare for the night. He sat in the back of the auditorium and never even looked at us. We practiced in a theater downtown, and the seniors' parents were responsible for transporting them to the day's rehearsals and nighttime celebration. I guess Mary's dad had argued with our principal, who stood his ground and refused to provide transportation exclusively for Mary. After the ceremony, Mary walked up to me, and I congratulated her. Her dad was standing in the back of a crowd of parents and students milling around. I looked down at her.

"There's your dad. See you later. Good luck in the future," I said. When dad walked up and Mary turned, I looked him right in the eye and said, "Have a nice summer."

Chapter 31

GOT MILK!

Sholenda was a second-generation student at Harrogate High School. Her mom had been a special education student seventeen years before, and several aides remembered her. Her daughter was now there in twelfth grade, with several different labels she'd been given over the years. Drugs and alcohol were diagnosed more than once, but anecdotal intellectual disability was always given as the final result. Sholenda was heavy, with extremely large breasts. She only stood about five feet, two inches, but usually wore her hair in a large afro, which made her appear taller. Sholenda was fairly high functioning, and could converse on a large range of topics, although she preferred to talk about subjects that were totally inappropriate for school.

Sholenda had been sexualized from an earlier age. Most teachers and aides concluded she had been having sex with cousins, brothers, uncles, or a succession of her mom's boyfriends. She was still high functioning enough to have an instinctual sense of self-preservation and keep from talking about it to a teacher or aide. Although Child Protective

Services had been called several times throughout her school years, they weren't able to pin anything down. That year she turned eighteen, and Mom hadn't done anything to complete the paperwork for guardianship; no one involved in her school career thought that was a good idea anyway. The school tried several times to have an independent guardian appointed through the Department of Developmental Disabilities administration, but Mom, again, never followed up, so it never happened. Sholenda would try to interact with other students and was usually was rejected, but once in a while, a boy would actually give her his home phone number. Phone calls would start at all hours of the night. The next day, generally after a weekend, either the parents or the police representative would show up to complain. The principal would tell all the special ed personnel to watch her for several days to try to keep it from happening again. It turned out she made periodic calls to 911 from cell phones her mom had let the contract run out on. It was news to some of us that the phones continued to have the ability to call 911, though. One night at her home, the police found a dozen old discontinued phones in a drawer.

Sholenda wasn't above trying her luck with other disabled students within her sphere of influence. Peggy had been teaching for over twenty years in different states and was a wonderful special ed teacher. Peggy helped me on a daily basis learn to be a decent special ed teacher. She did her best with Sholenda, and had made very good progress with her the year before. Peggy's room had a strange setup; we figured at one time it had been a music classroom. She had two tiny closet-like rooms with built-in desks. Peggy used one for storage, and the other for kids who actually wanted to have a few minutes alone to work on a project or some quiet time.

Aiden was a student with Fragile X syndrome, also known as Martin–Bell syndrome. It is an inherited intellectual disability, especially among boys. It's in the spectrum of intellectual disabilities ranging from mild to severe, with physical characteristics such as an elongated face and large or protruding ears, and behavioral characteristics such as hand-flapping, and social anxiety. Aiden had this in spades. He was a beautiful, but extremely nervous, young man. Aiden was verbal, and understood at a fairly high conversational level. He used the room many times throughout the day, and sat quietly and worked on homework or a puzzle.

The aide later estimated they hadn't turned their back on Sholenda for more than a minute. They didn't know at first where she had gone. That wasn't unusual; she often walked out of class if left unnoticed for a moment or two. An aide walked down the hallway to see if she was, as usual, looking for someone to talk to. Another aide thought for a moment, and opened the door to see if Aiden was all right. Sholenda had her bra and shirt up, and was rubbing Aiden's face in her breasts. Aiden was moaning and blubbering. The aide yelled, and they both stood up.

Naturally, there not being enough space, they fell on top of each other, both yelling and crying at the same time. Peggy spent the rest of the day trying to contact Sholenda's mother and talking to Aiden's mom on the phone. The principal tried to schedule a meeting with both sets of parents, but was unsuccessful at getting Sholenda's mom to attend. Luckily for Peggy, Aiden's mom understood, and it was close to the end of the year, so she let it go with the understanding they were never to be alone again.

The next morning, Peggy arrived at school to find a poster (from the cafeteria) tacked on her door with the popular promotion slogan popular that year "Got milk?" Some bad person had inserted the word "chocolate" below the wording on the poster. They never did find out who'd done it. I used my same refrain that had worked in the military for over twenty years: "I have no knowledge of the incident, sir!"

The next year, Sholenda's story took a troubled turn. As she was moderately high functioning, Sholenda was barred from computers unless completely supervised. She was one of several students with disabilities I ran into over the years who could manipulate computers like nothing I've seen. Sholenda was not quite that proficient, but could still find inappropriate sites in a second or two. We didn't have any problems at school, but she was free to have at it while she was at home.

One Monday morning, I was walking down the hallway and heard yelling in the office. It was still a half hour before the bell rang, but many students were already at school.

"Somebody better do something here or there's going to be hell to pay!" Sholenda's mom shouted.

"Ma'am, please come in the office and we'll talk about this," our current principal tried to say.

"Somebody let this happen to my little girl and I want some answers!" She was wailing now.

When he saw me, he motioned me over and said, "Brant, could you go get Peggy for me, please?"

I took off and got her. I saw her after school and she filled me in on what had happened. They were in a meeting for two hours with counselors, social workers, and a security representative and district rep also. It turned out there was absolutely nothing the school could do for Mom. She had never gotten guardianship of Sholenda, even after being advised in IEP after IEP year after year since Sholenda was fourteen. Mom was hysterical for most of the meeting, demanding that the school take some sort of action.

The story was this: Late Saturday night while her mom was either not at home or asleep, Sholenda had gotten on their computer and gone into a chat room. The problem with this chat room was its purpose was expressly for hooking up with strangers to have sex. A group of local gang bangers sent a cab to pick her up, and she didn't get home until Sunday afternoon. Mom didn't notice she was gone until lunchtime Sunday, when she went into Sholenda's room and saw she wasn't there. No one else in the house had seen her either. A few hours later, another cab pulled up and dropped Sholenda off. Mom called the police, and when two policemen showed up and talked to her they asked Sholenda a couple of questions.

"Sholenda, how old are you?"

"I'm nineteen sir," she answered. Her mom said they'd raised their eyebrows at that.

"Did the men hurt you or make you do anything you didn't want to do?" one policeman asked.

"No, sir, I wanted to go and be with them."

"What did you do with them?" he asked.

"I had sex with all of them," she said, smiling. They raised their eyebrows again.

"Did you want - " he started.

"Yes, sir, I wanted to. I liked it."

"Thank you. I'm sorry, there's nothing we can do. Have a nice day, ma'am," they said, and were in their car and gone in less than two or three minutes.

Sholenda graduated that year, and the next year in November, dropped by to show us all her new baby boy.

Chapter 32

BULLSHITTING TYSON

Once again, I was asked to take on another difficult student. Tyson came to us from a treatment facility and foster care. Actually, he had been adopted, but had been deemed too violent to stay in the house and was moved temporarily to the treatment facility but was now in a new foster care setting. Tyson was in a complicated situation. He was African American, about five feet ten, wore thick Coke-bottle glasses, and was 180 pounds of sinew and muscle. He had the most complete flat affect of any student I had ever seen. Flat affect is having a lack of emotional expression. It usually is a symptom typically observed in people with schizophrenia, autism, depression, or those who've had traumatic brain injury. He spoke only with a staccato like rhythm.

Tyson had had many labels. It was documented he had been abused brutally and relentlessly as a child. Now he was in the system and groups of people were trying to help him. The first day I met him he was with his foster parents. They were, once again, some of the angels, albeit different, but still angels walking among us. They were an

African American couple with a child or two of their own. His adopted mother was still trying to get custody of Tyson, and the politics of the arrangement were never quite clear to me. He'd had several outbursts at his adopted home and was a threat to the other children living there. He was to only be in my class for about two hours a day, and to use me as his homeroom teacher, much the same way Babak did.

Things were relatively smooth for a week or maybe two. We call it a "romance period," and as it faded, I thought we'd be okay. I followed him the best I could, and checked in with his general ed teachers. He was trying, but was behind by several grades. Tyson operated at about a sixth- or seventh-grade level. Many of our students did, but he was quiet and polite, so it looked like we might be the right placement for him after all. Then he fell in love with one of the prettiest girls in the school. It was her boyfriend who alerted Sam, our security guard. Tyson was following her at lunch and was at first just standing twenty feet away, but then gradually moved closer and closer. When Sam learned of the problem, Tyson was right next to them. They tried to talk to him, but only got intense looks and stares, no answers. It was making them nervous. Sam asked for me to talk to Tyson while Sam was present. He came by during the period after lunch when he knew Tyson was in my class. We stepped outside under the ramada.

"Tyson, I want you to know that you're doing a great job here. We're glad you're fitting in so well, and were wondering if everything is going good with you?" I said to start the conversation. I wanted him to know we liked him. He just looked down.

"Is everything going okay?" I asked again. Nothing. I shrugged at Sam, and immediately thought we needed to have had the counselor or psychologist have this conversation, but I understood Sam needed to make sure the other kids were safe. He just picked up on what his job was.

"Well, one thing, we need to talk to you about, Tyson, is following the other kids, okay?" Sam asked.

"There's nothing wrong with you wanting to be near them and talk to them. We were thinking we could introduce you to them and you could learn their names," I said.

We got no response and Tyson kept looking down. I noticed his fists were clenching.

"It's just that when you walk up to them without saying anything, it makes them nervous," Sam said slowly. He was holding a large Big Gulp iced tea, probably from hurriedly having finished his lunch.

"Why you bullshitting me?" Tyson said through clenched teeth. He then breathed forcefully via his nose. He looked like an incredibly pissed-off nearsighted bull.

"What?" asked Sam. We looked at each other, not comprehending where to go with this.

"Why you bullshitting me?" he said again.

Without warning, Tyson swung one of his fists. It looked like it came from the ground, but while it was on the way to hitting Sam, it was partially deflected when it went through the Big Gulp, spraying iced tea all over Sam and me. Luckily, we had backed off a second before and Tyson never connected with Sam.

We immediately moved backward a couple of feet to get our bearings and give Tyson some room. He stood there, panting and breathing through his mouth and out his nose, blowing snot to the ground. Tyson was suspended for two days and an emergency meeting was held. His foster parents were great. Mr. Keeter decided to give him another chance, and we had two more weeks of quiet. Though Tyson would still follow the girl around, he kept his distance, but it was now becoming an issue again, as her boyfriend was probably feeling his pride at stake and was not going to being able to stop it himself. Sam told me he didn't want anything to do with Tyson, and the next time he'd simply call the police. It happened two days later. The boyfriend confronted Tyson and suffered a blow that was as painful to his pride as it was to his jaw.

"He said the last thing he remembered Tyson saying to him, was - can you guess?" Sam asked me later that day.

"Why you bullshitting me?" I knowingly guessed.

Tyson was kept out of school another three days. He spent another week in a treatment facility; we learned he'd assaulted a police officer when they responded to a domestic violence call at his home. The foster parents again asked for a meeting, and I had to hand it to them - they really wanted to help Tyson.

He was given some ground rules, and we had several close calls, but again, a quiet period prevailed for a couple of weeks. Then, I'm sorry to say, *I* lost it. We were on edge for a couple of days constantly. It was not a pleasant atmosphere. I talked to Bobby, the principal several times about the intense dynamic Tyson was causing at our school. I had cleared the classroom twice when he was melting down about a situation in one of his classes. High school was a tough place for him to operate without overhearing stupid teenage comments, and Tyson could perceive any trivial remark as a direct threat.

"It doesn't border on paranoia; it most definitely is," Sam said.

The next day, Tyson came into the classroom fuming and blowing his bull bursts. He was storming around the room, and I let him for a few minutes. I cleared the room and sent all the other kids and aides for a walk. I was standing toward the front of the room facing the back, watching Tyson pace and rage. I didn't notice our student mentor was still sitting in the far front corner of the room. He hadn't said anything while I was keeping a close watch on Tyson's movements.

"Is there anything I can do to help, Tyson?" I asked quietly.

"Why you bullshitting me?!" Tyson yelled getting very close to me. Inches. I braced for a punch. He did this once, maybe twice more. I can't actually remember. Suddenly I couldn't stand it anymore. Maybe it was the Vannatter clan in me coming out, or I merely snapped. I was never really scared of him, but I simply stopped being fearful of being hit. I thought I might lose a tooth or two or have a broken jaw, but I was done. Job lost or not.

"Tyson, the only one bullshitting here is you." I faced him. "I'm sick of it. Do what you're going to do, 'cause I'm not going to listen to *your* bullshit anymore, and believe me, it's going to be a fight you're not going to like." My voice was steadily rising. I stood back and raised my fists. "Well, do something, or back off. Don't ever threaten me again, or get up in my face – I'll kick your ass all over this room."

We stood there looking at each other.

He instantly deflated. Tyson lowered his fists as I did. I immediately felt like shit. I asked him to sit down and he did. Right then, I noticed the student mentor. He was sitting there in shock. I couldn't believe I hadn't noticed him before. I apologized, and he discreetly nodded. I felt exhausted from the emotional journey Tyson and I had taken together in those few minutes.

"Can you think about keeping this to yourself?" I asked the student mentor, thinking that would be impossible for a high school student.

He nodded. Right then, the bell rang and the mentor practically sprinted out the door. Unbelievably, the mentor did keep it to himself. I immediately called Tyson's foster family, and the dad told me he'd done the same thing I had, and he hadn't had trouble with Tyson again. "Don't worry about it," he said. "You have given Tyson an idea of what the real world is like. He's a bully, and will get away with it if we let him." I at least didn't have any big trouble with him again either. Mr. Keeter understood, or at least pretended to, and said, "We'll just wait to see what the fallout will be." There wasn't any. Tyson moved to another school the next year, and I understood he was doing okay. The counseling was kicking in and the problems were decreasing. I was glad to hear that.

Chapter 33

HERMIONE GRANGER

I don't know how many times I've heard a special education teacher bemoan the fact that not only are these kids given a disability, they are saddled with parents who are some of the worst you'd ever see; that the apple doesn't fall far from the tree. I've had some of the most loving, caring people in the world with kids that have some of the hardest, most profound disabilities, and then I've had some of what I call "the angriest people in the world." But given both of those gradients, is it possible that a higher being (or providence) would give kids a significant disability (cognitive) *and* a mental illness? Over the years I've learned the two are not mutually exclusive.

Elise came to us from a much larger high school. She had several problems, and had an SLD label (which stands for "significant learning disabilities"). Elise worked at about a fifth- or sixth-grade level. Abstract cognition was high on her ability awareness. Elise did not have a label that called for placement in a self-contained classroom, but knowing some of the other issues, which entailed some serious unfortunate inappropriate contact with boys, she needed to have close adult supervision. Schools don't have the personnel to watch every student that has "issues." We did what we could, and many times, didn't do something until it was too late. We did the right thing with Elise.

Elise was attractive in an unusual way. She had long, wavy coal-black hair and was shapely. She needed a teacher who could get away and find inventive ways to watch her at times, check on her progress throughout the day, and make sure she was monitored until we found a level playing field and routine that would work. Elise had issues with every one of her teachers. She would incessantly ask her teachers and other students to call her "Lex," the young girl from the first *Jurassic Park* movie. We had a meeting and our administration refused, even to mom, to call her anything other than her given name, Elise. Several times in the first weeks, I was in conferences about her actions and meltdowns. We came up with a plan for her to be in my class two hours a day. Elise should have had a three-year evaluation and gotten a different label, but it wasn't due, and our psychologist was overloaded as it was at that point in the year. Elise still needed credits for graduation in mainstream classes, and I was the elected fool to try and convince her teachers that giving her a passing grade (75 -80 percent, earned or not) wasn't the end of the world. This was simply because our school didn't have the resource classes available for Elsie. I spent hours of my life attempting, with some success, to persuade typical teachers that the school regulations and federal law under "special education" requires that either coursework be modified and/or accommodated to suit their needs. I always boiled it down to this: If you didn't or morally couldn't, pass a student with a disability the modification or lack thereof was on you. I had math teachers, especially, find this to be an absolute travesty.

"That isn't fair, and I can't in good faith give a student a passing grade unless they earn it," I had more than one teacher state.

"Well, the modifications are completely on you. That means changing your assignments, being prepared to show them to a lawyer if Mom or Dad chooses to go that route if you fail them." I'd say. "You know, you aren't taking a slot away from a student applying to MIT or Stanford, and you're not going to be responsible for them unfairly winning the Nobel Peace Prize in science." I knew it was against these teachers' competitive backgrounds, and was even a question of ethics, but this was what the reality is of our schools today.

I was convinced Elise needed more testing; I felt more was going on than significant learning disabilities and she wasn't eligible for another two years. In my heart I could tell she was on the fine line between slow and intellectual disability, and didn't have the capacity to do better. It wasn't avoidance behavior making her act the way she did, but I couldn't persuade our psychologist to do the evaluation early. Of course, she wasn't the one that had to to deal with Elise from day to day, or hour to hour.

Elise talked to herself and had imaginary conversations with people in her favorite movies and TV shows. Once or twice in classes, she would let loose with a blood-curdling scream for no apparent reason, scaring the shit out of the kids and her teacher. When groups of kids were standing around at lunch before school, or even during passing periods, Elise would run up to them within a foot or two and stop suddenly, frightening them. Inevitably, they would startle and sometimes respond with yelling or shoving, and a whole process of discipline would result. She couldn't explain why she did these things. She lived with an adoptive mother who was a strange woman. But in most of these situations I felt she at least had someone.

Elise had been in several foster homes before she was adopted, and I always wondered what had happened to her there. Her mother worked long hours, and Elise was left alone at the house much of the time. We got through our first year, and she was due to come back the next year as a junior. The first day of the new school year I was called up to the office, and my department head was there with the principal. They were standing inside his office with the door open. Elise's mom was there, and so was Elise. I said good morning and nodded to everyone. Mr. Keeter handed me a note.

> To whom it may concern:
> In my capacity as Ms. Morrison's psychiatrist with Elise Morrison under my care, I advise all students and faculty, including administration, to refer to Elise as "Hermione Granger." It is in Elise's best interest, and I support we continue this practice until I instruct otherwise. Thank you for your assistance.
>
> Dr. John Turk

Mr. Keeter looked at me and waited for what I assume was a response. I didn't have one forthcoming. I shrugged.

He looked around the room and said, "I'll do no such thing until the superintendent of the district orders me to." With that he walked out of his own office and down the hallway. We all stood there for what seemed like another minute.

"The doctor says you have to," Elise whined.

"We don't have to do anything remotely ridiculous as this," our current department head said as she walked out.

"Who is Hermione Granger?" I asked.

Chapter 34

TEACHERS WHO HAVE LOST IT

Most bad teachers take themselves out of the equation after a year or two, despite what talking heads on the news, or pundits worrying about how unions are destroying our education system, say. It's stressful, for one thing, and the starting pay is horrible, for another. I have witnessed a couple of bad teachers, or teachers that couldn't handle the stress of being *on* all day, everyday. It isn't like sitting in a cubical in an office, or any other job I can think of. Students come at you all day, every hour, unless you're lucky enough to get a planning period and lunch.

One day on a Christmas break grading day, as I was walking down the hallway back to my class, I walked by Mr. Johan and Ms. Walker, who were talking very somberly, heads bent and close together. Right before I turned the corner, I heard her raise her voice and shout, "I did not call that girl anorexic!" Ms. Walker had had several shouting matches and meltdowns during that school year. This last minor one wasn't something that surprised me in the least. It was one more in a long string of incidents. The last one was during a grading day (no students), when I heard shouting and yelling outside my door. This was unusual due to the fact no kids were at school, so I didn't expect it. I cracked the door and saw Mr. Johan, the technology teacher, scrambling away, looking back over his shoulder. Ms. Walker was chasing him, hurling insults and profanity after him. He was trying escape.

"You don't do shit here, and I can't get my computer fixed and working, and all you can do is tell me you'll put in a work order for district people to come out here!"

I ended up not being a great fan of Mr. Johan, either. His class was interesting, and a couple of my kids had his class different times throughout the day. He had acquired more equipment than any computer teacher I'd seen before or since. Mr. Johan would project new movies on a huge screen from somewhere like Singapore or Thailand the same week they were released. We were about the same age and had music history in common. He'd secured an excellent grant from the state and had computer equipment piled up all over the cavernous computer room. If I mentioned I liked a certain or obscure group: - The Flying Burrito Brothers, Canned Heat, or Johnny Winter - the next day, Mr. Johan would have a double CD burned for me. It was nice. I had spent two years in Britain, and since they don't have the same copyright laws we do. I'd picked up many bootleg CDs, and it was long enough ago that cassettes weren't unheard of. I ventured to several record fests or fairs. In conversation, I told him about some Beatles bootlegs I had bought on cassette. They were from the Abby Road studios, and much of it wasn't even released on the Anthology series in the 1990s. I possessed about ten cassettes worth of the Beatle's talking and introducing songs to each other. It was Beatle freak heaven. At the end of the year, he offered to take the cassettes and transfer them to CD for me over the summer. I thanked him profusely and offered payment. He refused and said he was glad to do it.

Entering school the first day back for a week of teachers' meetings and classroom preparation, I was actually as excited as much for the school year as I was to have my Beatles tapes safely on CDs. 1 didn't see Mr. Johan anywhere around that first morning's meeting. Noah, our speech pathologist, sat next to me and said, "Brant, have you seen the computer lab?"

"No, what's up?" I asked.

"Follow me," he said.

We walked down the hallway, and when he opened the door, I stood there in shock. It was almost empty and only had a portion of the computers and equipment that had previously been loaded up to the ceiling on two of the walls. Wires and computer cables stuck up all over the floor and ran to nothing.

"What happened?" I asked.

"I'm not sure exactly, and I don't think anyone else is either. He's gone - Johan's gone, man," Noah said as he smiled.

"What do you mean, gone?"

"Gone, man. No one knows where he is, and it looks like he was running stuff in one door and out the other to his car during the year, and then this summer, he had a key and came in and cleaned the place out. There's a big investigation going on."

I didn't know what to say, and along with feeling bad for our students, who didn't have a decent computer lab for several weeks, I was pissed off about my tapes being gone along with everything else. Later in the year, our librarian heard he was up on the Navajo reservation. We never learned if charges were filed or what. She also had his email. I sent him a message to please send me back my tapes and that I would pay postage; and I asked what, if anything else, I could do to get them back. I never heard from the bastard.

The next year about four months into school, I was subjected to another laughable moment when a new teacher next to me in one of our portables flipped out. We had had an order for new desks in for some of the classes for a long time, and I had forgotten about it. That morning about nine o'clock, I was pushing a student in a wheelchair back to class with an aide who had helped me do the toileting when I noticed something funny. We saw several desks and a table on the ground behind the other portable, but they were scattered on the ground in front of our stairs, not lined up or in some type of order. I looked at my aide and said, "That must be the new desks and stuff, but tossing the old out the back door isn't right. I'll call Mr. Johnson and let him know what they're doing. It needs to be cleaned up."

"Yeah, you're right. That's horrible," she answered.

Right then, we heard this yelling and smashing noise coming from the other side of the building. I gave her the student and walked around the side, where I saw tables getting pushed out the door over the stairs and railing, and then crashing down on the ground. Behind it was Mr. Stuart, looking crazed and dazed at the same time. I'd started cautiously walking toward his room, when I heard a noise behind me. Mr. Johnson was running out the back door of the school towards us and was motioning for me to stop.

"It's okay, Brant, I got it," he said as he ran past. Right behind him was Sam, who looked at me, smiling and shaking his head.

I went back to my room, where two of my aides were watching from the stairs deck. We saw a half dozen students walking out and going with Sam into the main school building. A minute later, we saw Mr. Stuart come walking past our room and going right out onto the boulevard that runs past our school. He kept looking over his shoulder and laughing as he went. Mr. Johnson came calmly walking out a minute later. Mr. Stuart was a first-year teacher and we had heard he was having a hard time. He would always be standing outside his door with a student, talking intensely, and I always wondered what was going on *inside* his room while he was talking to the kids outside.

Sam said Mr. Stuart was actually an excellent history teacher, but had some really strange ideas about classroom management, and it didn't seem to be working.

That day, he started acting really weird and saying things that didn't make any sense to the students in his first period. A couple of kids went to the office and asked for someone to do something. Mr. Johnson was in a meeting and Sam was tied up with another behavior problem but planned on getting there as soon as he could. Lately he had been dropping in on Mr. Stuart several times a day. During second period, Mr. Stuart sat there saying nothing and then suddenly got up and started pushing chairs, desks, and a table out the back door, muttering, "See how you like school without any place to sit, you munchkins." Several students had run to the office, and that's about the time when I walked up.

We never saw Mr. Stuart again.

Chapter 35

A MOM WHO HATED TEACHERS AND SCHOOLS

I started as a teacher of the visually impaired in 2006. I had been working on the certification for two years, almost full-time, while also working full-time; four classes every summer and two semester classes during the year. I didn't need another master's degree, so I finished with a certification. I was an itinerant going from one school to another. One of the first students I picked up was a middle-school boy with cerebral palsy. Most students with cerebral palsy have a visual impairment, which is classified as cortical visual impairment (CVI). It can be devastatingly serious or mild, depending on the student. CVI is a decreased visual response due to the neurological problem affecting the visual part of the brain. Typically, a child with CVI has a normal eye exam, or has an eye condition that cannot account for the abnormal visual behavior. It is the most frequent cause of visual impairment in children born with cerebral palsy.

I gave Logan's mom one of my much-used titles of "Most Outraged Parent in the World." She demanded much of her son's teachers. He used a wheelchair and could talk slowly with much effort, but almost as conversationally as a typical middle-schooler. He was loved and taken care of; his parents took him to activities outside of school, sporting events, and trips. They spent an inordinate amount of time talking to him about a variety of subjects, like football and politics. When first meeting Logan, one would think he was extremely bright, and in many senses he was. Logan was extremely polite and pleasant. But once again, I was seeing a parent who would not allow her son to be tested. Hence, the only label he had during his school years was visual impairment and orthopedic impairment. Logan attended typical classes with a one-on-one aide. His mom's name was Judith and she would not ask the teacher - in this case me - but went right to a bureaucrat at the district level to demand that I be there on his first day in school. I would have gladly been there had she simply asked me.

While working with him the first couple of weeks - twice a week was what he was scheduled for and what I continued - I came to realize his issues were not with his vision. I called it, as I did with Granger, the physicality of cerebral palsy. Learning what his aide and his classroom teacher were going through was a rude awakening for me. His mom constantly berated his teacher, and before his first Individual Education Program meeting in November, he had been through two aides. With the third aide, I brought in eight-by-twelve cards with math problems in black letters on a fluorescent-yellow background. I held them only about two feet from his face, and first asked him to identify only the numbers on the cards. Logan was able to do this with no problem. I then showed him simple one-up problems, such as four plus one. He would think for a moment or two.

"Can you read what the numbers are?" I asked.

"Yes," he answered.

"What?"

"Four plus one," he said.

"What is the answer for that, four plus one?" I asked

"Five!" he shouted. I did this about three times, with a different set each time, but only one up. I then showed him three plus four. He hesitated longer and looked around at his aide for help.

"Just do the best you can, Logan," I said. "It's okay, just do the best you can."

"Nine!" he shouted. I didn't tell him he was wrong, but continued with the same level of problems. He couldn't answer anything other than one-up math problems. His aide looked at me unbelieving and confused. I just nodded and talked to his aide later about what strategies to use for Logan in the classroom to aid his vision issues.

"I've never seen a problem with his vision," he said.

"I know. I'm learning that we simply have to make sure we provide him with large-print, colorful backgrounds, and so on," I said.

Judith demanded I schedule him for an appointment with our ophthalmologist that came twice a year to give our visually impaired students a functional vision assessment. Dr. Burns was an extremely nice guy and worked great with our kids, even those who had cognitive disabilities. As soon as I walked into the room where he was setting up his equipment, he looked up.

"Why am I seeing Logan Marston again?" he nearly roared at me, obviously agitated.

"What?" was the only response I had.

"I've seen him twice in the last three years. I don't need to see a student more than once every four or five years unless there has been a dramatic change to his vision."

"I'm sorry, I didn't know, and Mr. Brinkley told me to schedule him."

"I know, I know, it's Mom. I'll handle it," he said, interrupting me.

During the examination, he continued to be brusque with Mom and at one point, looked at me and then at her and said, "This kid has better vision than me, it's at least twenty-forty and I see no indication his cortical vision impairment is an issue. Further more I don't see him needing any services. His issue is not from the eyes forward. Logan's issue is from the eyes backward."

"Does he need Mr. Vickers?" she asked.

"I don't really believe so, no," he answered.

"I can see him on a consultation basis until his IEP in two weeks, and then we can change his service time, if that's all right with you," I told her.

"I think that will be all right," she said.

During the next two weeks, I dropped in on him and checked with his teacher and aide. I should have seen it coming, but didn't, and learned a hard lesson. The Individual Education Program (IEP) is like a legal contract, and whatever it states must be followed to the letter, or schools, teachers, and the district can be sued. Lawsuits and lawyers drive so much in schools. I was called on the carpet for not seeing Logan for my full two hours a week. I knew to not even make excuses, and not to use Logan's mom's own words in my defense. I just went to the IEP and didn't know that my issues were only the tip of the iceberg.

As I walked into the school the day of his IEP, I saw his teacher and Judith talking in the hallway – well - Judith was yelling, and his teacher was crying. She had her face in her hands and was sobbing. I continued to the conference room, where I counted twelve people sitting around the table. I knew several, but not everyone. There were two psychologists and at least two program specialists, whose jobs were to dispel conflicts such as the one in this room, which was growing by the minute. Logan's teacher had raised concerns about his ability to do grade-level work. She had the temerity to ask that he be tested so the school could help him work to his potential and not be stressed. I had had several conversations with her, and she was confused as to why Mom didn't want him to be helped with the proper placement and support. They came in the conference room and the yelling continued.

"How dare you have the unmitigated audacity to question my son's intelligence!" she shouted.

After a few minutes of this, I started to pick up my papers and scooted my chair back. I was not an administrator, and couldn't believe the ones who were there were not going to get control of this situation. I was just going to leave, type up a statement, and get Dr. Burns to write up something for me and tell my team someone else was going to have to see Logan. Luckily right then, the school's vice principal walked in, somewhat took control, and moved the meeting along.

As the team was presenting its recommendations to Mom, who shot them down one after another as they came up, I noticed a woman I had never seen before. I had heard about her; she was a cancer survivor and had been down for the count several times. I heard she just kept bouncing back, and was obviously in remission again. She was dressed like the comedian Moms Mabley. Her name was Ava, and she was sitting there taking it all in. I had no idea how well she had until she, among all her peers and the bureaucrats present, spoke up. Logan's progression, or lack thereof was in question.

"What are we going to do when he's a senior in high school?!" Judith shouted for the second time.

Ava leaned over, and in a soft but intense voice, said clearly and concisely, "Oh, honey, when he's a senior in high school, he's *still* going to be in the second or third grade."

Silence. No one had the fortitude to follow up or contribute to Ava's pronouncement. The silence continued for a long couple of moments, and abruptly Mom started talking like nothing had been said. I saw Ava a week or two later in the district offices, hugged her, and told her I was glad she was feeling better, and that she was my hero in that meeting.

"I know, but I just don't care. What are they going to do to me? I'm lucky to be here everyday as it is. That mom told me after the meeting she was going to take him out of that school, and maybe the district. Ha! Ha!" she said, laughing. "I told her to help herself."

Judith did take him out of that school and put him into the second of three middle schools over the next three years. So, due to geography he moved on to another teacher of the visually impaired.

The next two years, I missed the classroom. I never felt like I was working as hard as those days when I'd been in the classroom with my own kids. I got bored as an itinerant, and didn't feel like I was making as much of a difference in the kids' lives. Granted, it was at least half the work of a classroom teacher, but I didn't like waltzing in and out of a room and making suggestions and not being part of the total experience.

Chapter 36

MEETING ANOTHER ANGEL

Three years later, I left my itinerant position and went back to Harrogate High School. I simply missed the classroom. I wanted to have *my* kids, not be breezing in and out of a classroom for a period of thirty minutes a month. Jill wasn't there; she had moved to a high school close to where she lived, and when I returned to Harrogate from the teacher of the visually impaired gig, I was working with a whole new crew. The aide who helped the transition and made my next two years livable - no, more than livable, *absolutely wonderful* - was Bill. He had been a river raft guide in Colorado, but moved to Tucson with his fiancé, soon to be wife, and started a whole new career. He was one of the most enjoyable, funny, smart, and responsible aides I ever had.

Being at Harrogate without Jill seemed odd, and, at times, I regretted my decision. I was concerned I had made a tactical error. Bill could make those thoughts disappear. I needed his support and his reassuring attitude about daily decisions to get me through many stressful days. He was also truthful, and let me know when I was making mistakes.

That was something that was invaluable to a teacher in special ed, but rarely offered. Most aides don't feel comfortable in that role. Bill helped me realize what my station, my role in life, was, and without a doubt, that was in the classroom. He helped me get through times with a couple of the most challenging kids I taught. Bill's biggest assistance came through humor. I always said if we couldn't have fun in this job, it could kill us, and Bill filled in those hectic days with laughter.

Some of the most fun I've ever had in my life has been with special education kids and my aides. I've learned as an adult that belly laughs are few and far between. I felt very fortunate that these kids made me giggle, chuckle, guffaw, and laugh almost daily. They were not usually the butt of the joke, but sometimes they made their own, and when you work with special education kids you know you have a special relationship and have the right to laugh with them and enjoy their delight in ordinary things we take for granted. With Davey at Desert Hills, I'd look for him every day, and smile when I saw that he was smiling wildly, purely because he saw me walking up toward him. I came to relish that, and no matter how challenging the days were, every day I could reflect back on something that was worthwhile.

Liam was almost done with school. He was a gas. Liam could be stubborn, willful, and non-compliant with many school tasks set before him. He had to have constant praise and reward to get anything done, but in actuality, we learned, he didn't usually follow up with the need he bargained for to finish any academic work. He loved ordering from menus; I had collected a dozen from restaurants throughout the city. Managers would always help with a gift of an ornate menu when they were told it was for kids with disabilities to work on math and living skills. Bill and I did this lesson every Friday and we looked forward to it as much as the kids.

Liam loved ordering different types of food, sometimes a seven-course meal. Emma was equally as pleased to order with Liam.

They both were kids with Down's, and worked well together. Emma was funny; she wouldn't order anything but salad, and when I'd try to cajole her into something like what Liam was ordering - a burger with fries, a big plate of enchiladas, or pasta - she'd just roll her eyes at me like I was clueless. At the end of one ordering spree, by the time we got to dessert Liam had accumulated about fifty thousand calories. I never gave them fattening treats like some special ed teachers. My snacks consisted of fruit, plain popcorn, or crackers, and most days I felt lunch was enough. Many of my kids had weight problems before they came to my class. I couldn't, with a clear conscience, add to the difficulty parents had keeping their kid's weight down. For parents, the kids equate food with love, and I understood the issue and didn't want to contribute to the struggle. But in our class, the more Liam added to his order, the more addition he had to do, so I let him go to town. Emma, on the other hand, had ordered another salad, a side of fruit, and was puzzling over what she wanted for dessert.

"Emma, don't you want something good, like an ice cream sundae, or a big chocolate cookie with vanilla ice cream on top?" I stupidly asked.

She looked at me hard for a moment, shook her head in exasperation as she tapped her temple, and fairly shouted, "Helllooooooooo?!"

I looked over at Bill, and we both started laughing until we almost cried.

Every Friday, if the routine held up, I would watch Liam walk to his bus, and before they left I'd walk down the line so I could watch them depart. I had developed the habit years before; initially it was to keep an eye on Owsley, but I also had to watch for Liam as he drove by. This was for guileless enjoyment and love. The bus driver allowed him to open the window. He had learned to close it by the time they turned the corner, and would stick his head out a few inches to yell at me in a hoarse shout. Liam would put his hand up to his ear with the thumb and little finger out to replicate a phone.

"Call meeee! Ughhhhh, caaallllll meeee!" he'd bellow at me.

I'd return the gesture.

"We gooooooo to lunch! Calllll meeeeee!" he continued as the bus rolled away.

We were lucky enough to have a therapeutic pool at Harrogate. On and off, we'd employ a full-time lifeguard. They weren't technically aides, and worked in a different capacity, but were as much help, and had a gigantic responsibility. We had a couple different ones over the years, but for a couple of years we had a wonderful, funny guy in his forties. He also worked at one or two of the city pools in the evenings. We shared the pool with several other special ed classes from other schools. Jim was a little strange, but what was more important, he *got* our kids and could handle some of the behaviors that inevitably surfaced. We had our scheduled time, and an aide or two would swim with the kids. Every Tuesday, as I had time, I'd go down to help a couple of the boys change and come back when they were done. I liked talking to Jim. We talked music, politics and swimming. He was a swimmer, and when he discovered I'd swam in high school and played water polo, we found common ground. Most adults take conversations with peers and co-workers for granted. Teachers sometimes go the whole day without a meaningful exchange with an adult. There just isn't the time.

Garth was from another class. He loved me, as he did most adult men. Garth was nonverbal and had Fragile X syndrome. We just knew and accepted him as Garth. He probably had seen few men in his school history, and gravitated toward them. He always tried to get my attention, smiled, and pointed to me. He laughed constantly. Jim had a slew of toys, balls, noodles, and pool playthings. Garth loved throwing the Nerf balls back and forth. A couple of the balls soaked up water and couldn't hurt you if they hit you. One day when I was there, the game progressed to where Jim and I were on opposite sides of the pool and throwing the balls at Garth. The harder we threw the more he loved it. Garth would immediately pick them up and fire them back, fairly hard, but surely determinedly. He screamed with joy. Jim and I got caught up in the moment.

"Get him! Get him!" Jim yelled at me.

"Right over there! Good one!" I shouted back.

"Destroy 'em! Yeah, excellent!"

We went on for several minutes, but suddenly we stopped and looked at each other. I bent over in laughter.

"We've really come a long way in our lives . . ." Jim trailed off in laughter.

"Boy, *our* high school principals should see us now, two grown men throwing Nerf balls at a retarded kid," Jim said, hooting and catching his breath, and wiping away tears.

"Yeah, well, you do what you can," I said.

Garth was making noises and begging us to continue and not stop. I realized it was fine; he loved it and was having the time of his life - as was I.

Chapter 37

DR. EVIL WAS STILL AN ANGEL

Bill smoothed the road with one of my biggest aide challenges. The next year was when Dr. Evil came to us. She was an aide who had been in several other classes and couldn't get along with the other aides, or teachers, for that matter. Rose, a.k.a., Dr. Evil (Bill gave her that nom de plum), had a PhD and was working as a teacher's aide. The head of our department asked me before school started if I could possibly help her and the school out. I agreed to try. At the least, it was *literally* trying. We never could figure her out. She was smart, but in the two years we worked with her, we never could understand what her story was, and she, in turn, never did figure out the students. I never fathomed how Rose benefited from a PhD in education. I had aides who'd started with a GED and were miles beyond her in working with special education students.

This was where Bill came to the rescue. He buffeted Dr. Evil from the wrath of the other aides, students, and at times, me. I continually lost patience with her unbelievable ignorance of what our students were capable of, and at what level they could master academics. Bill frequently ran a blocking pattern when the other aides were out for blood. Rose had no social skills, and couldn't read the frustration in the other aides' faces when they were at odds with something she did or didn't do. She didn't have this unbelievable helpmate in the other two classes she was more or less bounced from. Bill saved her job, in our room and in the school. My department head thanked me several times for allowing Rose to have a home. I hope I always gave Bill the credit. I hope I remember correctly that I did.

I had to ask her to stop hugging Emma. This was a tricky common situation in special ed. Many of our students had learned at an early age to give and accept hugs. At the middle-school age, a teacher needs to wean them from that habit, though. It's sad, because sometimes they need it and expect it. But as they grow older, it's unacceptable. Rose constantly hugged Emma. It was a full-frontal body hug, and would last several seconds. It was an embrace a parent would give. I interrupted them a couple of times, and showed Rose how to give a very shallow sideways hug, and then suggested a handshake. She never got it.

"Rose, would you give any other high school senior a hug like that?" I finally asked one day.

"No," she answered.

"Well, Emma's twenty years old, and if someone else looked in the room and saw you doing that and didn't know Rose or you, what do you think they might think?" She looked at me blankly. "I'll tell you what they might think. It could easily be misconstrued as unhealthy physical contact between a teacher and a student. Regardless of how innocent it actually is, you need to *stop* it."

Her eyes got big and she walked away, muttering she was sorry.

"She'll get over it, man." Bill said as he walked up to me.

"Was it too mean? I try not to be, but she never gets it."

"I know. It was okay. She'll let it sink in for a while and then be fine," he said, patting me on the back. I needed it. He looked at me and said, "What I think you need is a hug."

I allowed Dr. Evil an hour in the morning to teach a variety of subjects. She covered science, social studies, geography, and history. The rest of us just kept our peace and our mouths shut. I never had a problem with introducing new or mainstream subjects to our students, but you had to be much more careful to not teach using a vocabulary above a student with a cognitive disability than you do when teaching to students at a higher level. The students in our class were able to grasp kindergarten and first-grade concepts. Tomas was our most verbal student, and could somewhat contribute to a lesson, albeit at a much lower level than Rose anticipated.

The day after Ted Kennedy died, Rose taught a class on his legacy. I kept making low sideways comments to Bill about Chappaquiddick, and we could hardly keep our snickering quiet. The kids had no idea what Dr. Evil was talking about. I thought about interrupting, as I did almost every day, but refrained when I saw how emotional Rose was in talking about one of her heroes. After a longer period of time than was meaningful for any student, I drew my fingers across my throat and circled my finger in the air to help her remember to review the one thing she wanted them to gain from the lesson. Tomas had spent the majority of the time circling in the back area in his wheelchair.

"So, what is something you can remember about Ted Kennedy?" Dr. Evil asked. No student probably remembered who or what she had been talking about. "Can someone tell me what they know about Ted Kennedy?" she asked again. Her voice seemed strained, and even a hint of frustration had seeped into her timbre. Once again, she didn't realize her lesson was probably for a senior honors class in political science.

As Tomas was wheeling by, he looked up at Bill and me, whistled, shook his head, and said in a loud commanding voice, "He's dead!"

Bill and I had to leave the room, we were laughing so hard. It was cruel, but once again, he later patched it up and made it better by talking to Dr. Evil and convincing her our laughter had nothing to do with her lesson; we'd purely been enjoying Tomas' participation. She bought it.

The next year, I put Bill in for the Teacher Assistant of the Year award. I did this for an aide every year, but this year, I really felt strongly about it, and knew I put my heart and soul into writing it. As much effort as I put into the writing, like most years, I immediately forgot about it, so I was more than pleasantly surprised when I found out Bill had won. I knew there wasn't another aide in the district who was more deserving than Bill. The awards ceremony was in the largest high school in the district. Arriving excited and looking forward to it, we all sat at a table together relishing the experience, but over the next few hours, the night dragged on and on and on. Bill kept unnecessarily apologizing to Cheryl and me. He was sitting there as miserable as I'd seen him. I think he was happy about getting the award, but this bullshit way administrators had of dragging things on seemed endless. Working all day and then sitting through several hours of every award under the sun, and for every possible position in the entire district, exhausted us.

"I bet right about now you're wishing you had never written that damn recommendation, aren't you?" Bill leaned over and said.

We laughed and laughed, and I was still as happy as I've ever been, seeing him get what he deserved.

Chapter 38

GLOVE SINGS THE BLUES

I can still strum a basic D chord and think of it as the most beautiful sound in the world. It resonates in my soul, and as cheesy as that sounds, not many things in this world are as true or enduring as the beauty of that major chord. On and off for over fifty years, my guitar has always been there for me. Learning a new song, a blues riff, or chord is still a thing of wonder. I've never been a performer, and I don't play for people, but the few who hear me play think of me as fairly proficient in the fingerstyle country blues genre. I don't have any natural talent. Playing the guitar has always been incredibly hard work, but when I'm thankful for the ability to play, I always remember one of the people I touched with my music.

Glove came to me from another special education self-contained class. It seemed to be happening more and more often. When one of my fellow teachers was having a problem with a student, the answer inevitably was, "Send them to Brant's class. He'll be able to handle them." I didn't mind Glove from what I'd seen of him. I knew he could be mean and get frustrated extremely easily. His foster brother, Tomas, was already in my class. Glove had cerebral palsy and was in a wheelchair; he could only make guttural sounds and had limited use of his arms. He didn't have enough strength to move his wheelchair independently for a long distance but he could maneuver it slowly around the classroom. It tired him, though. He was in a foster home, and we got the impression early on that he was in a cash-flow situation - either in foster care, or even adopted, for the money. We call them "farms."

He came to school sick, he came to school unwashed, and he came to school extremely tired – he didn't sleep well. Childhood Protective Services had been notified several times, but it never quite crossed the line of abuse to trigger any action. Glove was sick quite a bit. If there were a virus, a cold, the flu, or a cough going around, he'd catch it. Many kids with cerebral palsy don't have strong immune systems; they don't get a chance to build them up. We'd have Glove use what little strength he had to exercise and get a chance to learn something while at school. The problem was we only had these kids half the year, and that wasn't enough for them to be on a comprehensive program to actually get in the shape they needed to be in to remain healthy. It's a struggle for most typical kids, much less kids with cerebral palsy. There were times when we changed Glove's clothes and washed the ones he wore to school. If he had an accident, we knew he would never bring back the clothes we sent home with him.

Glove wasn't interested in learning or participating in anything academic. Glove would try for a short period of time, but would get bored quickly, and remain uninterested for the remainder of the period. If we tried to keep him on task, we could count on him melting down and eventually attempting to give us the finger by raising his hand, most fingers together, and shaking it with a scrunched-up face that didn't allow us to mistake his intent. He'd make sounds approximating words, but they were incomprehensible to most, especially out of context. After a while with him, I was able to understand him, to a degree, and could generally get it. "Ugggg yoooouuuu!" he'd wail. Glove could stay mad for hours. When that happened, and I saw him be incredibly rude to my aides, I would usually put him in the hallway with his wheels locked (he didn't have the strength to unlock them) until they both had a time out, and we'd talk it out and come to an agreement. He didn't have the right to tell us to fuck off, and we'd try to compromise when he felt he'd attended to an activity long enough.

His turnaround in my classroom was remarkable. It wasn't that I was such a better teacher than my peers, it was just that different teachers connected with different kids in various ways. Sometimes it worked. But with Glove it *was* something that I was doing. In a very short period of time, he was staying on task for much longer periods of time and putting a great deal more effort into learning what he could.

My singing is god-awful and I know it, but I will gladly play and sing for my kids in class, mostly alone. Aides know not to comment on my singing, and will actually tell me it isn't so bad. I don't care; most kids, I've found, can relate to the universal magic of music. Many love it, need it, and look forward to it daily, and several over the years have had it change their attitude about many aspects of school. The rest will tolerate it, and many times I can see their pleasure creep in, and that makes my day.

Glove loved it more than most. I made him a makeshift drum set by wrapping a couple of small sturdy cardboard boxes with towels and binding them with duct tape, then fitting them on a stand; I then let him go to town. He would howl. I would sing songs that I thought the kids would like, and eventually found that my kids had their own musical interests. As long as we could come to a compromise on something I could play and something they liked – it usually worked out. We went through dozens of songs before I stumbled on Glove's forte. Glove was a blues man. I played kid's songs – "House at Pooh Corner," "Puff, the Magic

Dragon" - and would usually slip in some Beatles ("Yellow Submarine," "Bungalow Bill"). I had a boy who loved Johnny Cash. I'd learn anything that they wanted, and was always pleasantly surprised when I found out they'd been exposed to some great old songs from parents, or even grandparents, uncles, or aunts. One day I was just picking, when I started the instantly recognizable riff in "House of the Rising Sun."

"Uuuuugggggg yeeeeaaaahhhh" Glove started moaning and pounding and rocking his head. Even with his limited quadriplegia, he could thump those drum sticks I got him it seemed, for hours. Somehow I actually remembered what I thought were the long-ago-forgotten lyrics. We both finished smiling and then laughing out loud. I asked him if he knew that song from somewhere and he just smiled and nodded vigorously. I wasn't sure if that was true, or that perchance he'd simply connected strongly with it. We could never play again without finishing up with "House of the Rising Sun." I'd look at him after doing twenty minutes of kids stuff for the other students and say, "Glove, are you a blues man?" He'd stretch out his head, and with an intense glare straight back at me, howl, "Bluuuuuueeeeeeessss!" And off we'd go. He learned to love several other blues-based songs, and I introduced him to other bluesy tunes, but his all time favorite was still "House of the Rising Sun."

Tomas and Glove both lived in the same home. Tomas was more cognitively aware. He was cute, talkative, and polite. He was also wheelchair bound with cerebral palsy. Whenever you did anything for him, he'd thank you profusely. The issues were numerous and varied, but there were always issues with every kid, for those two especially, though. The saddest days for me were Fridays, when we put them on the bus together to go home. They never went anywhere or did anything; in two years, I cannot remember either of them telling us they'd left the house over the weekend. One of us would ask every Monday morning, "How was your weekend, Tomas?"

"Boring," he'd say, smiling, "I'm happy to be back at school."

Several teachers who worked summer programs always went the extra mile to make sure Tomas and Glove were involved in everything the teachers could get them into. We bought them clothes, sent home extra food. They'd wear the same clothes three days in a row and I'd either have to make a phone call, or send a note from the nurse to please change their clothes. Tomas was still being tube-fed by his foster mom because she didn't want him to thrive; that meant growing bigger than he was. This has become more common in recent years, to keep the kids small and simpler to handle; less weight means lifting is easier. We taught him to eat small amounts clandestinely – strictly against her wishes. She had a doctor supporting her in this travesty. We never learned what happened to either of their biological parents. There were four or five kids in the home. The one thing that got to me the most was when Tomas came off the bus soiled. For some reason, it happened to him more than Glove. Many a morning, I'd have something to do, or have another student come in after I'd gotten them settled in the room, and would leave to check out what else needed to be done. I'd see one of my four aides, usually Bill, come barreling in with Tomas, making the sign for bathroom. The standard sign is making a fist with the thumb between the index and middle finger. It's also the letter *T* in sign language, but when you shake it, it means "bathroom." I could smell Tomas as I joined them on the way to the restroom. I could tell he was always extremely embarrassed, and usually, we didn't comment. When he'd soil his pants, they'd put him on the bus anyway, and have the expectation that the school would take care of it.

"Hey, big man, did you need to go before you got on the bus?" I'd ask.

"I sure did. I mean, I already did, and Mom said go on to school anyway."

"The bus monitor said Tomas told her he hadn't been changed since last night," Bill said as he was pushing the chair. Bill handed me gloves and looked for a diaper and towels.

One Monday, Bill came in with Tomas and looked at me askew.

"No Glove today," he said.

"Really," I answered. I looked at Tomas and he shrugged. "Is he at a doctor's appointment?" I asked. Sometimes, rarely, if he had an appointment, he and other kids might just come in an hour or so late. Usually, they scheduled that stuff for breaks or summertime, but I thought maybe something had come up.

"No, he's really sick," Tomas said.

"Wow, how sick?" I stupidly asked. I amended the question. "How long has he been sick?"

"*Really* sick, all weekend. He might have to go to the doctor," Tomas said.

Glove didn't show up all week. On Thursday I had our speech pathologist, Noah, who spoke Spanish, call and get some more information. We could communicate, but not well; just things like, "Please bathe them, or at least send them to school in clean clothes."

"They said he was really sick and it might be bronchitis or a really bad case of the flu," Noah reported. I thanked him and went on with the next two days. The music wasn't as much fun.

The next week, the same thing. God forgive us, but there are times when special ed teachers feel torn about between enjoying a break, glad that a parent or guardian is responsible enough to keep a sick kid home. Tomas informed us, and a phone call home confirmed that Glove was in the hospital. None of us felt that sense of relief concerning Glove; when he was at home; he wasn't having a good time. A hospital must have been scary for him. Early the following week, I went with Noah to visit Glove in the hospital.

Noah and I walked into his room and gasped together. Glove had pneumonia. He was lying on his side with tubes in his throat and an IV. Afterward, we told each other that Glove had recognized us and responded. Noah swore Glove had blinked and nodded when he'd heard my voice, (which is brash and raucous, hence not being able to sing well). I wanted to believe he knew we were there and cared. I went back to school shaken, and told everyone the facts, when visiting hours were, and what to expect. In the next two weeks, Glove went into a coma. I went two more times to visit and we held out hope he would recover and come back to play the drums to songs he loved. He didn't.

The day we learned he'd died during the night before, one of my aides broke down and cried.

"I was mean to him and got mad at him for getting mad at me when I was trying to teach him." She sobbed.

"It's okay, I cussed at him - maybe under my breath, but I did - and I'm not proud of it, but it's there," I said.

"I don't know." She stopped.

"I do. We were as much of a family to him as his foster people were. We're not just here to be teachers . . . " I trailed off, grasping for something meaningful in my own mind. It was the awareness that this job entailed more than just teaching and going home. It was a vocation that drew us in and made us something special to some of these kids. We couldn't deny it. But more than that, it made them special to us, and we're proud to know them and have them in our lives.

"Do you have brothers and sisters?" I asked.

"Yeah," she answered.

"Did you always treat them nicely and have a perfect relationship with them?"

"God, no, I - "

"That's it. We treated Glove like a family member, and got mad and got pissed off and we got happy and laughed, and now it's okay to cry." I just let the words pour out; I wasn't sure if they made sense, but I felt them in my heart and hoped Glove could hear.

I went to the memorial service with Noah. There were few people there and we had to jostle schedules to make sure everyone got a chance, as it was held on a school day, but we did the best we could. We didn't have much to say to the foster parents. Noah seemed to think that a couple of people sitting in the far corner might have been his biological parents, but we didn't find out for sure. When I glanced over at them, I thought that it was sad they'd never gotten to see him pounding like a madman on those towel-covered drums, wailing and singing his heart out - a blues man.

Chapter 39

BACK WITH AN ANGEL

Two years after I went back to Harrogate High School it was declared an under-performing high school because of test scores. Every member of our staff received letters of dismissal. The district had a job fair, and three of us (self-contained) special education teachers went along with five other teachers to find new jobs. They would put the school under the umbrella of Letter of Improvement, which meant the staff would be required to attend professional development workshops for a year, and be constantly observed at the same time. Lesson plans, curricula, classroom management, and every other aspect of our job would be under scrutiny. The general education teachers who went to the job fair couldn't stand the thought of being held responsible for the kids' grades, some of whom had been kicked out of one or two other schools. A couple of them had been sent to our school after being kicked out of a district alternative school. Behavior problems from elementary into high school that unfortunately continued well beyond were our norm. One of my jokes was, don't use the derogatory term "normal" unless you're referring to a student who doesn't have a parole officer. Many of the students didn't speak English, and a percentage of those weren't interested in learning it, either.

Having men and women in suits come in and bitch at teachers who had been busting their asses for years trying to help kids, only to be dumped on by a district that obviously didn't care until test scores, became two unacceptable issues. Most of these "professionals" hadn't actually worked with kids for decades, and most of them had never dealt with behavior issues like we had to daily. When I was walking into the job fair, one of the district program specialists was sitting at a table in the large cafeteria. She looked up at me and said, "What are you doing here?"

"I got fired," I answered.

"But you're special ed. You'll keep your job."

"Do you want to see my letter? It says I'm fired," I shot back.

"I know, but you'll get hired. Didn't Mr. Johnson tell you?"

"Do you want to see my letter?" I asked again.

"Well, it's just a routine."

"I have my letter right here, if you want to see it," I said.

All three of us were hired within the first half-hour.

When Harrogate was labeled underperforming and I left for Culver, one of my greatest professional joys was walking in the door and finding Jill there. She and I worked together for two more years. It was always a pleasure to work with her, and I depended upon her more and more.

Another of the most interesting aspects of my experience at Culver High was when I learned that Logan was attending. The high school had come to a compromise with his mom: Judith didn't ask as many questions, and the school passed him along with the help of a one-to-one aide who stuck it out for the entire four years of high school. His name was Kenny, and he did all the work and negotiated with all of Logan's teachers.

Once my class started, I learned that Judith had given hard and fast orders that Logan was not to be in my class for any reason. Unfortunately, mine was the only classroom that had a bathroom that could accommodate him. We had a large space and a changing table. Logan had grown, and was a strong young man in his wheelchair who probably weighed close to 180 pounds. Kenny could lift him and sit him down without help. But when Kenny wasn't there, I was the only one who could perform that task. Logan still didn't have a label, and none of my aides wanted anything to do with him. The were always castigated by Judith the next day, as Logan could verbally tell her what his day was like, and the aide didn't have the background to provide the assistance in his classes that he sorely needed, meaning they didn't want to do his work for him; it seemed incongruous to them, as it did to anyone else. Judith preferred a substitute teacher, anyway; she made those wishes known and demanded a sub most days. She didn't want him contaminated (my inference) by an aide from "that" room with the retarded kids. She had said she didn't want him in "that" room for any reason, and told Kenny to find another toilet facility for him. Graciously, Kenny ignored that inane remark. A substitute aide wasn't always available, though. Not once in two years was one obtainable who could lift him, except the job coach and he was busy most days. I did it, and after the first complaint, I simply told the principal to find someone else to help him in the restroom. She couldn't, so I continued to assist him in my restroom. I assumed the matter was settled with Judith.

My second year was Logan's senior year. Time had flown by. The state education board had made changes in policy concerning students with cognitive disabilities. They were discouraging keeping students in school until they were twenty-two. Unless an Individual Education Program team could show strong reason why a student should remain in school an extra year or two (namely, for job training or medical reasons), it was strongly encouraged that students should move on with their peers. Logan did not have a label signifying a cognitive delay, so the new rule would pertain to him; there was absolutely no reason for him to stay an extra year. As the year progressed, Kenny would fill me in on how the discussions went down.

"She had him tested at the city college remedial site yesterday," he told me in November.

"How'd it go?" I asked.

"The same as the state reading test went last month," he said, obviously feeling bad about it. "She argued that I should be able to read it to him and they just kept saying, 'Well, then it's not a reading test if someone reads it to him, ma'am. She flipped out, and he couldn't hardly begin it, much less finish it."

Judith had accepted the school's collusion with her son's inability to perform at his grade level so she didn't have to face the reality of his actual placement and disability. It was easier to remain in total denial. She had been telling Logan his whole life that he could be a doctor like his dad, or anything he wanted to be. His personal expectations were just echoing what he had heard from her his whole life. It broke your heart.

"She's demanding he be given an extra year to take part in job development with 'those' kids," Kenny said one day, laughing.

"Well, how'd that work out?" I asked.

"The psych said the only way he'd qualify is if they started testing now, and it would take a month or two, at least, because he needs one of 'those labels' to qualify for that program," Kenny said in February. "She didn't want to hear that; she's going to the district."

Judith lost the battle at the district. Logan was on track to graduate in May. She had several more fights with our principal, the psychologist, and the district administrators. She lost them all. She was having problems placing him in programs. In May, she tried to play her last card.

I saw Kenny walking around at lunch without Logan one day early in the week of graduation.

"What's up? Where's Logan?"

"I won't see him until grad night," he said.

"Is he going to walk?" I asked.

"Check it out, yesterday Judith tried to bribe Logan's counselor."

"No way," I said.

"Yeah, she asked how much it would cost her to change his grades so he could come back one more year. I think it's really hitting home that there's no place for him to go that she approves of. Man, she asked me last week if I would go to work one-on-one with him in the city college remedial program, and I had to tell her I couldn't give up my position or retirement here. I won't see them until Thursday night, but yeah, he'll walk."

"Yeah, DDD will either provide a note-taker or someone to provide personal needs - not both. If the student can't perform independently and study and write, they're out of luck. Note-taking means just that, not having someone like you, Kenny, do the work for him," I said.

I saw them all at graduation that Thursday evening. Kenny smiled at me, but Judith looked miserable. All I could think of was six years earlier, her screaming at Logan's middle-school teacher, and Ava, who had passed a couple of years ago by then, leaning over and saying, "Oh, honey, when he's a senior in high school, he's *still* going to be in the second or third grade."

Starting my new school was interesting. It sat well up into the foothills. It made me immediately agree with performance pay for teachers as the high school was "highly performing" several years in a row. The problem wasn't the students, but most times, the parents. I had reconnected with Jill, and she had negated retiring when she found out I was coming. It felt good. The first few days of a new year, teachers have no students and work on setting up the classroom and going to various meetings. Since I wasn't new to the district, I only had to attend a few meetings. Another plus, the head of our department was wonderful.

Because of the No Child Left Behind requirements, we had a hard time finding aides who were capable, but not overqualified for the position and pay. That situation is still happening today, and will continue as long as we hire administrators and bureaucrats who don't have the backbone to change an obvious problem. That first year we hired two young women, both recently out of school, whom I really liked, but I was worried they would move on as soon as something else came up. The other candidates weren't very impressive, and I argued for the older interviewees, but was out-voted. I was glad, in retrospect, that happened. They were both wonderful, and started out motivated and stayed that way.

They found out about my sense of humor when they got their first check stubs and couldn't believe how much was taken out in taxes.

"Wow, what a bummer," Debbie said.

"Absolutely," I said. "But don't worry, you only have about thirty or more years to work." They both just looked at me. "Well, you have to keep on working so your peers can occupy Wall Street and keep collecting welfare and food stamps, while you keep changing diapers and working your asses off."

"Very funny," they said in unison.

Debbie, I quickly learned, was a fan of *The Big Lebowski*. She'd watched it with her dad and had even attended a *Big Lebowski* festival. We went on and on quoting the dialog back and forth when we could. I started the same thing with a senior in Junior ROTC at Desert Hills High School, but told him we couldn't repeat it word for word. He understood. His mom got him the movie, and I thought, *What a cool mom*.

"Yeah, man, it uses the F word, like, 260 times. I counted," he informed me.

Debbie and I came to a compromise and substituted the word "fricking."

"Is it something you don't want to say in front of the kids?" she asked. "Most can't understand it anyway."

"Yeah, I know, but we treat them like they can understand every-thing we say and could possibly repeat it. It's just out of respect for who they are; plus, I don't want to get fired right now," I said, laughing.

One day, Jill told me there was a rug among the piles of junk in one of our huge closets; stuff had accumulated over the years and been left behind by several teachers. She mentioned Debbie was moving out of her parents' house, and Jill was wondering if I would mind if she took it. I said sure, but to have her ask me. I was thinking more about having Debbie learn to advocate for herself and not be afraid of me. I think I intimidated them both a little, being their first boss. I wanted them to feel comfortable in their job and role working with special education severely disabled young adults. One day at lunch as we were feeding the kids, Debbie came up to me and looked really nervous.

"Brant, I was wondering if, well, I saw that rug in the closet and was wondering if you use it."

"The big one that looks oriental and really nice?" I asked.

"Yeah, Jill says you don't really want it on the floor since you have a couple of better ones."

I couldn't believe fate had given me an opportunity like this; it was too good to be true. If you don't know *The Big Lebowski*, what I said next is repeated in the movie a dozen times, and Debbie should have seen this coming, but to my incredible luck, didn't.

"Well, you know, man, that rug, like, really pulls the room together."

Debbie smiled and walked away shaking her head, and said, " I should have seen that coming. I can't believe I didn't," she said laugh-ing. "Thank you."

Both Debbie and the other girl left the next year, and I was sorry to see them go, but they both moved on to bigger and better things. Debbie actually started teaching history at Culver, and the other aide went back for her master's. I wished them both luck, and was glad for the time we'd had together. I still had Jill.

Chapter 40

TWO MORE INCREDIBLE PARENTS

It was during my last year at Harrogate High when one night, I was watching TV and saw an unbelievable story on the local news. The police and the school district were interviewing an aide at Culver High for reportedly hanging an African American special education student up on a fence and leaving him there for an indefinite period of time. It sounded like a horrible transgression against a special needs student, and the news media were out for blood. Like most viewers, I thought, *Oh my god, how could something like this happen?* I rarely tuned into the news daily, but I watched a day or two for follow-up and didn't hear another word after that initial report. Something flashed from the back of my mind and I realized I knew the student.

His name was Isaiah, and he was a shaken baby. I worked with him as a teacher of the visually impaired. Shaken baby syndrome. I only met his father once; he was a huge man, and Isaiah's parents were divorced. Isaiah must have been shaken dreadfully, probably beaten. Several times, I wondered why his father, who abused him, was still working and living an independent life. We didn't know the absolute details, other than he was responsible for Isaiah's condition. This information was passed on down from several teachers, and no one I talked to had heard the story firsthand. Shaken baby syndrome (SBS) is often fatal, and causes severe brain damage, resulting in lifelong disabilities. Mortality among babies with SBS is extremely high; up to half the deaths related to child abuse are because of SBS. Non-fatal consequences of SBS include varying degrees of visual impairment (including blindness), motor impairment, and cognitive impairment. Isaiah had all these, plus several other issues. He was non-verbal and didn't have any useful vision, other than once in a while, when Isaiah would raise his head, smile, and gaze in the direction of whatever was making him happy.

Isaiah had seizures constantly. He took a half-dozen anti-seizure medications, and when the meds worked he slept most of the day. When they didn't, Isaiah would have multiple seizures within minutes. Every few days, Isaiah would have a grand mal seizure, now known as a generalized tonic seizure. When it happened, it would result in loss of consciousness and violent muscle contractions. The movements could not be stopped by restraining or repositioning his arms or legs. It was the type of seizure most people picture when they think of seizures. It scared most people shitless. That abnormal electrical activity buzzed through his brain and Isaiah would flop around, while the best someone could do was help him attempt to say in one place and not strike out or hit his head on the ground. Isaiah had had dozens of these seizures over his school career. Without his medication, Isaiah would have had seizures that would have eventually killed him. I remembered all this and more. The next year, I found myself in that same classroom, not as a teacher of the visually impaired but as the classroom teacher.

Isaiah was in diapers and needed to be spoon-fed. Throughout all that, Isaiah had a strong personality that showed in his smile. A mouth full of teeth, it radiated for all of us during the course of the day. When he was told we were taking a walk to the nurse's office to get his medication right before lunch, that smile would kill me. Several of us, including me and the nurse, spent our own money buying Isaiah almond butter, as he was allergic to peanut butter; actually, all nuts. We could only buy it at stores like Whole Foods and Trader Joe's. We never even talked about it such was our caring for him, to give him a moment or two of pleasure. I would sing several songs to him as we walked along that would put him into such a good mood, it was hard not to smile and laugh with him.

We had scrounged up a La-Z-Boy chair for Isaiah to chill out in most of the day. He would participate in activities for only a short period of time before falling asleep, and a regular chair at the table with the other students was always precarious with him falling asleep. Every morning, he and I went on a walk with a mission. It was a wonderful routine. Before it got too warm, we'd head out. I was big enough to walk him safely. With Isaiah, you had to use a controlled, guided walk, where you put your arm under his at a parallel angle to assist him in walking. That way he couldn't really go down without you preventing him from falling, as opposed to him going down alone and hard. Isaiah walked like a marionette puppet. He was gangly and loose. When he did walk, it was tenuous and uncomfortable for anyone but someone as tall as he was getting, close to six feet.

I established a route out the back of our classroom and around the baseball field. It was all grass and it bordered a golf course driving range, just on the other side of the baseball diamond. His mom loved the idea of him walking for forty-five minutes to an hour every morning. We discussed that it was safe, and he could practice walking by himself for a large part of the journey. If he did fall, it would be on grass. We walked the weeds and brush looking for errant golf balls, of which there were many, as the golfers on the driving range obviously weren't very good. We collected them daily, and every time I picked up a ball, I handed it to Isaiah and he would break into one of his ecstatic smiles - and my day was already made. We'd put the balls into a bag and carry them all back to the room. At the end of the month, Isaiah and I would walk around to the entrance of the range pushing a shopping cart through the gated community's residential area. We snuck though a break in the wall and poured the balls onto the grass near the driving range hut. We were always early enough no one was around.

I was walking with Isaiah one morning when - even today, I can't explain how - I lost contact with him for a second. We weren't quite yet to the grass area bordering the baseball field. Isaiah went down hard - face first. He was bleeding from his right arm, a thin gash of about an inch, and a spot on his forehead. I rushed him to the nurse's office, and she looked him over and bandaged him up. She called Mom and left a message explaining he had taken a fall. She hadn't determined that he needed to go Urgent Care or a hospital, but if Mom wanted him to, we would transport him immediately. I left a similar message, but also repeated how very sorry I was, and felt horrible. I never heard back, and left two more messages before the day ended. I didn't sleep that night, tossing and turning feeling alternately stupid for having allowed it to happen, and worrying about my career, but even more, for letting Isaiah's mom down and losing her respect. The next morning when the bus driver was getting him off the bus, I was right there asking what Mom had had to say.

"She said to tell you to quit calling and bothering her about Isaiah's little scratches, that she trusts you implicitly; and continue the walks and she'll talk to you in a few days. She's busy at work and knows you guys care for him as much as she does," he said, laughing.

Right when I'd started that year, the last year's teacher had come by for a visit and told me what had happened during the "hung on the fence debacle." An aide was taking Isaiah to the bus when a wheelchair went over a curb, and she needed to help the other aide immediately to right the chair and help the student. You couldn't leave Isaiah alone on a sidewalk, even for a moment. She had, in fact hung Isaiah on the fence using his backpack hook, but only for about thirty seconds, no more. Several people attested to that fact. Another aide had whipped out their phone and taken a picture of him as a marionette flopping. It looked horrible, but it was a decision the aide made in the moment to help the other student. Isaiah wasn't hurt, or left hanging for more than was necessary. The next day after being told the series of actions, Isaiah's mom immediately threatened with several lawsuits the news shows, the person taking a picture of her son without her permission, and anyone else who might release or continue this, what was in her estimation, a false story. She instantaneously forgave the aide and didn't want to hear anymore about it. I was lucky to have known her and work with her amazing son.

Talking heads in the medical community have recently recommended that the term Shaken baby syndrome be avoided and the term *non-accidental head injury* (NAHI) be used instead. In 2009, the American Academy of Pediatrics recommended the use of the term *abusive head trauma* (AHT) to replace Shaken baby syndrome. I like the term "abusive head trauma" better, but how about, "Some asshole beat the shit out of this baby" (SABTSOOTB)?

That same year, on the first day of school I was, as usual, running around with my head exploding, getting everything sorted out and scheduling the three students in wheelchairs whose parents insisted they were mainstreamed throughout the day. Arranging aides and where they had to be for every period, the most difficult task was to juggle their lunches as many, if not all, students were not independent during lunch. I can't remember what I was hurrying for that morning, but as I rushed out the door, I looked to my right and saw a woman helping an obviously severely cognitively disabled young man, who looked to have some serious orthopedic issues also. Our classroom was somewhat isolated, not for any reason other than it was an exceptional room for us to have for our students. But a student wouldn't be coming to our class unless they meant to. I stopped. The woman and I made eye contact and I said, "I have a feeling I'm meeting a new student."

She smiled and said, "Didn't they tell you about us?"

"No, but that isn't a surprise. Welcome," I said. "What's this young man's name?"

"This is Jake, and I'm his mom, Helen. I'm sorry, they were supposed to tell you. We registered a couple of days ago. Are you busy? Are you going somewhere now?"

"It can wait. Let's get you situated and settled in our room. I'll introduce you to an aide that will be Jake's best friend before the day's over. C'mon in. Welcome."

Helen frequently shared Jake's education history for the next two years. She always said most teachers, when getting a new student, especially unaware and on the first day would have freaked out, but I made them feel so welcome, she couldn't believe it. Helen was a wonderful parent, and their family treated Jake like they would have any child; he was loved and taken care of. Jake was high maintenance, but Helen made our job easy and understood what her son was capable of and what he wasn't. Jake needed to be fed. Most occupational and physical therapists would have him struggle every feeding period and it would be a mess. He was nineteen years old. I felt, as with many of my students, if he hadn't gotten it by now, why make him suffer? Helen agreed.

"I'd much rather have his food *in him* than all over him," she told me that first day. I had invited her to stay as long as she wanted to make sure she was confident in his placement and with us. I was right – she loved Jill, and could tell it was the right place for her son. Their daughter, who was a senior, would come by the room the last part of the lunch period and spend time with Jake. That was very unusual. Though some are, most typical kids may not be ashamed, yet still want some separation from their siblings, and would rather most of their peers not know who their brother or sister are. It wasn't like that with her; she obviously loved Jake, and talked and played with him, at least twice every week.

Later in the year, I fought a battle for Jake. We had been left a huge swing; its support beams rose almost fifteen feet in the air on a tripod. They were referred to as "sensory," or "vestibular," therapy swings. Many special educators, and especially those administrators who hadn't been in a classroom for years, didn't approve and felt the swings weren't age appropriate. Since Jake operated at a pre-K level, I was never sure what was considered "age appropriate" for him. He earned time in the swing after morning activities, and later in the afternoon after another round of activities. He loved it, and actually benefitted from the time to settle down and focus, and it quickly became part of his routine. The swing was old and started to tear one day. Jill was worried, as it really was important to him. I got on the internet immediately and ordered another one. Later, I found out Jill told his mom I had purchased it myself. I, and most teachers I know, constantly did things like that. It was for our peace of mind, as much as for the kid's. One day, an assistant special education department bureaucrat was visiting my class to talk to our school department head and me about an upcoming IEP with Jake's parents. She stood looking around the classroom, and I saw her eyes settle on the swing.

"Oh, so you have a swing," she said condescendingly.

I immediately perked up and said a little too forcefully, "You bet. He earns it, he loves it, and more importantly, Mom loves it. It's staying." Enough said.

This bureaucrat wanted to impress on us that because Jake was twenty, he should be forced out at the end of that year. Because of that ignorant statement about our swing, during our Individual Education Program meeting, my department head and myself mutually decided on our own to arrange it so Jake could stay another year. They had just moved to Tucson, and it would give Mom time to find a placement for him and let them get settled. A couple of years later, I got an email from his mom and it touched me deeply. She also thanked Jill and me for making sure that, since I considered the swing my property after buying the seat, it was hers to take home at the end of the next year.

Chapter 41

MY LAST CRAZY TEACHER

During that year, I shared two extremely large classrooms with another teacher, two rooms that were unused, abandoned, and formerly shop classes and were triple the size of a regular classroom. To get to the other class, one would have to walk through the room I occupied. When they did traipse through, it was so big you would hardly notice.

Ms. Mankoff was a short, heavyset woman who had been teaching for many years; the last ten at Culver High School, and it was only five minutes from her home. She would instruct the autism class, and I would have the severe and profound room. I only had four kids in my room at any time, and three or four were out and about. I had four or five aides. Within twenty minutes of meeting Ms. Mankoff she informed me at least four times that she was a vegan. Immediately after that, every time she mentioned it, I informed her I ate dog every chance I got. It took her a half day to stop enlightening me after one of the aides finally told her I was joking. This continued periodically for the next year.

Ms. Mankoff wasn't a very good teacher. She took care of the kids, but intermittently she would have some kind of a crisis and was either out or unable to work. Toward the end of the first year, the school could see that we were losing several kids to moving or graduation, and two classes weren't needed for the next year. It was quickly looking like one of us would be one too many for the small special education population. I had more qualifications than Ms. Mankoff, and it looked like the scales were possibly tipping in my direction. I had caused zero problems and had extinguished various fires, and several parents were happy with their kids' placement. Ms. Mankoff hadn't done either. The best was yet to come.

I was unaware one morning in early May that she had been called to the office and told she would be moved to another school. She cried, and seemed to take it as well as could be expected (the principal clued me in later). About mid-morning, I saw her walking to her room and I waved to her. She ignored me. I was used to that, and didn't pay any further attention as I continued to work with my kids. Maybe fifteen minutes later, one of her aides came sauntering over. He did this regularly, and would vent; he had asked several times to be moved to my room, but that would entail moving one of my aides, and I always appreciated that no one wanted to be moved out of my room.

"Hey, Mr. Vickers, can I ask you a question?"

"Yeah, and please don't call me 'Mr. Vickers,'" I answered again, as I did regularly.

"Hey, Ms. Mankoff is being fired, or at least, sent to another school. Did you know that?"

"I guessed it would happen, but I thought with her longevity, it might be me who was asked to move."

"No, they told her she doesn't have the certification for autism and what your class is, so she has to move."

"Well, I'm sorry to hear that."

"And I have a problem."

"What?" I asked.

"Well, she told me she was going to kill herself."

"Whoa! When? Now?"

"Yeah, she's sitting in there with her head in her hands and said, 'I'm going to end this and kill myself.'"

Right then, we both looked up and noticed Ms. Mankoff looking around the corner at us.

"Go up to the office right now. Better yet, call on your cell phone as you go, and make sure you get ahold of one of the principals."

He looked at me like he didn't want to get involved, and didn't want to go. I could understand, but it wasn't a choice.

"Go! Don't worry about what she thinks. You didn't do anything here. We can't ignore what she said. Go, man. Go."

A few minutes later, the principal, along with a security guard and the nurse, came running through my room. Ms. Mankoff had already slipped through the back door. They had to call her husband and the sheriff to go to her home. She actually came back to work after a couple weeks of counseling and a psychiatric evaluation. She had left two students in her room unattended while sneaking out the back door.

The second to last day of school, I was sitting in the dark working on my computer when Ms. Mankoff walked out of her room with a parent whose son was going to be in my room the next year. I had gotten to know him, and he was a darling, tall boy with high-functioning autism. My wife had actually worked with him while he was in middle school. They didn't know I was sitting at my computer; I hadn't turned on the lights when I'd come in from seeing the students off on the buses.

"I don't think he'll be good for Oliver," Ms. Mankoff said.

"Well, I don't know what to do," the parent said.

"I think you should look at moving him next year and get him out of here," she continued.

I immediately knew who and what they were talking about. I stood up and Ms. Mankoff looked like she was going to faint. She muttered a goodbye and practically ran back into her room. I walked up and introduced myself to Oliver's mom.

"Ma'am, I've gotten to know Oliver, and I know he'll be fine in my class. This is my thirteenth year teaching, and I'll do your son right. I promise you that from the bottom of my heart. Ms. Mankoff is very unhappy, and I'm truly sorry about how this turned out, but don't let her influence or talk you into doing something like move your son to another school after he's done so well here. I think you remember his former speech pathologist from Pacifica Middle School, Cheryl?"

"Oh yes, she was the best speech teacher he ever had. He talked about her all the time. I miss her."

"Well, we're married, and if I need any help, I can always ask her for advice."

"That sounds good."

And it was.

That next year, I realized my class was also going to close. We only had two self-contained students and four kids in wheelchairs. The kids in wheelchairs had one-on-ones, and were mainstreamed. It was said their parents had a lawyer on retainer and insisted their kids be fully included and attend typical classes. Two of them were very cognitively low, and didn't really need, desire, or benefit from full inclusion, but it was what the parents wanted. The school was compliant, and I saw the writing on the wall. I didn't want to be an inclusion specialist, and since I still had my teacher of the visual impaired certification, I applied to my next job. It would be as a classroom teacher with students who were blind or visually impaired, along with being intellectually disabled. I spent five years there, and have worked with the most wonderful staff and kids of my career. After Bruce, Jill and Bill, I never expected to have another aide I relied on and trusted who helped me to the degree they did, but Donna has stood out. That made all the difference in the world.